No Color Is My Kind

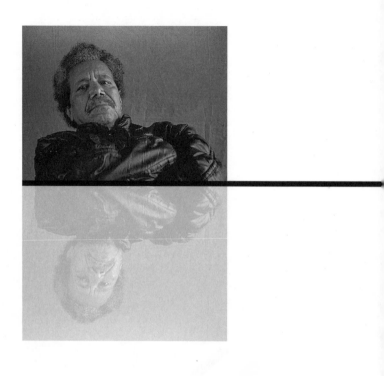

NO Color Is My Kind

The Life of Eldrewey Stearns
and the Integration of Houston

Thomas R. Cole

University of Texas Press   Austin

∞ The paper used in this publication meets
the minimum requirements of American
National Standard for Information
Sciences — Permanence of Paper for Printed
Library Materials, ANSI Z39.48-1984.

Library of Congress
Cataloging-in-Publication Data

Cole, Thomas R., 1949–
    No color is my kind : the life of
Eldrewey Stearns and the integration of
Houston / Thomas R. Cole.
        p.   cm.
    Includes bibliographical references
(p.   ) and index.
    ISBN 0-292-71197-2 (cloth : alk. paper). —
ISBN 0-292-71198-0 (pbk. : alk. paper)
    1. Houston (Tex.) — Race relations.
2. Civil rights movements — Texas —
Houston — History — 20th century.
3. Stearns, Eldrewey.   4. Afro-American
civil rights workers — Texas — Houston —
Biography.   5. Civil rights workers —
Texas — Houston — Biography.
6. Mentally ill — Texas — Houston —
Biography.   7. Cole, Thomas R., 1949–   .
I. Title.
F394.H89N426   1997
305.8'009764'235 — dc20   96-44105

In honor of my father,
Burton David Michel (1926–1953).

I never heard his story
from his own lips.

The words "A Man of Tender
Conscience" are engraved on his
tombstone.

Thomas R. Cole

I thank my parents,
Rudolph and Devona Stearns,
   and
I thank all those people who passed me by,
   Who left me room to see the sky,
And I thank that cast of thousands more,
   To whom I've paid my thanks before.

Eldrewey J. Stearns

Must I strive toward colorlessness?
. . . think of what the world would
lose if that should happen. America
is woven of many strands: I would
recognize them and let it remain so.
It's "winner take nothing" that is
the great truth of our country or
any country. Life is to be lived, not
controlled; and humanity is won
by continuing to play in the face of
certain defeat. Our fate is to become
one, and yet many—this is not
prophecy but description. Thus one
of the greatest jokes in the world is
the spectacle of the whites busy
escaping blackness and becoming
blacker every day, and blacks striving
toward whiteness, becoming quite
dull and gray. None of us seems to
know who he is or where he is going.

> Ralph Ellison,
> *Invisible Man*, 1947

I take great pride in the fact that I
am of European and African descent.
. . . I never owned a marriage license,
and I have sworn to God that I shall
never own anything beyond the bare
necessities of life. I want something
I've never had—the unmistakable
realization that I am an original
American. I am a racial hybrid.
Nothing more. No less. Perhaps,
true love.

> Eldrewey Stearns, 1983

Acknowledgments   xi

Introduction   1

Part One
Leader at Last

Part Two
A Boy from Galveston and San Augustine

Part Three
Wandering and Return

Photo sections precede chapters 1, 5, and 8.

As always, my wife Letha has been the primary source of support for my writing efforts. She has listened to me talk, think, and worry about this project for almost twelve years. Her skills as a psychiatrist and psychoanalyst were often crucial; but her quiet love, her forbearance, her loyalty, and her hardheaded midwestern practicality helped make an impossible task possible. My children, Emma and Jacob, have grown up hearing about and meeting Eldrewey and his family as if they were distant relations. I am grateful that they have never been afraid to demand my love and attention when it strayed too far from their needs.

Ever since I met Marc Kaminsky at a Gerontological Society meeting in 1984, I have been inspired, sustained, and instructed in our friendship. As a writer, poet, literary critic, gerontologist, cultural studies scholar, psychotherapist, and fellow Jew, Marc helped me face many problems. By introducing me to M. M. Bakhtin's idea of double-voiced discourse, and to James Clifford and George E. Marcus's anthropological work on reflexivity and the writing of culture, Marc opened up a new conceptual universe that enabled me to see how I could write a life story that acknowledges my own complex motivations, honors and respects Eldrewey's voice, and also claims the authority of careful scholarship. At many points when I felt lost, depressed, or unable to see the way forward, Marc reiterated his love for me, his belief in the project, and his faith in the tortoise's method of slow, painstaking, and unflinching confrontation with every bump in the road. I am grateful for all this, for his many critical readings, and for his example of devotion to the craft of writing.

This project began as a kind of experiment in the medical humanities — an experiment which I owe to my membership in the Institute for the Medical Humanities at the University of Texas Medical Branch in Galveston. I am grateful to colleagues, students, and staff at the institute for the help, tolerance, and guidance they have provided over the years. My good friend and institute director Ron Carson was skeptical when he needed to be and supportive when I needed him to be. In countless conversations over a decade of uncertainty, Ron's steadiness has been invaluable to me. I am grateful for his willingness to provide staff support and for his many readings of the manuscript.

No Color Is My Kind has benefited from the interest and support of many people. At a seminar where she commented on the last chapters, my colleague in psychiatry Jean Goodwin wondered out loud why so many people were eager to help. Perhaps, she suggested, people were drawn to Eldrewey Stearns as if he were a shaman who could suck out the noxious poisons of racism from their psyches. I think that there is much truth in this idea — and in the corollary that most of us are (or ought to be) recovering racists. Yet I have personally come to realize that attending to the pain of the "other" is not a substitute for attending to one's own pain and need for healing.

Many Institute students and faculty provided important criticism and feedback in noon seminars, in chapter readings, and in my graduate course on humanities and aging. My colleagues Chester Burns, John Douard, Ellen More, Bill Winslade, and Mary Winkler all contributed critical ideas and suggestions. I am also grateful for the interest and feedback of IMH students Craig Brestrup, Larry Wygant, Cheryl Viani, Faith McClellan, Faith Lagay, Kayhan Parsi, Deborah Cummins, Mary White, and Martha Holstein. In 1988, Pat Jakobi worked diligently for several months fashioning autobiographical chapters from early, raw transcripts. While our autobiographical route ultimately reached a dead end, these chapters contained essential material which was integrated into the biography.

Transcribing Eldrewey Stearns's life history tapes and other oral history interviews presented a host of problems. The earliest tapes were transcribed by Sheila Keating. I am also grateful to other secretaries in the institute who transcribed tapes over the years: Stacy Gottlob, Nina Fox, Dorothy Karilanovic, Kathleen Modd.

Karen "Bert" Bertonaschi spent one summer squinting at microfilm screens, looking for articles about civil rights in Houston's African American newspapers during the early 1960s.

The Kempner family played a critical role in keeping this project (and Eldrewey Stearns) alive. The late Harris Kempner personally paid Stearns a small monthly stipend to work on his life story for over two years. After Harris's death, his wife Ruth Kempner continued this contribution for an additional year. In addition, the Kempner Fund awarded substantial grants which allowed me to hire Raphaela Gonzales, who carefully transcribed over two dozen tapes.

In the fall of 1989, Eleanor Porter came to my office having recently retired as an editor at UTMB. She volunteered to transcribe several of the Stearns tapes and soon came to work part-time as my editorial assistant. Eleanor possesses superb skills as a transcriber and copy and production editor. She has transcribed dozens of tapes; organized all the visual and printed research and archival materials; devised the style for endnotes, abbreviations, and references; prepared the manuscript; and shepherded it through production. Eleanor is highly literate and highly emotional; her anger at Stearns's fate, her fierce advocacy on behalf of his voice, her suggested passages or wordings, and her commitment to the project are all embedded in this text.

I owe special thanks to Lisa Lambert, formerly the archives director at the Rosenberg Public Library in Galveston. When I was doing research at the Rosenberg Library, Lisa took an interest in this project. She arranged to set up an Eldrewey Stearns Archive which will hold the project's audiotapes and other primary research materials. In addition, Lisa — with the blessing of library director Nancy M. Smith — allocated scarce library funds for tape transcription. Dr. Cliff Houston, as University of Texas Medical Branch vice-president for multicultural affairs, provided funds to transcribe the final tapes. At this stage, Jonnie Michelletti performed yeoman work, transcribing many tapes which were extremely difficult to understand. These tapes illustrate the phenomenology of Stearns's illness in ways that appear only sparingly in this volume.

Many UTMB colleagues have helped shape this book. When he was president of the university, William C. Levin enthusiastically forwarded several grant requests and has maintained a keen interest in the project ever since. Over the years, many faculty and residents in the psychiatry department have attended to Stearns's life and his story: Robert White, Sharon Dott, Raymond Fuentes, Jaron Winston, Steve Mitchell, Joan Lang, Charlie Gaston, Russell Gardner, and Jean Goodwin.

I owe a large debt to my friend Bert Cohler, whose extensive body of scholarship on the life story and the study of lives has functioned as an intellectual crosswalk linking the territories of psychiatry, psychoanalysis, the social sciences, and the humanities. We had one of our best conversations about this project when no one came to a scheduled session on Stearns's life during a convention of the American Society on Aging.

Difficulties in my own life led me to seek help from several therapists during the gestation of this project. I am grateful for the care and thoughtful attentiveness of Charlie Gaston, David Freedman, and Stephanie Larsen, who helped me unravel some core emotional and conceptual knots.

I am also grateful to all those who spoke with me or granted me interviews regarding this book. Some will find their names changed in order to protect their expressed desire for privacy.

Devona and Rudolph Stearns allowed me into their household and their lives. I appreciate their trust and the tolerant cooperation of their grandsons, Roderick and Andre. I am also grateful to others from Galveston's black community: Edward Clack, Sally Coleman, Rose Bennett, Gloria Haywood, and Reverend James Thomas. I was new to oral history research when I began tracking the history of desegregation in Houston. Several people were particularly helpful: Otis King, Holly Hogrobrooks, Curtis Graves, Quentin Mease, Bertha Woodley, Reverend Bill Lawson, Cheryl Bright, Ester King, Judge Carl Walker, Jr., and George Washington, Jr. Louis Marchiafava, who heads the archival division at the Houston Metropolitan Library, and Tara Wenger facilitated the use of that library's visual and printed research materials. I learned much about Houston's African American community from the researcher and preservationist Pat Prather.

I appreciate the cooperation of photographer Benny Joseph, who allowed me to fish through thousands of old negatives in his attic. Mr. Joseph reprinted two dozen historic photographs from original negatives and granted permission to reproduce several of them here.

Kate Mayhern and Sandy Ogilvy of the Texas Southern University Law Clinic provided me with the information and strategy to appeal Stearns's first Social Security Disability decision.

Several of my historian colleagues have helped in various ways. I am grateful to Bob Abzug, Andy Achenbaum, Alwyn Barr, Howard Beeth, John Boles, David Chappell, Robert Fisher, Richard Fox, John Gillis, Waldo Martin, Merline Pitre, David Troyansky, and Cary Wintz. Jim Jones and I talked often about the fascinations and burdens of historical biography; his readings of early drafts and of the penultimate manuscript were especially helpful.

Chandler Davidson took the time to meet about the project and find his copy of Saul Friedman's unpublished article. I want to thank Tom Curtis for his reaction to the manuscript and for his efforts as scriptwriter and co-producer of the accompanying documentary video, "The Strange Demise of Jim Crow: How Houston Desegregated Its Public Accommodations, 1959–1963," available through the University of Texas Press.

I appreciate the reactions of other people who read sections of this book: Warren Carrier, Pam Diamond, Ronnie Dugger, Harvey Gordon, Margarette Gullette, Doug Ingram, Roger Kamenetz, Rabbi Sam Karff, Juliet Mitchell, Rod Olsen, Ruth Ray, Richard Seltzer, Marilyn Thompson, Matt Weiland, and Steve Weiland. I am especially grateful for the support and interest of Carter Williams and Frank Williams, who know in their hearts how the early death of a father affects one's life.

Eric Avery twice took time out from his work as an artist, psychiatrist, and activist to take photographs of Eldrewey and his family in Galveston and on our trip to San Augustine. I am grateful to Eric for these photographs, for his support of this project, and for introducing me to the photographer and artist Roger Haile. Roger spent a great deal of time and effort shooting, printing, and editing the pictures from two separate photo sessions in late 1995 and early 1996. A selection of Eric's photographs appear in Parts Two and Three and a selection of Roger's in Part Three. I am also grateful to Mrs. Devona Stearns for allowing us to use photographs which she personally took — or which are in her family collection — in Part Two.

Finally, very warm thanks to my editor, Shannon Davies. For eight years, Shannon has shown a steady, unwavering interest in the project and confidence in me. She facilitated the development and completion of this book with a light touch, a great deal of patience, and a firm sense of what it needed at various stages. In many moments when I felt confused or uncertain, Shannon responded with just the right blend of professional candor and personal support. Without her, I doubt that Eldrewey Stearns's life story would ever have found a publisher.

This is the story of a man whose soul is not rested. I met Eldrewey Stearns in September 1984. I was teaching at the University of Texas Medical Branch, in a weekly psychiatry case conference which introduced medical students to the characteristics of major mental disorders. As a historian and faculty member from the Institute for the Medical Humanities, my role was to highlight ethical, cultural, or historical issues in discussions that followed interviews with hospitalized patients.

This week's specialty was manic-depressive illness or bipolar affective disorder. The patient was a fifty-two-year-old black man who complained that although he felt very important, no one understood him.

"I haven't been happy since April 25, 1960," he told the psychiatrist. "I'm always depressed until a new woman or a new bottle comes into the picture." Stearns had been committed to the psychiatric hospital against his will and now felt confused. It was "mysterious," he said. "Everybody was being too nice." At first glance, he appeared to be a disheveled, vulnerable, and angry man whose life had unraveled under the stresses of poverty, racism, alcoholism, and mental illness. Yet his diction was sometimes learned, even elegant. Stearns claimed to have drunk enough liquor for twenty-five lifetimes, often blacking out and finding himself in jail. Though doctors had put him on heavy doses of lithium, he chose to "go off it in favor of booze." Previously an inmate at Austin State Hospital, St. Elizabeth's in Washington, D.C., and Jennie Sealy Hospital in Galveston, he had been brought to the hospital this time by the mental health deputies, who found him on the beach in a drunken stupor.

A psychiatry resident recalled seeing him twice in the crisis clinic prior to this admission. The first time he had been referred from the emergency room (he had come in complaining of abdominal pain) for his bizarre behavior. The second time he had tried to circumcise himself with a razor. Stearns announced how proud he was of this — a remark that brought only ridicule and defensive laughter from those who might have asked about the significance of circumcision for this "black" man whose great-great-grandfather was apparently Adolphus Sterne, a German-Jewish immigrant and a founding father of the Texas Republic.

Surprisingly, this histrionic, vulnerable, angry man spoke in eloquent phrases, though these did not always flow logically from one another. He claimed to have graduated from Michigan State University, to have received a law degree from Texas Southern University, and to have been the "original integration leader in Texas." Doubtful glances spread throughout the room. Stearns stated that he had already experienced everything one could desire in life. Marooned on Galveston Island, sleeping on a couch in his parents' living room, he had only one remaining wish: to write his life story and show the world how he "embodied the totality of man's experiences."

As soon as the patient left the room, the psychiatrist turned to diagnostic issues. "What are the positive findings on the mental status exam?" he asked. The ensuing discussion revolved around criteria for alcoholism and bipolar affective disorder.

"What should we make of the patient's own story, his desire to write an autobiography?" I asked, indignant at the omission of the patient's point of view.

"A typical expression of grandiosity, a symptom useful for diagnostic purposes," replied the psychiatrist.

"I wonder," I said hesitantly. "Perhaps the work of telling or writing one's life story might be a means of cure as well as a symptom." Silence. Was I so naive as to think that storytelling might be a means of healing this man's broken brain? Even more, the silence seemed to say, why would anyone want to hear about the life of a poor, crazy, aging black man?

My own academic interests in history, aging, and autobiography had recently sensitized me to the special potential of life stories for both historical research and psychological growth. According to one school of developmental theory, personal narratives bring the chaotic, disparate events of a life together in a work of productive imagination that transforms that life into a coherent unity. By imposing a kind of retrospective order on the unpredictable events of a life, personal narratives assist in the achievement of identity. Life stories also rely heavily on reminiscence, which is associated with increased feelings of well-being or ego integrity in later life.

But to be intelligible, life history has to be more than a purely subjective account of one's own life — it has to be "followable," understandable according to our Western belief that all narratives have a beginning, a middle, and an end related to each other in a meaningful manner. Might the long disciplined effort to create such a narrative have a positive effect on Stearns's inner sense of cohesion and self-esteem?

The next morning, as I walked to the psychiatric hospital, the power and historical significance of collaborative efforts like *The Autobiography of Malcolm X* and *All God's Dangers* ran through my mind. I knocked on the door at the end of the second floor hallway and told the aide who answered that I wished to speak with Stearns.

The aide took me down to the common room, where Stearns was alternately pacing the floor and looking out the window. I introduced myself and said that I had appreciated the chance to learn about him in the medical-student case conference. He told me that he had been invited there to lecture.

A short man, clothed in a bright yellow shirt and painter's pants, he looked at me with a fierce gleam through eyes that would later betray great pain and loneliness. Brown skin and salt-and-pepper hair stood out sharply against his yellow shirt. Deep triangular lines on either side of his moustache widened to a mouth spitting out rapid-fire sentences, punctuated by awkward silences.

"It sounds like you have an important story to tell," I said. "I'd like to help you get it down on paper."

"An interesting proposition," he replied, skeptically sizing me up. "I doubt you're up to it. . . . But then, I'm not exactly in a position to refuse."

While Stearns was still in the hospital, we began meeting in my office once a week. It soon became apparent that he literally could not write due to severe tremors; in the first few sessions he was unable to formulate an outline or a focus of his own. Each time he came in, it seemed that we had to test each other's mettle after the niceties of coffee and a pleasant setting wore off. Who was in control here? What did I want out of this? He spoke in large, grandiose expressions, waving his arms and raising his voice — a drowning man, I thought, struggling to keep from going under. Unaware of my own grandiose impulses, I assumed that I could throw him a life line and pull his story of suffering and heroism onto *terra firma*.

After Eldrewey was discharged, his father Rudolph began driving him to campus for our sessions. I drove him home when we were finished. Those first few weeks left me confused. Had I taken on too much? Where did my role as oral historian/editor end and my role as pseudo-psychotherapist begin? Stearns had refused to return to the hospital on an outpatient basis. He took his lithium irregularly, and he refused to believe that any psychiatrist or psychologist could help him. Yet he showed up at my office without fail at the appointed time every week.

Despite expressions of interest, none of the psychiatrists on campus were willing to see Stearns in my office. Raymond Fuentes, my friend and psychologist colleague, agreed to meet with us in my office each week to assess Stearns's condition and to provide emotional support and expertise. Later, when Raymond was admitted to the hospital for medical tests, Eldrewey remarked, "At least he'll find out what's wrong with him; I have to tell the whole story to find out what's wrong with me."

Punctually, this man, who seemed to have nothing but a suit of clothes and an old blue travel bag, came to my office to work. We began meeting twice a week to tape his recollections, which revealed an extraordinary memory and imagination. He had a vast treasure buried within. The question was, could we rummage around in that memory — arousing its terrible demons and painful disappointments — and return to the present with the story and the man intact?

After two months of searching for early memories amidst awkwardness and mutual confusion of purpose, we reached a brief moment of understanding that gave us both hope. Stearns remarked that working on this book was like going to school again. I asked if he thought he would learn about himself.

"That's right," he replied. "It's a soul-searching project, and I pray to God it will become an obsession like the sit-ins and the boycotts and all those other things in my previous life."

"But, Eldrewey," I interrupted, "Dr. Fuentes and I don't want it to become an obsession — we want it to become a part of your life and not an escape from it. Do you see what I mean?"

"Well . . . right now I can't separate the two. As I've said numerous times, I have already had everything God could give a man in one lifetime. Reliving my life to write this book is like heating up yesterday's soup. Anything I get out of this book or this life from now on is an unexpected, welcome bonus."

"What about the possibility that the book may actually be an appetizer?"

"To what?"

"To the next course in your life?"

"Well, then I welcome the main course. If I can get that much light into my life . . . there's a twinkle in my eye, and my heart skips a beat to see that you and others have hope when I myself have almost abandoned hope. I am almost a recluse. I go nowhere except around the house, a small five-room bungalow where I live among close relatives. I don't even interact with them; if it weren't for the TV, I would have no communication with the outside world. . . . So I look forward to seeing you every Monday almost as the flowers want for rain." I was hooked.

After several months of taping, Eldrewey seemed to be clearer and more focused. One cold morning in February 1985, he called the office. His father couldn't drive him because the car was not working and he had no money for cab or bus fare.

"Why don't you walk?" I asked. "Didn't they call you Rabbit for your quick feet when you were a boy?"

"Do you think I can make it in an hour and a half?" He surprised himself by walking those few miles in less than an hour. Feeling both elated and desperate for money, Eldrewey began thinking of ways to support himself while working on the book. He approached the prominent Galveston philanthropist Harris Kempner and requested financial support. Kempner called and asked me what this book was all about, since he could not understand everything Eldrewey said. I told him that I thought it a valuable project but could not confidently predict a completed manuscript. I typed up a proposal for six months of funding, which Kempner agreed to provide out of his own pocket.

During the spring of 1985, while we were meeting twice a week and taping his memories of the late 1950s, Eldrewey began to lose the thread of the story. The content of the sessions moved into grand pronouncements about his sexual prowess. He became increasingly disorganized, resumed his drinking, and began making sexual advances to female colleagues and office staff.

One day when he came in, his speech was slurred and his

breath reeked of alcohol. The session produced only incoherent ramblings on tape and frustration in me as I realized he was spinning out of control. Afterward, I drove him home and told him that I would not work with him if he came in again with liquor on his breath. He denied that he'd been drinking and insisted that it was none of my business. I replied that alcohol was off-limits at work; the office was a safe place to work and its rules had to be followed. "I am worried about you," I said. "I hope you will stop drinking and keep yourself together."

The following Monday he failed to appear for the first time. Instead, he began calling several women in the office, asking for dates. Frightened and angry, they turned to me to stop him. I began to wonder: why had I gotten myself into this project which sapped my time and energy and which my colleagues viewed as impossible and dangerous? I spoke on the phone with Eldrewey's mother, Devona Stearns, who had lived through many such episodes and knew what was coming. "Why does this book take so long, Dr. Cole?" she asked. She said she had to give Eldrewey money to go out and buy a beer. It was the only way she could have any peace around the house. He had stopped taking his lithium a few days ago; she was worried that he would become violent.

I then called Eldrewey, saying that I had missed him and hoped he would come for our next appointment. I repeated that the office was a place for work, not women. His calls to the women continued; their anxiety and anger intensified.

The following week I ran into Eldrewey in front of Gerland's grocery store on University Boulevard. He was walking aimlessly, without eyeglasses, drinking a beer wrapped in a brown paper bag. He wore a dirty light blue shirt, half-tucked into mud-splattered pants. He walked up to me smiling and chattering, shook my hand.

The next day I called him again. "I am worried about you. I think you need help," I said.

"All I need is some warm pussy, preferably your wife," he answered and hung up.

I called Dr. Sharon Dott, a senior psychiatry resident who was following his case and said I thought he needed to be hospitalized. She said she would wait until Monday, when he was scheduled to call her.

That weekend, the phone rang in the middle of the night. My wife Letha, a psychiatry resident on call, was needed at the emergency room to see a patient who had been brought in by his father. It was Eldrewey, floridly psychotic after several days without sleep or lithium. "How can I help you, Mr. Stearns?" Letha remembers asking.

"You could give me some of that warm pussy," Eldrewey answered. Yet within a few minutes he agreed that he needed to be admitted to the psychiatric hospital. He turned to my wife and said, "This must be very difficult for you."

During his first weeks in the hospital, Eldrewey barely acknowledged me when I visited. He was furious with me for having interfered with his sex life and for advising him not to drink. "If I had a gun, I'd plug you right now," he said. For the first several visits, which lasted five to ten minutes, I simply said I was glad to see him and hoped that he was feeling better.

One day I brought him a bathing suit so that he could go swimming with the other patients. Slowly, he softened and even expressed pleasure at my visits. For me, it was a relief to see the redness disappear from his eyes, to watch his face regain a shape of inner coherence. I mentioned looking forward to resuming work on the book. He looked at me with fear and amazement.

During the following two weeks while I was away, Eldrewey continued to recover. From New York I sent him a postcard of the Statue of Liberty, then under repair. On that vacation, I came across a passage from the Gnostic Gospels that articulated my hope for our project: "If you bring forth what is within you, what is within you will save you. If you do not bring forth what is within you, what is within you will destroy you."

Before leaving town, I had reluctantly agreed with Ron Carson, our institute director, that Stearns's presence in the office was causing too much disruption and should not continue. During my absence, the office was moving to a new location in the magnificently restored Ashbel Smith Building (better known as "Old Red"). Eldrewey knew this and was looking forward to working there. Rather than upset him by announcing that we could not work in Old Red, I decided to wait until returning from vacation.

When I got back to town, Eldrewey had just been released from the hospital and nobody knew where he was. He had apparently decided to find an apartment. I went to the locked ward and asked if anyone knew where he was living. A medical student who had taken a liking to him said she thought he had rented a room at 24th and Avenue H.

I drove to that corner, got out, and began knocking on doors. Nobody had heard of Eldrewey Stearns. After two hours poking around a Galveston neighborhood called "the jungle," I found his landlord, known as Red. "Oh, yeah," he said. "He rents an unfurnished room from me for twenty-five dollars a week. Nice guy. He lies out here on the front lawn sometimes, drinking beer and talking to himself."

"Where is he?" I asked.

"He left here about an hour ago. Said he was going to some Old Red building down there at the medical school."

"Oh shit . . . Thanks."

By the time I got back to Old Red, Eldrewey was already gone. He had knocked on the door of the office suite, saying he was there for an appointment with me. One of my colleagues came to the door. "Eldrewey," he said in a loud voice, "let's step outside here for a minute."

A shouting match ensued in the hallway. Stearns insisted that he was there for an appointment with me. My colleague responded that I was out of the office, that others had already told him to stay away, that he was frightening people and should not come where he wasn't wanted.

"Who the hell are you to tell me what to do?" demanded Stearns. In the meantime, another colleague, alarmed by all the commotion, stepped out into the hall and quietly persuaded Eldrewey to leave. When I arrived at the office, I was greeted with barely contained fury. "He's harmless," I insisted, without convincing anyone. My shouting colleague was still shaken from the intense confrontation. Angry myself and fearing a major setback, I left again to find Eldrewey.

After another hour of driving up and down the hot streets between the medical school and his apartment, I finally spotted him, walking with that light-blue travel bag. Relieved, I pulled over, rolled down the window, and motioned to him to get in. I apologized for the rude reception he had gotten, saying how glad I was to see him. He seemed less upset by the incident than I was.

I asked him what had happened. He said that when he had

heard someone call him by his first name, he thought it was a welcome, rather than a sign of disrespect from a man he had never met. "I had been looking forward to showing people the new Eldrewey Stearns over there in the new office." I told him that we couldn't work in Old Red due to his earlier behavior. While in the hospital, he had fantasized himself as a king in the castle of Old Red.

"I owe you an apology," he said.

When we resumed our work, it was August 6, 1985 — the fortieth anniversary of the atomic bombing of Hiroshima. Stearns picked up the thread of the narrative right where he had left off, on the verge of his intense career as an integration leader.

part ONE

Leader at Last

Eldrewey Stearns appears before Houston City Council to protest police beating, August 1959. *Houston Chronicle* photo.

Texas Southern University student protesters sitting in at Weingarten's Store #26 lunch counter, March 4, 1960. *Houston Post* photo, courtesy of Houston Public Library.

Lunch counter closed during sit-in protest. *Houston Post* photo, courtesy of Houston Public Library.

Reverend Bill Lawson, Director of the Baptist Student Union at Texas Southern University, ca. 1960. Photo by Benny Joseph.

Texas Southern University President Sam Nabrit, ca. 1960. Photo by Benny Joseph.

South Central YMCA Director Quentin R. Mease, ca. 1960. Photo courtesy of Quentin R. Mease.

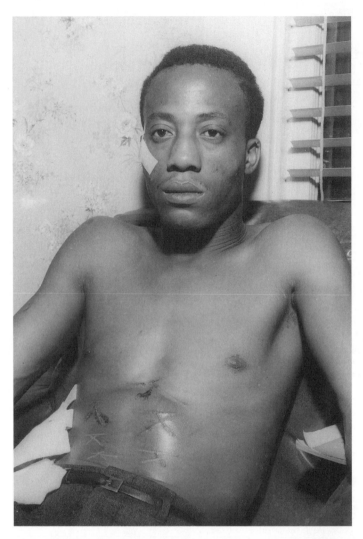

Felton Turner, revealing two sets of the letters "KKK" carved into his abdomen, March 7, 1960. Photo by Benny Joseph.

Curtis Graves (far right), attending a student protesters' ceremony. Eldrewey Stearns (left) presents an award to Felton Turner, March 1960. Photo by Benny Joseph.

Attorneys Hamah King (left) and George Washington, Jr., meeting to raise bail money for student demonstrators, ca. February 1961. Photo by Benny Joseph.

Attorney George Washington, Jr., opening the door to Houston City Council chambers, ca. August 1961. Photo by Benny Joseph.

Quentin R. Mease, James Brooks, and A. E. Warner (front row, right to left) firing Colt .45s at ground breaking for the world's first domed stadium, January 3, 1962. R. E. "Bob" Smith (back row, right) and Harris County Commissioners look on. Photo courtesy of Quentin R. Mease.

Quentin R. Mease (front left), Jim Jemison (far right), Hobart Taylor (second from right), and other African American community leaders take a look at construction of the Harris County domed stadium, ca. fall 1962. Photo courtesy of Quentin R. Mease.

Progressive Youth Association members being honored at the Antioch Baptist Church, May 14, 1961. Photo by Benny Joseph.

Flyer inviting African Americans to a mass meeting in support of the Progressive Youth Association. Photo from scrapbook of John Bland.

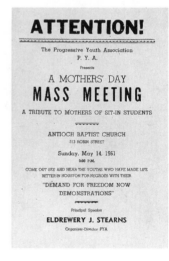

ATTENTION!

The Progressive Youth Association
P. Y. A.

Presents

A MOTHERS' DAY
MASS MEETING

A TRIBUTE TO MOTHERS OF SIT-IN STUDENTS

ANTIOCH BAPTIST CHURCH
313 ROBIN STREET

Sunday, May 14, 1961
3:00 P.M.

COME OUT SEE AND HEAR THE YOUTHS WHO HAVE MADE LIFE
BETTER IN HOUSTON FOR NEGROES WITH THEIR

"DEMAND FOR FREEDOM NOW
DEMONSTRATIONS"

Principal Speaker

ELDREWERY J. STEARNS
Organizer-Director PYA

Marquee of the segregated
Majestic Theatre in downtown
Houston, 1963. *Houston
Chronicle* photo.

John T. Jones, publisher of the *Houston Chronicle*, looking
at a portrait of his late uncle, Jesse Jones. Photo ca. 1960,
courtesy of Houston Endowment.

Holly Hogrobrooks (left) receiving an award from Eldrewey Stearns at Antioch Baptist Church mass meeting, May 14, 1961. Photo by Benny Joseph.

Attorney George Washington, Jr. (left), seeking advice and financial support for the student protesters from Theodore Hogrobrooks, Sr., ca. 1961. Photo by Benny Joseph.

Bobby Beasely (back to camera) leading student protesters, attorneys (upper right), and veteran labor leader/activist Moses Leroy (lower left) in the "Battle Hymn of the Republic" on the steps of the Riesner Street Jail, ca. 1961. Photo by Benny Joseph.

Police Chief Carl Shruptrine, ca. 1960. *Houston Chronicle* photo.

Eldrewey Stearns (center), flanked by students, speaking to attorneys George
Washington, Jr. (left), and Hamah King at Riesner Street Jail, ca. 1961. *Houston
Chronicle* photo.

I cruised [along] . . . noticed a cop on my tail. . . . A young white cop. . . . "Where's your wallet?" I had a wallet without a driver's license and with a picture to beat the band of a white girl—bright and white. . . . The race problem was a sex problem then, now, and as long as we have different races, black and white and yellow. . . . I left the Doctors' Club as Eldrewey Stearns. I would return as a full-fledged Raceman.

Eldrewey Stearns

At 2:30 A.M. on Sunday, August 23, 1959, two white Houston police officers were out investigating a burglar alarm ringing at the B & B Package Store near the 700 block of Elgin. Suddenly, they noticed a young black man driving a gray 1952 Dodge with defective tail lights. Officers J. T. Cole and J. P. Bujnoch jumped into their police cruiser, pursued the Dodge, and brought it to a stop at San Jacinto and Holman. The pale light of a last-quarter moon seeped through scattered storm clouds. Soft, wet breezes from the Gulf of Mexico stirred the heavy summer air. It was a tense moment. Hours earlier, patrolman John Wesley Suttle had been killed by a hit-and-run driver. And Houston's African Americans were beginning to protest police brutality.

What happened over the next few hours is a matter of controversy. The driver of the 1952 Dodge, Eldrewey Stearns, was hauled off to jail, where he was held until about 7:30 in the morning — unusual treatment for a traffic violator. Stearns claims that he was arrested because he had a white girl's picture in his wallet and that he was verbally abused and beaten in jail. The officers noted that Stearns had no driver's license and said that he was belligerent. In an investigation held later, Cole and Bujnoch claimed that the phone lines to the police station were jammed with calls following the death of Officer Suttle: since they could not verify Stearns's identity and record by phone, they took him to the police station.

Stearns had just gotten off work as a cocktail waiter at the prestigious Doctors' Club in the heart of the Texas Medical Center. He was twenty-seven years old, enrolled at the law school of Texas Southern University (TSU), engaged to be married, and itching to become a civil rights leader. When the club closed around 1 A.M., the maître d', Eddie Marx, asked him for a ride home. Stearns felt proud to be taking a white boss home in his car. Marx, a recent German immigrant about Stearns's age, was new to segregation and to the club, which had an all-white membership of about 500 and a virtually all-black service staff.

Marx, who didn't yet have a car of his own, took a particular liking to Stearns. "He spoke to everyone, he was very intellectual, and very bright," Marx remembers. "On many occasions, we sat and talked about how black people were treated in the United States and what he thought was wrong." Stearns was a favorite of the Doctors' Club clientele, just as he had been a favorite at the elite Artillery Club in Galveston, where he had worked during his teens. He was used to being treated with respect by wealthy whites, with whom he was invariably efficient, witty, and gracious. Scorned by anyone — black or white — he quickly became enraged and unpredictable.

After he dropped Eddie Marx off that night, Stearns noticed "a cop car on my tail" in the rearview mirror. "Pull over there, boy!" he remembers a policeman shouting. He had no driver's license, and his wallet contained only a Michigan State alumnus card, a picture of a white girl, some handwritten notes, and a traffic ticket issued to a client from the Doctors' Club.

"From up north, huh, nigger? One of those northern niggers we see? Whose picture is this?" asked one of the cops.

"She's my girl friend," Stearns answered defiantly. He said he was a law student and that he knew his rights: their job was to issue him a ticket and let him go on about his business.

"We got a new nigger on our hands here," said one officer, placing a call back to the station. A few minutes later, Stearns recalls, the other policeman shoved him into the police car, saying: "Who the hell do you think you are, telling a white man and a police officer about the law?"

In those days, white police officers often roughed up Houston blacks and then charged them with resisting arrest. Eyeballing a white woman or "talking back" to a white policeman frequently earned a beating and a trip to the "hole" at the city jail. Houston's blacks had a reputation for being docile, but the beginnings of protest were in the air. Two weeks earlier, an African American attorney, Aloysius Wickliff, had publicly called for an end to police brutality against blacks in Houston. After Stearns's arrest and beating, Wickliff demanded an investigation on behalf of a black civic and political group known as the Harris County Council of Organizations (HCCO).

The following Wednesday was "Pop Off Day" at the City Hall, a weekly time when citizens came before the mayor and City Council to air grievances and pitch their causes. Newspaper, radio, and TV reporters always attended. Stearns seized the moment. He had been an effective debater at Michigan State University and relished verbal combat. He asserted that he had been beaten like a dog for not saying "yes, sir" to officers Cole and Bujnoch. White Houstonians were not accustomed to highly articulate blacks demanding their rights in public. As he warmed to his topic, "I saw the bulbs popping and photographers moving up closer and closer to the platform."

Yet Stearns knew better than to acknowledge what he considered the real cause of his arrest and beating — the white girl's picture in his billfold. "I had too much going for me otherwise: a battered mouth and body as proof that they had beaten me and debased me, degraded me to the level of an animal."

"The white press ate it up," he remembers. In the summer of 1959, Stearns was a handsome, young black law student — dressed immaculately with his signature bow tie, horn-rim glasses, and a Phi Kappa Delta golden key on his lapel. At the City Council meeting, most of the questions came from Louie Welch, a sympathetic and politically ambitious city councilman who later became mayor of Houston. Mayor Lewis Cutrer, according to Stearns, "turned redder than a Texas branding iron" and ordered a complete investigation of the incident. Welch insisted that the investigation be conducted by the City Attorney's Office, rather than the police department.

Back at the Doctors' Club, Stearns became something of a celebrity to the blacks and a source of embarrassment to the white management. As Stearns tells it, when he arrived for work after the City Council meeting, he was met by a bartender named Dudley. "You are a star, Stearns," he said, nervously polishing the bar with his white rag. "They want to interview you. That fella there. His name is Dan Rather."

Not long out of Sam Houston State College in Huntsville, Rather was setting up for the interview in his long-sleeved white shirt. "We came to do a story on your trip to City Hall today," he said. "Can you do it?"

Of course I can do it, thought Stearns, who had been waiting for just this opportunity. "I was wearing my cocktail waiter uniform, a little white jacket rimmed in purple. . . . I felt like I was in Hollywood." During the next several years, Houston's civil rights movement took to the streets, and Eldrewey Stearns emerged as its most prominent spokesman. His charismatic verbal ability alarmed many white Houstonians who were accustomed to the quiet moderation and legal strategies of most older black leaders. Stearns aggressively violated the unwritten code of civility that governed public conduct in racial matters.

Stearns had made several specific complaints: that he was called a "nigger" by almost all the police officers who talked to him that night; that he was not allowed to call his lawyer, Carl Walker, Jr., immediately; that he was thrown to the floor in the booking office by policemen who pulled off his shoes, glasses, and ring and took everything out of his pockets; and that he was grabbed and beaten on the way to his fifth floor cell. Stearns remembers:

> **I was on my way to jail, with a billy club in my side. There I was relayed to two other rednecked peckerwoods. They hit me across the head, in the neck and chest, stomach and legs. Then two other jailers took me to a dark room upstairs across from the drunk tank and proceeded to kick my brown ass once more. One of them kept giving me a grin that reminded me of a jackass eating cactus through a picket fence. I thought the night would never end. . . . Deep down inside I wanted them to beat me more to make a stronger case. But I kept screaming, "Stop! Don't hit me no more."**

All the police officers involved denied under oath that they called Stearns a "nigger" or used excessive force. They all testified that Stearns was uncooperative or belligerent. The city jail records indicated that over 140 people were booked on August 23; Stearns was one of only three labeled "very belligerent."

According to Lieutenant Earl Maughner, who handled the booking office that night, Stearns was sent up to cell D-1, the "drunk tank," at around 4 A.M. because his attorney had not yet come to the station and he could not post a bond of $35. Maughner testified that Stearns violently refused the routine procedure of removing his shoes to reveal any contraband material or weapons. He remembered forcibly removing Stearns's shoes, but using no more force than necessary.

Other officers testified that Stearns had to be physically carried out of the elevator and into the cell. Officer Joe Oakes claimed that Stearns was "hollering" and lecturing the officers that "all these colored men in cell D-1 were here, not because of any wrong they had done, but because society had caused them to be here."

Stearns remembers being thrown into the drunk tank and asking inmates if they would be his witness. "But my voice fell on deaf ears. It was as quiet as a mouse pissin' on cotton." Yet when Edgar Pfeil took the testimony of Tex Taylor, Eugene Fred Mayberry, and Booker T. Coleman—three black men incarcerated with Stearns that night—they remembered plenty of noise. Tex Taylor said that he couldn't see anything, but he heard a loud scuffling in the hallway and Stearns was hollering, "Oh, oh, oh, please, please turn my hand loose. Don't do that!" Fred Mayberry said that he rode the elevator upstairs with Stearns and that before they got to the cell one of the police officers told Stearns to "step into the room here and when you come out you will do what I ask you to."

"No, I am not going in there!" Mayberry recalls Stearns shouting, "Because you're gonna take me in there and beat me up again." Then, according to Mayberry, an officer came up from behind, put both hands under Stearns's arms and around his neck, and forced him into the room. From the front, another officer hit Stearns in the stomach and kicked him a couple of times. Mayberry, still standing in the hall, watched through the open door as the two officers beat and cursed Stearns, who eventually walked into the cell. Booker T. Coleman testified that there was a loud commotion and struggle lasting five or ten minutes. He claimed that two officers forced Stearns down to the floor, holding his arms behind his back, but that he never saw them hit or kick Stearns.

After attorney Carl Walker, Jr., posted his bail, Stearns was released. "I made a beeline to the highest ranking police officer on duty," he remembers.

The station was busy with blue uniforms of the white captors and black, brown, and yellow faces of prisoners. "What is your story, boy?" Inspector W. J. Burton asked. He leaned back and listened. I hadn't learned yet that when people are not saying anything they are not neces-

sarily agreeing with you. He was just waiting for me to shut up.

For ten minutes, he said nothing. "You are confused, boy," he said finally. "These are white men in Houston that you are dealing with. You did not answer 'Yes, sir' to them, I understand, and talked about your constitutional rights. This is Houston, Texas, boy. You are lucky. From what I hear you still got your head on your shoulders. The best thing you can do—hear me well, boy—the best thing you can do is get your little black ass out of here and never look back."

Inspector Burton denied having made those remarks to Stearns. "I attempted to explain to him that everyone didn't have the command of the King's English," Burton told Pfeil, "and that in many instances southern people referred to Negroes as niggers. And that I would think from what he told me that he didn't have a great deal to complain about. . . . I couldn't find where he had been mistreated."

The publicity surrounding Stearns focused considerable scrutiny on race relations in Houston, the largest city and home of the largest African American population in the American South. The city attorney's investigation into Stearns's charges was finally released in late January 1960. Prepared by Edgar Pfeil, the report was based on statements obtained from two dozen people and contained 785 pages of testimony. It effectively debunked the claim of police brutality—not by proving that Stearns was not beaten but by establishing he had been "belligerent," leaving the unmistakable implication that he got what he deserved.

It is impossible to determine exactly what happened the night of August 23, 1959. The officers' denial that they used excessive force is difficult to believe. Stearns's version of the story may be exaggerated. By the standards of the 1990s, however, what happened to Eldrewey Stearns that night was unquestionably police brutality—regardless of his outbursts. But for Houston in the late 1950s, Stearns's verbal aggressiveness automatically branded him a troublemaker, against whom violence could be used with impunity.

The *Houston Post* story of February 26, 1960, "Student's Claim of Brutality Denied," leaves the impression that the police officers were victims and Stearns was the aggressor. It fails even to mention the testimony of the black inmates who witnessed the beatings. Pfeil's report was circulated to the City Council, mayor, and Chief of Police Carl Shuptrine. No action was taken. When the City Council announced the outcome of its investigation, the issue dropped like a stone. The police department was off the hot seat. But the arrest and its aftermath had launched Stearns's career as a "raceman" who soon galvanized many who would otherwise have stayed on the sidelines in the fight against Jim Crow in Houston.

Shortly after Stearns's confrontation with the Houston Police Department, he was fired from the Doctors' Club. A few weeks later, he was kicked out of his apartment near TSU by his roommate, Otis King, who later became a Houston city attorney and then dean of the TSU Law School. Every Sunday morning at seven, the landlady, Mrs. Schneiderson, came to collect her weekly rent of $7.50 each. Occasionally, when Stearns said he had no money, King paid the rent or put Mrs. Schneiderson off for a few days. He hated being leaned on or embarrassed, but didn't mind covering for Stearns once in a while. They were both working odd jobs and going to school at the same time. But one weekend in late 1959, Stearns went too far.

That Saturday, King spent the morning at the law school library and then had lunch with Stearns at the Groovey Grill — a favorite campus restaurant and bar, operated by Faurice and Jessie Prince. The Princes, who had no children of their own, acted like parents to many of the TSU students who took their meals there. At lunch, Stearns told King that he'd been working some catering jobs and that he had plenty of money for rent the next day. When King came back to the Groovey Grill for a nightcap around 10 P.M., Stearns was still there drinking away the rent money. The next morning, Mrs. Schneiderson came at seven. "Okay, Drew, where's the rent money?" King recalls asking. "And he sort of rolled over and said, 'I don't have it.'" King was furious. As Stearns remembers it, he couldn't pay the rent because he had just lost his job at the Doctors' Club. Whatever the reason, King told him to get his things together and leave. It would not be the last time that Stearns had no place to live.

Stearns moved in with Billy Survance, his future brother-in-law, and soon went to work for Quentin Mease, executive director at the South Central Young Men's Christian Association (YMCA). Mease, a native of Iowa and decorated Air Force veteran of World War II, had come to work for the Houston YMCA in 1948. Quietly but persistently and firmly, he pushed for a new facility in the black community, which had traditionally used worn-out equipment in old rented buildings. It took until 1955 to open the South Central Y, which was located on Wheeler Street in the heart of the TSU campus.

Under Mease's directorship, the South Central Y became a vital center of community activity, housing a kind of Negro Rotary called the Business and Professional Men's Club. In fact, during the late 1950s and early 1960s, the South Central Y was virtually the only place in Houston where white politicians, businessmen, and professionals regularly came to "do business" with influential blacks. Mease, who by 1960 was becoming one of Houston's most respected and influential African Americans, believed that the time was right for tearing down the walls of segregation, but he preferred to work behind the scenes. He knew that Stearns's radicalism and his urgent sense of mission could help energize a basically conservative and fragmented African American population.

Stearns remembers his first assignment at the South Central YMCA: "to appear before this [Business and Professional Men's] club and tell them about my ass-kicking rendezvous with white policemen that unconstitutional night, as I called it. Mr. Mease introduced me. A Reverend Malone, pastor of the large St. John's Baptist Church, sprang from his seat to protest my getting out of line." Dr. B. A. Turner, a dean at TSU, came to Stearns's defense. Mease became a mentor for Stearns, introducing him to powerful blacks and whites throughout the city.

In the five short months between Stearns's arrest and the City Council's release of the Pfeil investigation in late February 1960, the racial climate in the American South changed irrevocably. A new form of protest — the sit-in — ignited the student phase of the civil rights movement. On February 1, four young men from North Carolina Agricultural and Technical College sat down at a segregated lunch counter at a Woolworth's dime store in Greensboro, North Carolina. "We do not serve Negroes," they were told. Instead of leaving, the four students remained; the next day they returned with more protesters who quietly occupied the lunch counter. The sit-ins spread like wildfire; by mid-April, the Student Non-Violent Coordinating Committee (SNCC) was launched in Raleigh to guide the growing movement.

The quiet dignity and restraint of young African Americans demanding their rights posed both a moral challenge and a genuine economic threat that whites could not ignore. Ingeniously, the sit-ins silently broke through the old code of civility in race relations, which prized peace and goodwill while suppressing rage at the indignities of segregation and second-class citizenship. Moreover, the sit-ins, like the earlier Montgomery bus boycott and other forms of direct action, signaled a new reality — that whites could no longer dictate the terms of negotiating power between the races.

As the sit-in movement spread through the Deep South, Quentin Mease was taking the pulse of Houston, which had a reputation for cultural backwardness and political conservatism. "Houston," wrote John Gunther disparagingly in 1947, " . . . is, with the possible exception of Tulsa, Oklahoma, the most reactionary community in the United States. It is a city where few people think of anything but money."

As if to confirm Gunther's harsh judgment, Houston hosted a particularly virulent Red Scare in the 1950s, when anyone advocating social change was quickly marginalized with the label "outside Communist agitator." Driven by an ethos of free enterprise, and still dominated by a small circle of self-made white developers and oilmen, boom town Houston was the nation's seventh largest city in 1960. Its population had more than doubled every twenty years since 1900.

Houston's business leadership was fervently committed to private economic growth — and to protecting the city's reputation as a place of opportunity. "Houston is a city on the move," wrote *Houston Chronicle* reporter Saul Friedman in an unpublished article on race relations in the Bayou City, "so preoccupied with growth that it has not had time to discover its character. It is a city in search of its character. It is therefore pretentious, and terribly conscious of its image. More so, perhaps, than any city in the nation." It was so self-conscious, in fact, that *Chronicle* publisher John T. Jones never allowed Friedman's article to be printed.

Despite Houston's image as a booming metropolis, the city's African American population — almost one-quarter of the total — still lived as second-class citizens. More by custom than by law, blacks were segregated within or barred from white establishments such as hotels, theaters, restaurants, public schools, colleges, parks, jails, and hospitals. In downtown Houston, a black man bleeding in the street could not get service from the driver of a white ambulance. While racism in Houston was not as harsh as in deep East Texas or many areas of the Deep South, segregation accomplished its major goal of preserving a servile black population.

Friedman's extensive research showed that in the early 1960s the average family income for African Americans in Houston was $3,386, barely half that for whites. According to the 1960 census, one in every nine whites held a professional or technical job; the rate for blacks was one in fifty-four. Blue collars, maids' uniforms, overalls, and waiters' clothing were the predominant dress of Houston's black workers.

On the other hand, Houston's African Americans had rates of home ownership, levels of income, and business opportunities that compared favorably with those of blacks in any southern city — and certainly with the conditions in deep East Texas and Louisiana that many of them had left behind. The National Urban League congratulated Houston when it learned that the number of blacks earning more than $4,000 annually rose from 1,000 in 1949 to more than 17,000 in 1959.

Moreover, blacks in Houston and Harris County had a successful legacy of fighting segregation in the courts. Working with attorneys Thurgood Marshall and James Nabrit, the Texas State Conference of the National Association for the Advancement of Colored People (NAACP) undertook a long and expensive campaign to undermine the legal bases of segregation. In 1940, Dr. Lonnie Smith filed suit in federal court against the election judges in the city's Fifth Ward, who had prevented him from voting in the Democratic Primary election. Four years later, the United States Supreme Court held in *Smith v. Allwright* that the state Democratic Party's all-white primary — the so-called Jay Bird

Primary — violated the Fifteenth Amendment of the Constitution. After *Smith*, lawsuits all over the country were filed challenging various discriminatory voting schemes.

In 1945, the Texas Chapter of the NAACP decided to challenge segregation in educational institutions. It carefully picked its venue, plaintiff, and attorneys. Heman Sweatt, a Houston mail carrier, applied to the only public law school in Texas, the University of Texas (UT) at Austin. Though clearly qualified, he was denied admission, pending the state attorney general's opinion on whether a black could be admitted to the University of Texas.

In 1946, the attorney general ruled that Texas must either provide an equal education program for Sweatt or admit him to UT. The state created a makeshift black law school in Houston for Sweatt, who declined to attend a transparently unequal school. Sweatt's attorneys, Thurgood Marshall, W. J. Durham, and James Nabrit, then filed an appeal with the United States Supreme Court.

While the parties waited for a Supreme Court decision, the Texas legislature allocated $2,000,000 to acquire the campus of Houston College for Negroes and establish Texas State University for Negroes, later Texas Southern University. In 1950, the Supreme Court held that Texas had not provided Sweatt with the educational equivalent of the University of Texas, effectively opening its graduate and professional schools. Black Texans henceforth had opportunities for professional education in an integrated setting — and Houston had gained a separate university with substantial funding.

Eldrewey Stearns had followed the Sweatt case closely. In fact, Heman Sweatt's brother, H. L. Sweatt, had been Stearns's physics teacher and mentor at Central High School in Galveston. After his graduation from Michigan State in 1957, Stearns was denied admission to the University of Texas Law School in Austin. He enrolled reluctantly at the law school at TSU, which he dubbed "Separate But Equal U." At TSU, Stearns came across other, mostly younger, students who were also impatient about the slow pace of change in race relations. Holly and Ted Hogrobrooks, Earl Allen, Curtis Graves, Charles Lee, Bobby Beasely, Otis King, Herbert Hamilton, Deanna Lott, Eddie Rigsby, Jessie Purvis, and others were tired of waiting for the legal system to work. They would soon form the nucleus of the small but effective student protest movement in Houston.

Buoyed by the legal victories of the 1950s, yet frustrated by the intransigence of the white establishment, these students were increasingly critical of their elders' tactics. In 1954, the Supreme Court had ruled that segregated public schools violated the Constitution. Yet six years later Houston's school system had not budged, despite the school board election of Hattie Mae White, who in 1958 became the first black since Reconstruction elected to significant public office in Houston. Some students thought that most black church leaders had been essentially bought off by white politicians and business interests. They began to see the NAACP Legal Defense Fund as an organization that provided a handful of comfortable jobs for lawyers but few practical benefits to the larger black community.

Stearns quickly emerged as the most militant and vocal of this small group of students, who were preparing to take risks their parents never dreamed of. Most had not been exposed to the raw bigotry, lynching, and physical intimidation that their parents had survived or witnessed. And they were too young to remember the terrible race riot of 1917, when about one hundred members of an all-black infantry regiment stationed at Camp Logan marched to town and fought a running battle with white police officers, citizens, and other military units. Memories of that awful night left black and white Houstonians over age forty with a palpable fear of race war.

In late February 1960, Stearns came to work at the YMCA one night while Mease was supervising preparations for an NAACP dinner. Stearns walked to the lectern, picked up the microphone, and began reciting the Gettysburg Address. "How's that sound, Mr. Mease?" he asked. "Well, Drew," Mease responded, "that's pretty good, but why don't you quit sounding off and organize students here, like they're doing over in North Carolina and Georgia?" The following morning, H. L. Zachary introduced Stearns to four TSU undergraduate students — Holly and Ted Hogrobrooks, Eddie Rigsby, and Jessie Purvis — who were already meeting daily in Room 214 of Hannah Hall to plan a Houston strategy. That night at work he announced, "Mr. Mease, meet the leader of Houston's Student Protest Movement."

Stearns and this small group of TSU students were also goaded into action by Senator Lyndon Johnson's disparaging comment that Texas "nigras" were too complacent to engage in public protest. When Holly Hogrobrooks brought the newspaper carrying his comments to 214 Hannah Hall, Johnson's clever words hit their mark: the group immediately planned a sit-in for Friday, March 4, 1960. Their first target was the lunch counter at Weingarten's Store #26 on Almeda St. near the TSU campus. Joseph Weingarten, the Jewish owner of the supermarket local chain, had recently been honored by B'nai B'rith for his humanitarian and community service. At Store #26, Weingarten's customers were mostly black; students thought he would be vulnerable to pressure to integrate his lunch counters there.

Stearns and this small group planned a careful, nonviolent protest. Believing that media coverage was their best protection against violent attacks, Stearns said he would call the radio and TV stations as well as the major white newspapers: the *Houston Post, Houston Chronicle*, and *Houston Press*. He contacted George McElroy, who was working at the black weekly the *Informer*. McElroy promised to send photographer Lloyd Wells and suggested that Stearns contact the police — a piece of advice that proved invaluable. Holly announced that her father, Theodore Hogrobrooks, Sr., would post bond for anyone who might be arrested. Reverend Charles Lee, a thirty-two-year-old Methodist chaplain on campus and a veteran of the Korean War, counted the lunch counter stools, found the nearest phone booth, and planned the travel route.

On the evening before the first sit-in, Reverend Bill Lawson and his wife came home to find the lights on downstairs in the Baptist Student Center. Lawson, then director of the Baptist Student Union and professor of Bible at TSU, was perplexed: no student activities had been scheduled that night. The anxious students described their plan and asked him for instructions in nonviolence. "I was horrified by the idea," he recalls. Although Lawson emerged as one of Houston's preeminent civil rights activists, he initially played a conservative role. "If there was anybody who was supposed to be in line and nonradical," he remembers, it was a black man hired in 1959 by the Southern Baptist Convention to work in a state university. Lawson advised against the sit-in demonstrations. He reminded the students that many of them were on financial aid. They came from families that had never been in trouble with the law before, and they were risking the possibility of being hurt, thrown in jail, jeopardizing their chances to get good jobs.

"We're not here to ask your *permission*," responded Stearns. "We're *going* to sit in. We've got our plan all ready. We came to ask you to instruct us in nonviolence. If you don't want to, just tell us and we'll find somebody else."

"And so I stammered and stuttered . . . trying to tell them something about the hazards of this kind of unprepared, unarmed confrontation, and they walked out of the Baptist Student Center and left me there. And I still didn't know that a page in history had turned."

That night was a long one for Stearns, who stayed at the home of Clarence and Flo Coleman, who was eight months pregnant. Stearns couldn't sleep; he fretted that the plan would fizzle, that he would lose his nerve. "The faces of the four students stuck to my mind like crazy glue. . . . I had given them my word that I would lead them. I needed only to act out the role of a leader. I walked the floor like an expectant father in front of the maternity ward waiting for the cry of his newborn babe."

The next morning, it was still not clear that the protest would actually take place. Lawson's warnings had discouraged many students, and Stearns worried that those remaining might get cold feet. Most TSU students knew nothing about the protest. Many were indifferent. Some were frightened or hostile. One female student spit on Eldrewey as he handed her a leaflet. "Get that shit out of my face," she responded. "You and all those other damn fools are going to get killed and start trouble for us all." Stearns was virtually alone in pushing for direct action. "Nobody thought the melon was ready for plucking in Houston," remembers Charles Lee, "except Eldrewey Stearns. He just figured, you gotta pluck it, you gotta do it, you gotta go."

Stearns and Holly Hogrobrooks spent all morning on campus

recruiting and instructing potential demonstrators. They circulated a leaflet containing a list of Do's and Don'ts obtained from Fisk University students. These included:

—**Do show yourself friendly on the counter at all times.**
—**Do report all incidents to your leader.**
—**Do remember the teachings of Jesus Christ, Gandhi, and Martin Luther King (Negro minister and leader of resistance to segregation, notably the boycott of segregated bus service in Montgomery, Alabama, several years ago).**
—**Do feel that you have a constitutional and democratic reason for what you are doing.**
—**Don't strike back or curse if attacked.**
—**Don't speak to anyone without stating your purpose for being in the movement.**
—**Do sit straight and always face the counter.**
—**Do refer all information to your leader in a polite manner.**
—**Do continue if your leader is discouraged and placed in confinement.**
—**Don't laugh out.**
—**Don't hold conversations with floor walkers.**
—**Don't leave your seat until your leader has given you permission to do so.**
—**Don't block entrances to the store and aisles.**

That afternoon at four, thirteen well-dressed students assembled at the flagpole in front of the TSU administration building. It was a small group, uncertain and still wavering. Stearns choreographed the scene to inspire the students with the symbolism of freedom. They held hands around the flagpole, as the Stars and Stripes above waved in the warm March wind. Someone sang the "Star-Spangled Banner." Stearns remembers seeing one white face — the face of fellow law student Roger Ash — in a circle of anxious students. "I stood there like I'm facing a . . . mirror of people, but in that mirror was also a white face there. . . . And I said, 'All you black niggers, negroes, whatever, you can be just as . . . white as this white boy if you come with me.'" They broke into pairs and marched three feet apart down Wheeler Avenue to Almeda. As they walked toward Weingarten's, four more students joined the march, raising their number to seventeen: Holly Hogrobrooks, Ted Hogrobrooks, Eddie Rigsby, Jessie Purvis, Eldrewey Stearns, Charles Lee, Earl Allen, Curtis Graves, John Hutchins, Clarence Coleman, Deanna Lott, Guy Boudois, Roger Ash, Bernice Washington, Jimmy Lofton, Harold Stovall, and Pat Patterson.

Stearns left the group to phone the white press and police. Roger Ash was the first person to step inside Weingarten's front door. The black students filed in and anxiously approached the lunch counter. Charles Lee, eldest of the group and a war veteran, sat down first. The others followed his lead. When the TSU students sat down and politely asked for service, store manager Mert Bang was himself seated at the counter having coffee. White customers left without finishing their meals. By then, a crowd of about a hundred TSU students was milling in and around the store. Demonstrators promptly filled all thirty stools at the counter.

"Who is your leader?" Bang asked several students.

"I'm my own leader. I just want a cup of coffee," answered one.

"All I ask is some service. I'm just seeking my democratic rights," replied another.

Mert Bang called the headquarters of the supermarket chain and received instructions. Within a few minutes, he returned to the counter with two yellow placards reading "Lunch Counter Closed."

"There won't be any violence here," Bang told a reporter, "not as long as I can get in the middle."

Fear of violence kept everyone on edge. Yet the sheer uncertainty of the situation had its humorous side as well. After the signs were tacked up over the grill, no one in the large crowd knew quite what to do. "Many stood around," remembers Holly Hogrobrooks. "Spectators stood around. Within fifteen minutes the law enforcement officers got there, and they stood around. Everybody stood around!"

Three Weingarten officials arrived shortly and invited several students upstairs into a closed conference. A *Houston Post* reporter later heard one student ask: "Are you going to serve us or are you not? That's the whole thing. I don't think you can afford not to—you've got too much money involved." The students walked out of the meeting and back to the closed lunch counter around 5:30. They remained quietly seated until the store closed at 8:30.

At six o'clock, Houston's television and radio news programs reported the first sit-in west of the Mississippi River. The student demonstrators were ecstatic: they had gotten media attention, proved that they could mobilize other students, disrupted a segregated business, and avoided violence. Stearns and several others headed for the Groovey Grill to plan their next move.

Charles Lee, whose wife worried when he didn't come home to their two children until that night, was particularly concerned that students understand the risks they were taking. Lee, who himself carried a .45 pistol for protection, realized that successful sit-ins required strong, disciplined nonviolence. He insisted that each lunch-counter demonstrator be willing to die rather than retaliate if attacked. Those who could not comply with this rule were given other assignments: providing rides, running errands, making phone calls, creating signs. Stearns and Curtis Graves took charge of ensuring that all participants were neatly dressed. They decided to work in shifts of four hours each.

News of the first sit-in not only swelled the ranks of the demonstrators, it also brought out the segregationists. The next morning, well-known oilman and segregationist leader J. M. Wren got to Weingarten's before the demonstrators did. Driving his Cadillac up to the curb, Wren entered the supermarket and purchased some cigarettes. "I'll be back later to see if anyone is loitering," he said on his way out.

About fifty demonstrators arrived in the middle of the morning. Several carloads of young whites dressed in work clothes walked into the store and eyeballed the students at the lunch counters. A green sedan pulled into the parking lot with a Confederate flag hanging from its antenna. A scuffle between whites and blacks not involved in the protest broke out; young black James Gates received a knife wound in the back and was treated at the Veterans Hospital.

That Saturday morning, Curtis Graves drove a small group of protesters to the nearby Mading's Drug Store. Although the press and the police had been called, they were not present when the students arrived. The manager posted a "Fountain Closed" sign, but students remained seated at the lunch counter. The students sat quietly, reading books and magazines; some got up and were replaced by another shift. Jessie Prince brought juice and doughnuts from the Groovey Grill.

Around noon, two carloads of white toughs from Galveston pulled into the parking lot. They had heard about the demonstrations on the preceding night's news and driven fifty miles up the Gulf Freeway to confront the protesters. Several of the whites entered the store. They began walking back and forth behind the students, taunting and jeering. "I said to myself that I will look forward," remembers Curtis Graves. "I will not turn around. I will take the knife or whatever comes and I will not strike back."

Just at that moment a police officer walked through the door followed by Lloyd Wells, photographer and writer for the *Informer*. The policeman, Graves recalls, "didn't say a word. . . . He just walked through the drugstore and kind of circled in and out. . . . And at the same time (and back in those days photographers had press cameras that had the great big flashbulbs in 'em) flashbulbs were going off. . . . And it diffused everything, tranquilized it."

Meanwhile, unbeknownst to the students, Police Chief Carl Shuptrine had already made extensive plans to prevent violence and decided not to arrest protesters. Both undercover and uniformed officers were sent to each demonstration. Police cars with trained dogs were ordered to remain in the area but out of sight.

This response to sit-in demonstrators and their segregationist opponents contrasted sharply with official reaction in other areas of the South. After black students at Alabama State staged a mild sit-in at the state capitol cafeteria on February 25, Governor John Patterson demanded that Alabama State president H. Councill Trenholm expel all the students involved. "The citizens of this state do not intend to spend their tax money to educate law violators and race agitators," he told Trenholm. "And if you do not put a stop to it, you might well find yourself out of funds." Trenholm complied. Nearly 4,000 African Americans rallied to protest the governor's threat. In Nashville, after two weeks of demonstrations, the downtown merchants demanded arrests if the demonstrations continued. On February 26, police there arrested over eighty demonstrators, after failing to stop whites from attacking protesters with rocks and lighted cigarettes. In Orangeburg, South Carolina, 400 students marching downtown to a sit-in were met with tear gas, water hoses, and mass arrest.

When the Houston sit-ins began on Friday, March 4, no one knew how strong the resistance would be. Dr. Samuel Nabrit, the president of Texas Southern University, was in Atlanta attending a meeting of the Council of Southern Universities. Over the weekend, Ralph Lee, a white banker on the TSU board, told the press that the sit-ins were going so smoothly that Nabrit must have engineered them. Lee demanded that Nabrit put an end to the demonstrations. When Sam Nabrit returned home on Sunday, newsmen asked him to respond to Lee's allegation. He refused.

On Monday morning, Nabrit met with Mack Hannah, Houston's wealthiest black and chairman of the TSU Board of Regents. Hannah — the cigar-smoking 300-pound financier who headed the Standard Savings and Loan Association on Dowling — was already on the phone with Governor Price Daniel every morning to keep him informed of the situation. After meeting with Nabrit, Hannah called Carl Shuptrine along with several key board members. He assured them that the TSU administration had no role in the protests and would cooperate to prevent any bloodshed or property damage. Chief Shuptrine then called Nabrit and indicated that the students informed him before every demonstration. He thought the students had violated no law and were well behaved. They exchanged private phone numbers.

By Monday afternoon, many more TSU students eagerly joined the group, which then called itself the Student Protest Movement. The SPM decided to continue demonstrating every day and added the Henke & Pillot supermarket on Crawford to the list of targets. Like Weingarten's, and Mading's, Henke & Pillot quickly shut down its counter. Plainclothes officers wandered through all three stores. Someone phoned in a bomb threat at Henke & Pillot, but investigators turned up nothing.

That night, twenty-seven-year-old Felton Turner was stopped by two masked whites who ordered him into their car at gunpoint. They had been hired, they said, because "those students at Texas Southern University were getting too much publicity." Turner gave to a news reporter the following account of what happened next:

When I was in the car they beat me with a chain. . . . When we got to the field, the tallest man said, "Give him the works." That was when they beat me with a chain again, and the short man cut me with a knife. I was afraid they would kill me. So I acted as if I was unconscious. But I could tell they were cutting some kind of design on me. . . . The tall man climbed into the tree with a rope. They tied my hands and knees and pulled me up [by my feet] until I was resting on my head and shoulders.

After his kidnappers left, Turner worked himself free, walked to a nearby night watchman's shack, and called the police. When he looked at his body in a lighted room, Turner saw two sets of the letters "KKK" gouged into his stomach. The incisions were one-sixteenth of an inch deep and three and one-half inches high.

Turner's grisly and highly publicized experience sent shudders throughout the state. Senator Ralph Yarborough called for swift legal action and condemned the violence as "a disgrace to Texas, America, the Christian ethic, and Western Civilization." Stearns immediately saw the public relations bonanza in Felton Turner and issued him an award on behalf of the Student Protest Movement.

When it became clear that the sit-in movement in Houston was not going to fold, Mayor Cutrer and others increased the pressure on Nabrit. While presidents at other state universities capitulated to white politicians, Sam Nabrit stood firm. A Ph.D. in biological sciences from Brown University and former member of Dwight Eisenhower's National Science Board, he was already a figure of national stature. (Nabrit was later appointed to the Atomic Energy Commission by President Lyndon Johnson.) Moreover, his brother, attorney James Nabrit, had worked with Thurgood Marshall on the NAACP lawsuits in Harris County that defeated the all-white primary and opened up the University of Texas Law School.

On Tuesday, March 15, Nabrit called together a general assembly of students and faculty to make his views public. He began by saying that he was not afraid to lose his job. He and his wife could afford to live on their savings if necessary. Nabrit viewed the issue as one of citizenship rather than of academic policy. The students had violated no laws or TSU regulations, and he had no desire to control their activities. "If all the other students in the South are viewing segregation as unjust and morally wrong, then there would be something wrong with our teaching, if our students thought otherwise," he said. "Our view then is that it is the democratic right of students to seek remedial measures for social injustices within the framework of law. *We stand with our students.*"

We decided to march on City Hall . . .
to stir up some fire under the mayor's
Biracial Committee. . . . Inside the
Student Union I stood on a table. . . .
"We must go down there and show
them that we are not tired." . . .
I never looked back to count or
discount as we made our way to City
Hall. . . . [W]e approached angry white
faces. . . . A reporter asked me,
"Stearns, how many people are behind
you?" To which I answered, "All those
not in front of me are behind me."

Eldrewey Stearns

In its story on Nabrit's TSU speech the next day, the *Houston Post* failed to mention his ringing endorsement of students' democratic right to protest. Instead, the *Post* focused on the conciliatory comments that Nabrit apparently made directly to the press after the speech. He told reporters that students had successfully dramatized the issue of segregated eating facilities. He was quoted suggesting that it was time for negotiations to take the place of demonstrations. Nabrit said that he'd been in contact with Mayor Cutrer and Police Chief Shuptrine, both of whom assured him that they were working on behalf of a peaceful and orderly solution. He underscored this as a victory by pointing out that other southern cities had not reached the point of negotiations until after arrests and considerable violence.

While Nabrit supported the goals of the sit-ins and the students' right to nonviolent protest, he was also keenly aware that his state-funded university campus depended on the goodwill of powerful whites. As student protests spread and attracted increased publicity, the mayor and others leaned on Nabrit to squelch the movement. Nabrit balanced conflicting pressures and loyalties with great finesse: he supported the movement and its goals while cooperating with the mayor's efforts to contain militant student leaders. He publicly supported the students' democratic rights to protest yet quietly decided that the movement's headquarters should be removed from the campus.

During the same week he delivered his speech on the sit-ins, Nabrit called Charles Lee and informed him that students could no longer use TSU facilities to plan their protests. He simultaneously assured Lee of his personal support and promised that no student would be expelled for civil rights activities as long as he was president. Lee immediately contacted Quentin Mease, who encouraged the students to use the nearby South Central YMCA as a planning and staging area for demonstrations. Mease was already an effective mentor for Stearns. Locating movement headquarters in the South Central Y increased Mease's influence, allowing him to serve as master strategist, steadying hand, and bridge to powerful people in both the African American and the white communities.

After the first week of demonstrations, Cutrer and city attorney Richard H. Burks began a series of early morning briefings with members of the Houston Police Department. A native of Mississippi, Cutrer had grown up believing that white supremacy and segregation were simply the natural order of things. Nevertheless, remembers Sam Nabrit, he made a concerted effort to "lay aside personal prejudice and act as a Christian." Cutrer told police officers that their job was "to see that people conduct themselves in a peaceable manner, regardless of race or creed." He reminded the men of their "grave responsibility" and urged them to act based on law rather than emotion. "The eyes of the world have been on Houston the last week to see if we can handle this calmly, intelligently, and fairly," said City Attorney Burks.

On Monday, March 14, Mayor Cutrer came to the TSU campus. "He came, as you can imagine, with a police patrol and everything else, horns honking . . . to indicate his power." Nabrit had arranged a meeting between the mayor and student leaders in the TSU board room. "I think his first intention was to try to frighten them directly, since he couldn't do it by his public communication," remembers Nabrit. The students were not dissuaded. Next, Cutrer offered to set up negotiations if the demonstrations ceased. Nabrit asked the dean of students, Dr. J. B. Jones, to arrange a meeting at City Hall between Mayor Cutrer and student leaders. Jones contacted Charles Lee, Eldrewey Stearns, and Earl Allen and told them that the mayor wanted to meet with them downtown. On Tuesday, as Dr. Nabrit was speaking about the demonstrations to over 3,000 students and faculty on the TSU campus, Mayor Cutrer met at City Hall with Dr. Jones, Lee, Stearns, and Allen.

The student leaders came to the meeting expecting to work out a compromise directly with the mayor. Instead, Cutrer informed them that they were subject to arrest if they continued to demonstrate after being asked to leave lunch counters. Stearns and Allen said that they had no intention of halting the demonstrations. Lee, however, began having second thoughts. After concluding that this meeting was designed to intimidate them, Allen got up to leave. Dr. Jones asked them to stay. "We're gonna continue to do what we're doing because he [Cutrer]'s not givin' an inch," replied Allen. "He's just tellin' us what we can't do."

After this meeting, the press spoke to members of the group individually. Cutrer said he had requested an end to the sit-ins "to assist in removing any cause that would result in violence, which we are trying so desperately to avoid." The mayor saw his job primarily in terms of protecting the peace in a city where free enterprise reigned supreme. In Houston, supporting property rights meant supporting the practice of segregation. Cutrer's position was that a lunch-counter proprietor had the legal right to serve or deny services to anyone. J. B. Jones pointedly clarified TSU's position: "We have no official responsibility in this matter. The university is neither fostering nor promoting the activity." Allen told reporters that students hoped to meet with officials of stores with closed lunch counters to discuss a solution.

That evening, the next phase of the plan to contain student militants unfolded. TSU administrator Dr. B. A. Turner invited students Allen, Stearns, Graves, Boudois, and King to his house for dinner. Boudois, an undergraduate student from Haiti and the most militant of the group, immediately sensed the purpose of the dinner. When Turner raised the issue of the demonstrations, Boudois interrupted and asked if he would mind serving dinner before discussing the sit-ins. Surprised by this brash request, Turner agreed but asked why it was made.

"I feel that I'm going to disagree with what you have to say," Boudois replied, according to Otis King. "And after I have taken exception to what you have to say, I would not feel comfortable eating your food, and I'm very hungry. So can we go ahead and eat? Then I can disagree with you."

After dinner, Turner got right to the point: "You have dramatized the situation, now let someone else resolve it." He suggested that negotiations with older adults were taking place behind the scenes. "You guys have done a magnificent job. . . . Now it's time you young people step back and let us negotiators move in and handle it." Politely but firmly, the students told Turner that they would not back off, despite his view that the demonstrations threatened the university's funding.

After the group broke up for the evening, Stearns and Graves went back to Stearns's apartment. Fear and loneliness set in again. While both wanted to continue demonstrating, they were discouraged by the TSU administration's efforts to rein them in. "We didn't know what the hell was going to happen," Graves remembers.

Stearns was frightened by the sudden realization that he had no one to protect him. He called his young physician friend, Dr. Herman Barnett, and told him that he was totally consumed by the movement, that he wasn't eating or sleeping and was afraid that he would die. "What do you expect me to do?" Barnett shot back. "Someone has to die for it." Next, Stearns went to Dr. Nabrit with his fears: "I'm willing to die for the movement, but I don't want to get hurt." As it turned out, he was denied this wish. Eldrewey Stearns was destined to become not a martyr but a deeply wounded and forgotten casualty of the movement.

That night, Stearns and Graves talked openly about the possibility of dying. Stearns called it "the crisis" — living through the decision that integration was important enough to die for. Graves's mother had called from New Orleans to ask whether he was safe. Stearns had talked to his mother in Galveston; Devona Stearns was proud of her son. She had no inkling of the toll the next few years would take. Feeling a strong need for adult protection and leadership, Stearns and Graves decided to call Martin Luther King, Jr., and ask him to come to Houston. At a speech in Durham, North Carolina, King had recently endorsed the sit-ins. He was the first established leader to praise the student protesters:

What is fresh, what is new in your fight is the fact that it was initiated, led, and sustained by students. What is new is that American students have come of age. You now take your honored places in the world-wide struggle for freedom. . . . If the officials threaten to arrest us for standing up for our rights, we must answer by saying that we are willing and prepared to fill up the jails of the South. . . . And so I would urge you to continue your struggle.

Graves had known one of King's chief lieutenants, Andrew Young, since their days together at a YMCA summer camp in New Orleans. He called Young, who gave them King's phone number. They reached King in Atlanta. For about twenty minutes, they recounted the story of their demonstrations, their fears and uncertainties. "We laid all the stuff at his feet," Graves remembers. "And when it was over we were quiet, to wait for him to say what he was gonna do for us, you know, 'I'll be in on the next plane . . . I'll send Andy Young. I'll send somebody.'" But instead, King took them both by surprise. "Very quietly, very calmly, he said, 'I'll tell God about it.'"

Stearns and Graves hung up the phone and stared at each other in silence. "Was he really gonna tell God about it? Was he on his knees right now? We were trying to figure out what was going on," Graves recalls. "We thought that we had wasted our long distance telephone call and that he had either given us a double shuffle or that he was really in touch with God. We didn't know which one it was. . . . Eldrewey and I were just looking at one another, saying 'What the hell do we do now?'"

While Charles Lee and Bill Lawson were inclined to halt the demonstrations and work toward a negotiated solution, Stearns worked at fever pitch to expand the number of targets and participants. The following week, about 150 students moved boldly beyond the relative safety of their TSU neighborhood and began sit-ins at downtown stores on Main Street, the domain of Houston's white business establishment: Foley's, Grants, Walgreen, and Kress. They followed a precise and orderly schedule, arriving at 3 and leaving promptly at 4:30. Despite Cutrer's announcement that students could be arrested, lunch-counter operators shut down their counters rather than call the police. With this bold and disciplined move downtown, the students regained the initiative; for the next few weeks, the elements of surprise and momentum were on their side.

One day in mid-March, student firebrand Guy Boudois came across the news that the Argentinian ambassador, Emilio Donato del Carril, would be visiting Houston on Friday, March 25. Boudois called Stearns and they decided to send a group to the City Hall cafeteria: either the students would receive service or they would succeed in embarrassing the city. Boudois rented a room from the honorary consul to Haiti and TSU professor of history, Dr. J. Reuben Scheeler. "Doc would leave his consular information and notices . . . on his desk," Holly Hogrobrooks remembers. "And Guy, in the process of cleaning up his offices, would happen to see these. And somehow we would happen to know which ambassador was coming in, when and where. And we would be able to meet him with a demonstration. Nobody could ever figure out how we were getting that kind of information."

Historically, both the City Hall cafeteria and the County Courthouse cafeteria had been closed to blacks. No one had tried to integrate either facility since April 1956, when Matthew W. Plummer, then an investigator for the Harris County district attorney's office, and four other African Americans sought to enter the courthouse cafeteria as customers. Plummer and attorney Henry E. Doyle had filed a lawsuit to open the courthouse cafeteria and were attempting to eat in a public facility where they worked. Coming down the stairway to the basement facility, Plummer was slugged by staunch segregationist J. M. Wren. "It's trash like you that is causing all this trouble," Wren shouted at Plummer, who retreated silently. "The good niggers don't want this, and neither do we. It's tramps like you that are part white that are causing this trouble. We don't want you people." Wren charged that the NAACP was a Communist-backed organization aiming to take over the county courthouse. "If you're going to have a riot, let's have it now," he shouted. The group — composed of Plummer and Doyle, Lillie Marie Alonzo, attorney Francis Williams, Robert Ford, and Nina McGowen, a reporter for a black local weekly, the *Informer* — quietly turned around and walked upstairs to the main floor. Plummer later charged Wren with assault, but an all-white jury found him not guilty.

Four years later, the cracks in the edifice of segregation had widened considerably. Stearns called John "Doc" Miller and asked him to assemble a large group of students to picket City Hall at 9 A.M. on Friday, March 25. He also contacted Mayor Lewis Cutrer and informed him about the planned sit-in and picketing. Cutrer told Stearns that he would not take sides, that the issue was between the students and the merchants — a weak argument, since the cafeteria was housed in a building owned by the city.

Miller called about fifty students and instructed them to meet early Friday morning at the YMCA. Thirty actually showed up at the Y and were driven down to City Hall with picket signs reading "Don't Get Angry — Think!" and "We Want a Freedom Sandwich" and "No More Back-Door-to-Go Service." Stearns and Otis King led them on a march around City Hall, singing, "What a friend we have in Jesus / Oh, what needless pain we bear. . . ." Half a dozen white students from Rice and the University of Houston joined the demonstration, bringing the number to about thirty-five.

About ten minutes after the picketing began, the Argentinian ambassador and consular officials arrived; looking a bit confused, they walked past picket signs and made their way into the building. After several hours, Miller led several students inside the building to the cafeteria. They sat down at a table and waited. White patrons, mostly city employees, angrily got up and left. A crowd began milling around outside the cafeteria, looking in through big glass windows. The manager, Mrs. Elenora Russell, called Mayor Cutrer, but he refused to talk with her. Mrs. Russell then called councilman Louie Welch, who was upstairs in the council chambers. She was afraid of getting in trouble if she served the students, she told Welch. "Serve them," Welch responded, "because if you don't you are going to get into trouble. They are citizens of the city and this is a city building, so serve them." Mrs. Russell told Welch that the crowd of people outside the cafeteria was getting bigger. He said he'd be right down.

Meanwhile, Garvin Berry, a reporter for the *Houston Press*, received a phone call from a City Hall employee: "You better come on down here to the cafeteria. We've got a student demonstration here and we're fixin' to have some trouble." Berry came running down the steps from the press room on the third floor at City Hall. Then the elevator door opened and councilman Louie Welch elbowed his way through the crowd. "Get those niggers out of there," someone yelled. "Here comes the councilman, he'll throw them out," yelled another. "So he came elbowing through," Berry remembers, "pushing all the way and he looked in there" and saw the black students sitting alone at one big long table. "And he looked around. . . . And he said, 'Well, we don't *all* have to be damn fools, do we?' And he walked in, picked up a tray, went over and sat at a table beside 'em and started talking to 'em. And defused the situation."

By 4 P.M., about twenty-five black students had been served coffee, soft drinks, and cheese crackers. "This was our first home run," Guy Boudois told a reporter for the *Houston Post*. The students, however, were in for a very long game, and many of the strongest players were not yet on the field.

While many whites supported integration of the City Hall cafeteria, they apparently didn't make up for the lost business of those who boycotted. The following day, Mike Russell, the owner of the cafeteria, in an attempt to get his white customers back, announced that he would not integrate his facility. Serving the students didn't produce integration anyway, he told reporters. "It was just a matter of the Negroes coming in and the whites staying out." Russell said that he received so many calls protesting cafeteria service to blacks that he had gone fishing over the weekend to get away from the telephone.

Meanwhile, Louie Welch called Stearns and asked him not to send students back to the City Hall cafeteria. "Russell said he will call you and said he'll make it worth your while," Welch added, according to Stearns. When Russell called, he appealed to Stearns's heart as well as his pocketbook. "I have two boys in college and I know you've been to college. . . . You know how I feel about this?"

"I certainly do, I understand how you feel about this," answered Stearns.

"Well, I'll make it worth your while," Russell continued, according to Stearns, " . . . if you will just pull back your people and tell them to please lay off me and go and fight the mayor." Stearns replied that he could not promise anything. It is unclear whether Russell actually paid him off, but the demonstrations at City Hall ceased even though the cafeteria reverted to segregation.

By the third week in March, the students were having more impact than the city had anticipated. The mayor came under growing and conflicting pressures to act more forcefully. The demonstrations were still receiving front-page press coverage and had begun to hurt the sales of several downtown businesses. Both the Houston Council on Human Relations and the Houston Council on Education in Race Relations (HCERR) urged Cutrer to appoint a biracial committee to study the problem. Reverend George J. Aven, president of the HCERR, wrote to the Retail Merchants' Association (RMA) asking that the merchants accede to the students' "reasonable and legitimate requests." Aven called on the retail merchants to take part in public meetings of "Houstonians who are concerned that our community continue to grow and prosper free of the disorder and violence which took their toll on business and community life in Little Rock," where President Dwight Eisenhower had sent federal troops to quell violence and enforce high school integration in September 1957. On behalf of the Retail Merchants' Association, W. J. Wallace replied that he supported the idea of a communitywide committee and stood ready to provide the mayor with representatives from the RMA.

Of course, various groups defined "the problem" differently: for the downtown merchants, it was the disruption of business; for the student protesters, it was the outrageous practice of segregation; for many older African Americans, it was how to support progress toward equal rights without jeopardizing jobs and other previous personal and collective gains; for the city's administration and power elite, it was how to avoid violence and embarrassment — how to maintain Houston's image as a booming, progressive southern city, ripe for investment and international trade.

Shortly after the demonstration at City Hall, Charles Lee got a phone call inviting him to a meeting with the mayor and several leading figures: Jack Valenti, then public relations assistant to the mayor; Leon Jaworski, then head of the Houston Chamber of Commerce and partner in one of the city's biggest law firms; and Reverend L. H. Simpson of the Pleasant Hill Baptist Church, the most prominent preacher in the African American community and a vocal opponent of the sit-ins. This group convinced Lee to try to halt the demonstrations; in return, the mayor would agree to appoint a biracial committee to study the situation and make recommendations.

Although he didn't recognize it at first, Lee soon understood that the city would protect him. Many mornings that spring, when he left his house on Barbee Street for the day, he'd see a man sitting in an unfamiliar car parked across the street. His wife was tailed when she went to her mother's house three blocks away or took their children to school or music lessons. When Lee went to file a complaint for harassment, he was told that these men were undercover agents assigned for his protection. Hobart Taylor and Jack Valenti confirmed this and assured him that his family would not be hurt.

As soon as Lee decided to pursue the path of negotiation, he contacted Bill Lawson, Eldrewey Stearns, and Earl Allen. Within a day, they had drafted and signed a letter to the mayor, stating that they would stop demonstrating if the mayor appointed a biracial committee. Stearns and Allen were reluctant to sign the letter, feeling that the committee was simply a delaying tactic designed to keep students from demonstrating until they went home

for the summer. Nevertheless, Lee and Lawson prevailed on them
to sign the letter to the mayor, which read in part:

> **You have been, we feel, generous and lenient in this entire crisis—as generous as a Caucasian without the experience of segregation can be—and we believe that the City of Houston has been the most discreet and judicious in the current wave of Southern crises.**
>
> **But there is another side to the coin. We are determined. We may lose jobs or friends or life, but we will not lose purpose. You have implied that if the demonstrations were stopped you might appoint a committee to talk with us. Once before we stopped but no actions were taken. Nevertheless, we will gladly stop again if we may have confidence in negotiations that will be in good faith. . . . It is not now, nor never has been, our intention to do with brute action what ought to be accomplished through civilized negotiations.**
>
> **Frankly our feet are tired, our families are unhappy, and we are behind in our lessons.**
>
> **We want to comply with your proposal to come to gentlemanly terms at a conference table with city merchants.**

Even as Mayor Cutrer prepared to appoint a biracial committee, he reiterated his view that local government had no obligation to resolve the disputed issues. The sit-ins, he told a press conference, were "an economic rather than a civil rights campaign," and merchants had to make their own decisions. "The laws of our state say that private enterprise should have freedom of choice in determining customers they wish to serve."

On April 7, 1960, Mayor Cutrer appointed forty-one Houstonians to a "Citizens' Relations Committee," which he insisted would be strictly advisory. Francis Williams, then president of the local NAACP chapter, welcomed the formation of the committee but withheld judgment about its workings. The committee included businessmen, professionals, and religious, labor, civic, and educational leaders. Roughly one-quarter of the members were African American; they included local physician Dr. A. W. Beal; the dean of students at TSU, Mrs. Ina Bolton; TSU students Charles Lee and Deanna Lott; Reverend John Moore; Dr. Samuel Nabrit; Reverend L. H. Simpson; prominent entrepreneur Hobart Taylor; A. E. Warner, president of the Negro Chamber of Commerce; and attorney Aloysius Wickliff, president of the Harris County Council of Organizations, an umbrella organization of black business, professional, and political interests. Prominent whites on the committee included George E. Dentler, president of the Houston Restaurant Association; attorney Leon Jaworski; Dr. Lewis McAdow, president of the Association of Ministers of Greater Houston; Dr. Hyman J. Schactel, rabbi of Congregation Beth Israel; Howard Tellepsen, developer and chairman of the Port Commission; Jack Valenti, the mayor's press secretary; and W. J. Wallace, secretary-manager of the Retail Merchants' Association. Other members included representatives of the American Legion, the League of Women Voters, local television stations, students from Rice, St. Thomas, and the University of Houston, and Felix Tijerina, a restauranteur and leader of the League of United Latin American Citizens (LULAC).

Like their counterparts in Atlanta, many of Houston's business leaders believed that they could wait until students went home for the summer vacation and return to business as usual in the fall. These intentions gradually became obvious even to conservative blacks, many of whom eventually came to support the tactics of direct action. Leon Jaworski was particularly determined to stop the demonstrations, which he thought harmed the city's image and threatened to erupt into violence. At the beginning of the committee's deliberations, Jaworski called for secrecy and asked the members to vote on a statement condemning the students for trespassing on private property. He was shocked when a majority voted against him.

TSU student Deanna Lott told the committee that the city had a moral obligation to treat blacks with the same respect and privileges accorded to whites. She and others backed A. W. Wickliff's demand for immediate municipal desegregation. Jaworski called for a vote on Wickliff's motion, which carried by a margin of nineteen to three. Then, according to Nabrit, Jaworski "really lost his marbles" and swore the committee to secrecy until he could talk to Mayor Cutrer. "He wanted to make sure that nobody knew what had transpired in there and it never got any press."

After several frustrating meetings, Wickliff wrote a passionate memorandum to fellow members of the Citizens' Relations Committee. Wickliff said he was "greatly disturbed" by the committee's failure to recommend integration. It was a matter of "ordinary human dignity," he argued, for "Negroes in Houston" to enjoy the "rights and privileges that go along with being a real American and a real Texan." Mayor Cutrer never even announced the Citizens' Relations Committee votes.

Meanwhile, Stearns and Lee jockeyed for control of the student movement, which quickly lost steam during the moratorium on the sit-ins. In countless meetings at the Groovey Grill, Earl Allen mediated a constant tug of war between the impulsive Stearns and the military Lee. "Eldrewey was *the* leader. We all understood that," remembers Allen. "Charles Lee was recognized as part of the leadership, but the inspiration behind the whole movement was Eldrewey. Eldrewey could inspire a group of people. When he spoke, he spoke with inspiration. Charles Lee was heavy-handed. People would listen to him, but they soon tuned him out."

Most TSU students were willing to give the committee time to work. Stearns — impatient, angry at losing control of the movement, and determined to keep up the pressure — gave the committee less than a week. He complained to Quentin Mease that he'd been tricked into signing the letter. "I told Quentin Mease what I was going to do. I was going to destroy the whole thing and he said, 'No . . . just take your time and think it out. You'll think it out.' And sure enough, I did, and that was the day I wrote them an ultimatum."

On April 11, Stearns, Otis King, Leo Craig, and Fanny Lovelady sent Mayor Cutrer a letter, stating that if the lunch counters were not integrated within two weeks they would begin demonstrating again. Charles Lee told *Houston Post* reporters that the ultimatum was issued by a splinter group which did not represent the sentiment of the student body. The African American *Pittsburgh Courier* not only carried Lee's remarks, seconded by Deanna Lott, but also printed Stearns's view of the situation — that the organization had "unanimously expelled" Lee because he had accepted an appointment on the mayor's committee. "All for Integration? Houston Student Leaders Battling among Selves" ran the *Pittsburgh Courier* headline.

During the moratorium on demonstrations, Stearns flew to Raleigh, North Carolina, to take part in a Youth Leadership Meeting organized by Ella Baker of the Southern Christian Leadership Conference (SCLC). Baker, who had been a community organizer in New York during the Depression and a field secretary for the NAACP during the 1940s, feared that the caution or self-interest of older leaders might put too many restraints on the new student movement. Roughly 150 students from nine states poured onto the campus of Baker's alma mater, Shaw University. In her opening address on April 15, Baker urged students to develop their own separate organization and to broaden their efforts beyond the lunch counters to the entire segregated social structure. James Lawson, a theology student who had been expelled from Vanderbilt for refusing to withdraw from the movement and was already a nationally known teacher of nonviolent tactics, served as "dean" of the conference.

In his keynote address, Lawson criticized the NAACP for being preoccupied with lawsuits and fundraising; the older leaders, he argued, seemed uninterested in their most important resource: "a people no longer the victims of racial evil, who can act in a disciplined manner to implement the Constitution." Martin Luther King took the podium and declared that the sit-ins were not only a blow against white racism, they were also a revolt against "the apathy and complacency of adults in the Negro community . . . who indulge in buying cars and homes instead of taking on the great cause that will really solve their problems." King made three recommendations: a national organization (which became known as the Student Non-Violent Coordinating Committee); a campaign of "selective buying" to punish segregated variety-store chains; and a cadre of volunteers willing to go to jail rather than to raise bail or pay fines. Above all, King emphasized his philosophy of nonviolence.

The Raleigh trip gave Stearns exactly the boost he needed to continue the struggle in Houston. During a layover at Idlewild Airport in New York, he picked up a white-and-gold dinner plate that he planned to use as a prop in a speech aimed at reigniting the student movement. He returned home late on April 24, the date he had set for resuming demonstrations if Houston's lunch counters had not been integrated. Well past midnight, Stearns let himself into the South Central YMCA. Forgoing sleep, he typed up and mimeographed a few thousand leaflets announcing a mass meeting at noon the next day. He spent the morning passing out leaflets and building support for the rally.

About two hundred students filed into the YMCA gymnasium at noon on April 25. Most were just as hesitant and confused as the original seventeen had been on March 4, when the movement was launched at the TSU flagpole. Otis King and Earl Allen spoke first on behalf of the "New Negro" militancy and argued for resuming the demonstrations. Allen then introduced Stearns as the leader who had done more for Houston than any other man. Stearns walked to the podium and held up his dinner plate: "This plate symbolizes that today we shall eat," he shouted. He recounted King's powerful message from the Raleigh meeting and called on the students to take to the streets again.

The crowd was still roaring its approval of Stearns's rousing oratory when Charles Lee came to the podium. "Wait a minute, you all," he insisted, according to Stearns. "We're not going anywhere. You're not going anywhere. We can't go downtown because we're not ready." Lee, who had been in charge of logistics, pointed out that they had no organization—no prearranged target, no transportation, and no schedule. The crowd sat back down. Bill Lawson then addressed the assembly. "We've waited for four hundred years," he reminded them. "To avoid violence, we can wait a little longer." Lawson, who enjoyed enormous respect from the student body, encouraged them to back off and let the negotiations proceed. If the students would slow the pace down, he argued, things would work themselves out.

After Lawson spoke, students began talking quietly among themselves. Stearns understood the prudent reasoning of Lee and Lawson, but he realized that his power and influence were at stake. "I had given an ultimatum," he remembers. "God, nobody else . . . [would] help me if I turned around then." Several people stepped up to the podium and said they weren't going to demonstrate. The crowd began filing out of the auditorium. "If you're not with me, then God's with me," shouted Stearns as the room emptied out.

At the end of the meeting, only a handful of students remained. Guy Boudois, Otis King, Curtis Graves, Holly and Ted Hogrobrooks, Jimmy Lofton, Charles Guidry, Jessie Hughes, and several others remained loyal to Stearns, even though it appeared that Houston's student protest movement, not yet two months old, was mortally wounded, if not dead. "Well, Drew, buddy boy, we can't go now," said Boudois. Stearns refused to admit defeat. "I felt it necessary for me to be this spiritual force, this moving force that kept them going," he remembers. "The only thing that saved me that day was Holly Hogrobrooks. She came forth and said, 'We're the splinter group all right, so let's be a splinter in their side.'"

Sitting in the YMCA lobby, while the other students waited on benches inside the gymnasium, Stearns convinced Boudois to stick with him; they decided on a new name to resuscitate their organization — the Progressive Youth Association (PYA). The two went inside and rallied the troops around their new strategy. Boudois thought that demonstrating on Main Street was too dangerous and, with characteristic savvy, suggested the Greyhound Bus Station at Texas and Prairie, where the employees were already threatening to strike for higher wages.

Curtis Graves led a quickly assembled group down to the bus station, a place frequented by poor whites who might not take kindly to the demonstrators. They expected to be jailed by nightfall. Stearns called the press. He and Otis King stayed at the YMCA, waiting to line up a bail bondsman and an attorney. "And Curtis called," remembers King. "And we thought he was gonna say, 'Hey, I've been arrested,' or 'We're being arrested.' . . . [Instead] he said in a very dejected sounding tone — Curtis has got a deep voice — 'Drew, they're feeding us.' And we just whooped, because he was disappointed! And he didn't realize then . . . how momentous this was, that the whole tactic had *worked!*" They left the YMCA, ran to the Groovey Grill, and asked Mrs. Prince to turn on the television. On the six o'clock news, local reporter Dan Rather quietly announced that Negro students had been served at the Greyhound Bus Station.

The April 25 victory at the Greyhound Bus Station breathed new energy and life into the movement. The PYA became a formal organization with officers, community advisors, letterhead, and paid memberships. Stearns appointed himself executive director. Annual membership cards sold first for fifty cents or one dollar, later for two, five, and ten dollars. On the back of the membership card, the Progressive Youth Association, whose very name was an offense to Houston's conservative political atmosphere, listed the following purposes and objectives:

1. **Total integration of all facets of American life.**
2. **Civil and Political Education.**
3. **Inter-Racial Communication.**
4. **Education for individual competence.**
5. **Improvement of economic status.**
6. **Attainment of recreational facilities.**
7. **Promotion of good will through public relations.**
8. **Propagation of Spiritual and Democratic ideals.**
9. **To obtain better job opportunity.**

The PYA included students from TSU, Rice, and the University of Houston as well as community members. Stearns initiated a public relations campaign to promote his own visibility and that of the new organization. Quentin Mease continued to open doors for him both among the black middle class and in the white community. Drs. Herman Barnett and C. W. Thompson brought Stearns to the all-black Houston Medical Forum. He also appeared regularly at churches and community organizations to raise money for rent, telephones, demonstration materials, and the like.

The same day that Stearns had sent his ultimatum letter to the mayor, he had also written to Harry Graves, dean of the TSU law school, requesting permission to withdraw. Though he remained in touch with Quentin Mease every day, Stearns quit his job at the YMCA and devoted himself entirely to the movement. Although enrolled since the fall of 1957, Stearns had never concentrated on the study of law; he was often on probation for marginal grades and missed classes. His strengths and weaknesses as a student were well captured by James Blawie, a former teacher from Michigan State who wrote in support of his application to the TSU law school:

> Mr. Stearnes [*sic*] is a man of high intelligence and considerable wit. He is a born public speaker—a crowd-pleaser, you might well say. At Michigan State, he had his finger in every pie, belonging, to my own knowledge, to about every major club on campus and being active in them. As a

student, Mr. Stearnes was somewhat of a disappointment, not in that he did not do satisfactory work (he was a high C, low B student) but in that he could have done so much better if he had expended the least effort. He has a breadth of vision and a scholar's mind, if he can be kept at work. . . . If he can concentrate his efforts, he should stand high in his class.

For reasons that later became sadly apparent, Stearns was never able to channel his remarkable powers into a sustained course of academic study or work. For the next several years, however, in bursts of incredible energy, audacity, and brilliance, he devoted his powerful intellect and charismatic speaking ability to fighting segregation. He was a mercurial figure, apparently sociable but also aloof; he projected an imposing persona, yet people also felt that there was something strange about him. Earl Allen remembers the powerful and confusing impression Stearns made during their first conversation:

I don't know how long he talked, but it seemed like it must have been a couple of hours! So when I got through with him, I said, "Eldrewey, you know what?" (And I think this is when our friendship developed.) I said, "Either you are a genius or you're a damn fool. . . ." So we hit it off, and I always admired him because he was such a visionary, a go-getter. . . . He was ahead of his time, anyways. I was in-spired. I was moved by it. No question about it.

Many people saw Stearns's unwavering boldness as selfless devotion; after all, he gave up his job at the YMCA and — temporarily — his place in the law school for no apparent personal gain. Other people began to view him as a con man who said he was raising money for the PYA but seemed to pocket much of it for himself. Actually, both views were correct. The trouble was, at certain moments, Stearns was literally selfless — unable to perceive any boundaries between himself and the movement. This was at once a source of unusual creativity and of seriously distorted perception. Thinking about the mass of students who defected from him at the YMCA auditorium, for example, he remembers his refusal to accept defeat: "I became a movement

within a movement in other words. That became my movement. . . . I felt then if I did not honor that ultimatum . . . then I
was dead. There would be no Eldrewey Stearns."

The success of the PYA and the obvious footdragging of the
mayor's Citizens' Relations Committee led Reverend Bill Lawson
to reconsider his views on the tactics of direct action. He suggested that the students consider a boycott and offered his home
as a place to make strategy as well as picket signs. The PYA announced that their next activity would be a well-publicized one-
day boycott of selected downtown stores. Veteran railroad labor
union leader Moses Leroy and others suggested that the PYA join
forces with the NAACP. The students — unwilling to take a back
seat to their elders — declined a joint effort. Targeting Foley's,
Kress, Woolworth's, Walgreen, Grants, and Weingarten's, the students made and circulated signs asking African Americans to boycott these stores on May 7, which they christened "No-Shopping
Day." On the evening of May 6, Drs. Herman Barnett and C. W.
Thompson accompanied Stearns to black nightclubs, where he
announced the next day's boycott.

Although it was largely a symbolic action, the boycott attracted
considerable interest in the black community. It was followed by
picketing the next week, when noticeably fewer African Americans shopped at targeted stores. On May 21, 1960, the fledgling
black *Forward Times* newspaper — which tended to avoid conflict
and emphasize positive accomplishments — noted that the Houston Public Library, city buses, and Jeppersen Stadium had quietly
integrated. Meanwhile, Weingarten's store #23 located at 5810
Lyons Avenue, in the heart of the mostly black Fifth Ward, ele-
vated two employees from stock checkers to cashiers. "The importance of this move," wrote the *Forward Times* reporter eu-
phorically, "is that another invisible barrier has fallen. . . ."

The mayor's Citizens' Relations Committee, however, produced little to cheer about. Whites on the committee were dis-
mayed at their inability to control the revitalized student movement, which was gaining new support in the black establishment.
Wickliff and his allies on the committee held firmly to their call
for immediate municipal desegregation. The May 10 meeting
ended with noisy verbal exchanges after the committee chair,
J. P. Hamblen, refused to bring any motions to a vote. No further

meetings were called, and the mayor disbanded the committee in early June.

On June 19, the *Forward Times* threw a party for Foley's black employees on Juneteenth, the annual African American celebration commemorating the day that news of Lincoln's Emancipation Proclamation arrived in Texas. It was a curious scene: the PYA was outside picketing against Foley's segregated practices; downstairs in the basement, black employees were celebrating Juneteenth under the auspices of the *Forward Times*, which was trying to enhance its visibility as well as its revenues from Foley's advertisements. Freddy Goodall, who was both an employee and a PYA member, joined the picketing rather than the celebration. Stearns was offended by the *Forward Times* party; he made a special appeal, urging blacks to cancel their credit accounts and stop patronizing Foley's and other segregated businesses.

Although no one knew it at the time, when Stearns and the demonstrators reached Foley's, they met their match. This biggest downtown department store was the turf of Bob Dundas, then in charge of Foley's entire advertising and public relations campaign. Dundas had been working at Foley's since 1925. He was a hard-bitten, old-fashioned political fixer and lobbyist who played for keeps and worked faithfully with the city's ruling elite. Dundas was a complicated man: driven by personal ambition, committed to the welfare of the city, and haunted by fear of racial violence. Born in 1904, he was barely a teenager the night of August 23, 1917, when the telephone operator called his home in a panic: the "nigger" soldiers at Camp Logan were rioting and shooting. Dundas's father grabbed his gun and went downtown to protect the city. Later, Dundas went to the morgue and saw the bodies of sixteen whites — including five policeman — who had been killed in the insurrection.

In 1960, Dundas could see that a federal solution would ultimately be imposed on the city if Houston didn't act on its own. "I was tired of all the pussy-footing around by all these other groups," he remembers. After the failure of the mayor's Citizens' Relations Committee, Dundas shouldered the role of primary broker in behind-the-scenes discussions in the white business community. Motivated by personal ambition, fear of violence, a sense of community responsibility, and the financial interests of

Foley's, Dundas worked tirelessly. After several months of strong-arming, economic leveraging, and moral suasion, he secured an agreement that seventy lunch counters in supermarkets, drug-stores, and department stores would be silently integrated during the last week of August. Not only did Dundas broker the arrange-ment with lunch-counter operators, but he also made sure that there would be no press coverage of the historic event.

Dundas was in constant communication with John T. Jones, Jr., publisher of the *Houston Chronicle* and president of the Hous-ton Endowment, which controlled the vast local real estate and commercial empire accumulated by his late uncle, Jesse Jones. To the dismay of the southern traditionalists on the Board of the Endowment, Jones supported and encouraged Dundas. A con-templative man of enormous power and few words, Jones favored desegregation for two simple reasons: it was good business and it was good citizenship. He promised that neither the *Chronicle* nor radio station KTRH, which the endowment also owned, would breathe a word about lunch-counter integration for ten days.

Dundas got similar promises from Oveta Culp Hobby, who owned and operated the *Houston Post*. Next, he approached Jack Harris, formerly General Douglas MacArthur's chief of informa-tion during World War II, then in charge of the Hobbys' televi-sion and radio stations, KPRC-TV and KPRC-AM. Harris had been wooed to Houston in 1947 by Governor William Hobby and Oveta Culp Hobby, who later served as secretary of Health, Edu-cation, and Welfare in the first Eisenhower administration. Dun-das knew that his plan could still fall apart and didn't know what to expect from Harris. "Have you ever been in a race riot?" Harris asked Dundas. "It's the most horrible thing I've ever seen. Don't worry, I'll take care of the whole damn thing. You forget about it. There won't be a peep." Dundas, who was then handling the en-tire news blackout by himself, was immensely relieved. "I could have kissed him," he remembers.

Not everyone thought that the blackout was a good idea. George Carmack, editor of the now defunct *Houston Press*, ac-cepted the blackout reluctantly, after Dundas threatened to pull Foley's lucrative advertising from his paper. Carmack "was a tra-ditional newspaper man," remembers John T. Jones, Jr.: " . . . if you got news, publish it. He was the editor, but his business manager sat on him enough so he *was* quiet. But Carmack never did agree that he did the right thing." Jones, on the other hand, felt that it was necessary to suppress the news to accomplish integration without violence. He knew the truth of the old banker's adage: "When peace reigns, interest runs."

When it came to integrating Foley's lunch counter, Bob Dundas left nothing to chance: he personally wrote the script, assigned the parts, and directed the stage production. He called Sam Nabrit and asked him to assemble a group of orderly students. He arranged a police escort for them. After the students arrived at Foley's, he kept policemen at the door and relied on private bodyguards to handle the situation inside Foley's.

Dundas, who was threatened by segregationists more than once during this period, personally warned white toughs off the premises. A partition was placed between the counter and the glass window, preventing passersby from viewing the scene. Students were not allowed to come and go on their own. Herbert Hamilton remembers trying to sit down at Foley's with a white protester named Jim Daniels: "As I walked through the door, two other guys grabbed me from behind and just picked me up and walked back with me. . . . they was trying to protect me from the police, from the people who was there, but they just picked you up and threw you out." On the day when the simultaneous integration plan went into effect for all downtown lunch counters, Dundas made sure that the students were served plenty of food, whether they could afford it or not.

While the downtown merchants and media were executing Dundas's plan, Eldrewey Stearns was in St. Paul, Minnesota, where he attended a congress of the National Student Association, along with 300 other leaders of the sit-in movement. One afternoon, someone handed him a copy of a paper which carried a story on the integration of lunch counters in Houston. Elated, Stearns flew home immediately. "I thought it would be jubilation, almost like fanfare in the streets," he remembers. Instead, he came back to discover that no one knew what had happened. He called Dan Rather, who refused him air time and explained why there would be no news coverage. Infuriated, Stearns complained that he was being robbed of the fruits of all his hard work. "So?" asked Rather.

The Dundas plan simultaneously accomplished two things that had eluded Mayor Cutrer's Citizens' Relations Committee: it integrated the lunch counters and it ended sit-in demonstrations by eliminating the reason for them. The news blackout — which was really an extension of an earlier decision to keep news of demonstrations off the front pages — was so effective that Houstonians only learned about the lunch-counter integration from outside newspapers, radio, and television broadcasts. Even the weekly newspapers in the black community — the *Forward Times* and the *Informer* — failed to carry news of an event that seemed not to have happened.

I saw in the Dome Stadium that it would bring about integration. . . . We had jeeps to go out in the white community. . . . It would be a black driver and a white announcer announcing, "Come vote. Don't fail to support the greatest wonder of the world, the Dome Stadium!" Out in the black neighborhoods, the white boy would be driving and a Negro doing the talking on the loudspeaker, and this is something they hadn't seen, so that got their attention. . . . We won the thing.

Eldrewey Stearns

On September 2, 1960, the Austin-based *Texas Observer* noted Houston's oddly momentous change in racial customs: "Last week, without a line of publicity in any Houston newspaper or over any Houston radio or TV station, lunch counters, in about 70 supermarkets, variety stores, and drug stores were integrated. . . . Newsmen in Houston readily acknowledge that the Houston press had suppressed the news that sit-ins . . . there have succeeded. . . . This resulted in a strange anomaly. Texans everywhere but Houston read about lunch-counter integration. The wire services sent out routine stories which included references to the Houston press clam-up."

In its issue of September 12, *Time* magazine ran a blistering story entitled "Blackout in Houston." The *Time* columnist had little sympathy for suppressing the news in order to protect public safety. "For all their intentions of doing good by stealth, the *Post*, the *Chronicle*, and the *Press* would certainly have found life simpler had they lived up to a motto engraved in stone over the entrance of the Houston *Post* building: LET FACTS BE SUBMITTED TO A CANDID WORLD."

Although John T. Jones gave his blessing to the blackout, he did not intend to allow the *Houston Chronicle* to remain what it had been in the 1950s — a mouthpiece for the city's aging oligarchy, out of step with many in a growing metropolis of a million people, over twenty percent of whom were African American. The afternoon *Chronicle* was losing ground to its rival, the Scripps-Howard *Press*, as well as to Oveta Culp Hobby's morning *Post*. In September 1960, Jones took steps to reverse the paper's decline. He spent almost two days in the Rice Hotel interviewing William P. Steven, a newspaper editor known for invigorating papers in Tulsa, Oklahoma, and in Minnesota. The two men liked each other, and Jones offered Steven the job as editor-in-chief. Before he accepted, Steven wanted to know where his future boss stood on the issue of integration.

"You know, John, there is one thing that troubles me about working in the South that you ought to know. I feel that integration is an essential fact in the demonstration of democracy. I think it is necessary for the full development of the economy. And I think it is the only way to make our foreign policy mean anything in a world of mostly dark skins."

"The *Chronicle* supports the law of the land," Jones replied, according to Steven. "The only trouble I'll have with you is that you may want to talk about it too much." A moderate Republican and friend of Lyndon Johnson, Steven took over the paper and rejuvenated it until 1965, when he was ousted along with Jones by a right-wing coup at the Houston Endowment.

The news blackout and unilateral desegregation of lunch counters quickly sucked the wind out of the PYA's sails. Even influential blacks were taken by surprise. "Negro leaders weren't really included in the negotiations," Sam Nabrit told reporter Saul Friedman in 1965. "The students instigated the movement and the white-power structure decided among themselves to desegregate. And we brought it to the rest of the [Negro] community."

Throughout the fall of 1960, business was slow at the new PYA office in the Afro-American Insurance building, 2206 Dowling. Texas Southern University students starting a new semester were more interested in their studies and in the Nixon/Kennedy presidential election than in the sit-in movement. During the summer, senator and presidential candidate John F. Kennedy had won over many young blacks with a campaign statement supporting the sit-ins: "It is in the American tradition to stand up for one's rights, even if a new way to stand up for one's rights is to sit down."

Back in March, when Eldrewey Stearns and Curtis Graves had asked Martin Luther King, Jr., to join their movement in Houston, King had refused with the ambiguous reply: "I'll tell God about it." In October, King's brother was among the students who asked him to join a sit-in demonstration in Atlanta. This time he agreed.

On October 19, King joined eighty student demonstrators at Rich's department store, where his family had shopped all their lives. He was the first to be arrested. Senator Kennedy placed a personal call to Coretta Scott King, then pregnant with the couple's third child, and expressed his concern. A week later, Robert Kennedy called and urged Judge Mitchell to release King on bail. The next day, Martin Luther King emerged from his first prison experience. He talked about jail as a personal test of faith. His father talked politics: "I had expected to vote against Senator Kennedy because of his religion," said the conservative Baptist

Martin Luther King, Sr. "But now he can be my President, Catholic or whatever he is. It took courage to call my daughter-in-law at a time like this. He has the moral courage to stand up for what he knows is right. I've got all my votes and I've got a suitcase, and I'm going to take them up there and dump them in his lap." Kennedy's support of King may have been the key to his narrow victory over Richard Nixon.

In Houston and Harris County, the Democratic Party, which had a strong biracial organization, hired PYA members to pass out leaflets, solicit volunteers, and urge people to pay their poll tax ($1.25) in order to vote for Kennedy. In November, the Kennedy/Johnson ticket carried 85 percent of the black vote and 51 percent of the white vote in Harris County.

After the presidential election, Stearns, Graves, and Otis King began looking for ways to jump-start the student movement. At the Wheeler Street office of attorneys Washington and King, they found what they were looking for. George Washington, Jr., and Hamah King, who were roughly the same age as Stearns and already practicing law, eagerly embraced the Progressive Youth Association. Their legal strategy and self-sacrificing defense work helped refocus the movement and shaped it decisively over the next two years.

George Washington, Jr., was born in Dallas in 1929, the last of seven children whose parents came from sharecropping families in East Texas. Washington grew up admiring the powerful African American attorney W. J. Durham, who served as Thurgood Marshall's chief NAACP lawyer in the Southwest. He attended historically black Huston-Tillotson College in Austin between 1946 and 1950, while *Sweatt v. Painter* (the NAACP suit challenging segregation at the University of Texas Law School) was wending its way through the courts.

During his years at Huston-Tillotson, Washington worked nights at restaurants and hotels on Congress Avenue in downtown Austin. "I saw Durham come from Dallas with teams of lawyers," he remembers. "We used to peek through the windows in the Travis County Courthouse and see Thurgood Marshall there examining the Regents and officers of the University of Texas, pressing the Sweatt case to conclusion." Shortly after the Supreme Court ruled in favor of Sweatt on June 6, 1950, Washington applied for admission to the University of Texas Law School. He was admitted within weeks and in 1954 became the second African American to graduate from the law school in Austin.

Hamah King (Otis King's older brother) was born in Texarkana in 1931 and moved into Houston's impoverished Fifth Ward — popularly known as "the Bloody Fifth" — at the age of ten, when the sulphur company where his father worked transferred him to Houston. The family lived in a low shotgun rent house on Lyons Avenue owned by an old black Baptist minister, Jessie Dale. Hamah enrolled at TSU (then Texas State University for Negroes) in 1949 and graduated in 1953. Drafted immediately into the United States Army, King spent the next two years as an instructor in operational radar systems in El Paso and returned to attend law school at TSU in the fall of 1955. By June of 1958, King had graduated from law school, passed the state bar, and joined the ranks of about thirty African American lawyers, most of whom (men like Clarence Jackson, Carl Williams, Weldon Berry, Matthew Plummer, Francis Williams, and Robeson King) worked in downtown offices in the Prairie Professional Building above a large Weingarten Supermarket on Prairie Street.

In the late 1950s and early 1960s, young black lawyers in Houston lived on the edge of poverty. "You were dealing with a double prejudice," King remembers. "It wasn't only that white and Hispanic clients would not hire a black lawyer. Blacks themselves did not have confidence that a black attorney could manipulate the system." In those days, King says he might have gone hungry if his wife hadn't been teaching school. In the fall of 1960, King joined the firm of George Washington, Jr., and Andrew Jefferson, who left within a few months to become an assistant criminal district attorney in San Antonio.

Washington and King moved their office into a renovated house on Wheeler Street, next to the Groovey Grill and across from the TSU campus. They were perfectly situated to provide legal support and a steadying hand to Stearns (who was Hamah's age and only two years younger than George) and the Progressive Youth Association. George and Hamah considered themselves too old to participate directly in the student movement. As lawyers, they'd be wasting their talents and jeopardizing their careers by sitting in with students. Yet they were too young to be part of

Houston's black establishment and they felt excluded from the small coterie of established black ministers and lawyers who jealously guarded their turf and their contacts in the white community.

Washington believed that the NAACP was becoming a comfortable "legal bird's nest." King felt that many black leaders had been bought off by politicians who came around only at election time to seek votes and then disappeared until the next election. "At the time I was young and fiery and ready to go and felt that they were standing in our way," King recalls, referring to the established black leadership. "It was our perception that they were serving their own self-interest . . . particularly as it related to politics."

In December 1960, the Supreme Court, in *Boynton v. Virginia*, prohibited segregation in waiting rooms and restaurants that served interstate bus and rail travelers. Washington quickly realized that the student movement could be revitalized by creating local test cases. He advised Stearns and Otis King to organize waves of sit-in demonstrations at the Union Station restaurant on 501 Crawford. Union Station was a train terminal owned by the Houston Belt and Terminal Company.

Although the restaurant clearly fell under the legal jurisdiction of interstate commerce, owner James D. Burleson refused to serve blacks. "I'm running a white restaurant, not a Negro restaurant," he told a reporter. "If I were running a Negro restaurant I would be off down around Lyons Avenue." Given Burleson's stance, Washington assumed that student demonstrators would eventually be arrested at the Union Station cafeteria — thereby increasing public visibility for the movement and providing a test case to vindicate the constitutional rights of African Americans in Houston. The following summer another Texan named James Farmer, executive director of the Congress of Racial Equality (CORE), would use the same strategy to launch the Freedom Rides.

The first arrests in Houston took place almost a year after the first sit-in at Weingarten's. During the last week in February 1961, the PYA began sending groups of students, including whites from Rice and the University of Houston, to sit in at the Union Station cafeteria. Burleson tried everything to keep them away — he closed for a few hours or locked the doors when he saw them coming. But as soon as he reopened, a new group of students appeared. On Friday evening, February 25, a waitress served coffee to a light-skinned protester named Edwin Conway, who was sitting alone in a booth. "We got it!" said Conway, flashing a victory sign to the others. The waitress quickly snatched the coffee away. An exasperated Burleson called the police and filed charges of loitering against fourteen students, who were arrested and taken to the police station. King and Washington bailed out the students, paying $10 bonds posted by the Houston Medical Forum.

The next night, about seventy TSU students filed into the cafeteria around 6 P.M. and asked to be served. Again, Burleson called the police. Sergeant C. E. Marks arrived on the scene shortly and offered the students an option: leave or go to jail.

"What will the charge be?" asked Holly Hogrobrooks.

"Loitering," Marks responded.

At 7 P.M., police began rounding up the remaining forty-eight students. The atmosphere was lighthearted. Officers and demonstrators kidded and joked with each other.

"We came here to eat and I guess we'll eat in jail. What's the menu up there?" asked one student.

"Pinto beans." Marks grinned.

"With corn bread?"

As they were herded into patrol cars and paddy wagons, the students sang songs, amending the lyrics to "God Bless America . . . my segregated sweet home." The mood was relaxed.

"We laughed going into the paddy wagon," remembers Curtis Graves. "We laughed as we were booked that night. We laughed as we were fingerprinted. We laughed as we were put in the holding tanks. We laughed about the whole thing because we thought this was the way we would finally get attention for the process." Led by Stearns, the students decided to refuse bail and remain in jail until their trial, set for the following Monday.

The arrests quickly galvanized new support among middle-class blacks who were protective of their youth and angry at the implication that their children were criminals. Stearns was determined to push his advantage. Demonstrations at Union Station continued, and more targets, including the City Hall cafeteria and downtown theaters, were hit. Student enthusiasm soared.

"When the kids were endangered [by arrests]," Washington remembers, "all the parents got excited about how far this was going, and how long they were going to last. The students were just *driven*, they were completely unmindful of personal safety, of the hours, and we became concerned about their studies. . . . so we attempted to moderate the frequency of their sit-ins. And they smarted under that. . . . It became an exercise and an adventure for them, accompanied with such zeal that even Eldrewey could not control it."

At the court hearings for the first arrests, George Washington asked cafeteria operator James Burleson why some customers were denied service.

"I refuse to serve certain kinds of people I feel are detrimental to success in my business — drunks, for example."

"In addition to drunks, whom else do you refuse to serve?" asked Washington.

"I refuse to serve Negroes because it would hurt my business," Burleson responded. "I have a separate table for them in the kitchen." Judge Joe Harris fined each of the arrested students $25 for loitering.

On the morning set for arraignment of the students arrested at the second Union Station demonstration, George Washington failed to appear. Curtis Graves and the other forty-eight students sitting in the courtroom were stunned. Unable to pay bail, they were taken to the cell block A of the Harris County Jail to serve their time. Built to accommodate around forty people, cell block A now housed almost one hundred. At first, Curtis Graves thought they'd be in jail for only a few hours. That night, they slept on the floor and on dining-room tables.

By the second night, Graves still hadn't heard from the attorneys. "I had really hit my low point," he remembers, "because I felt that they had abandoned us. . . . the food was bad and there were bugs in the place. It stunk and there were no toilet seats, and none of us had ever been exposed to anything like this before. . . . They literally fed you beans and fatback every day."

Much to their surprise, these students were treated as celebrities by other prisoners in the segregated jail. Many inmates gave up their bunks and mattresses for them. One veteran prisoner took Curtis Graves aside and gave him some paperback books. "He pumped me up and he said, 'You know, it's going to be all right. . . . You're doing this for a cause.'" Unbeknownst to Graves, Washington had deliberately left the students in jail, realizing that their incarceration would help fundraising efforts in the community. Quentin Mease prevailed on the Harris County Council of Organizations — a strong black political organization that met regularly at the South Central YMCA — to raise bail money. Five or six days later, Washington came down to the jail and posted bond for all the students.

In the first eight months of 1961, the student movement in Houston rose steadily toward its zenith. The Progressive Youth Association moved boldly on several fronts. Students continued sitting-in at Union Station and at cafeterias in the County Courthouse, City Hall, and Reisner Street jail. They initiated "stand-in" demonstrations and picketing at segregated theaters downtown — Loew's, the Majestic, and the Metropolitan. And they began picketing companies that wouldn't hire African American cashiers, sales personnel, and managers.

In March, a white student named Jim Daniels joined the PYA. A studious and quiet young man, Daniels threw himself into protests at Union Station, various theaters, the Southwestern Bell Telephone Company, and City Hall. Then enrolled at South Texas Junior College, Daniels transferred to Texas Southern in June, following abuse from whites who considered him a traitor to his race. He was beaten several times both in and out of jail until, he remembers, "I became acquainted with a few friendly thugs who arranged that I would not be hurt."

Throughout the spring of 1961, Stearns pushed the PYA toward new targets and expanded goals. Meanwhile, Quentin Mease was receiving pressure from Bob Maloney of the downtown YMCA and Chet Ridge of Community Chest, who objected to the South Central YMCA being used as a staging area for PYA activities. With his usual combination of diplomacy and disarming firmness, Mease kept both men at bay. He also had to contend with the fears of blacks. One afternoon, Jim Jemison, an African American businessman and chairman of the South Central Board, watched in horror as PYA members and police cars filed out of the parking lot past angry whites on their way to a downtown demonstration.

"Quentin, I don't like this," complained Jemison, a major do-nor and fund-raiser for the Y. "You see all those bulls out there. And they might blow up this building."

"Jim, I'm here," replied Mease. "The ladies are in the office, the maids are upstairs. The janitors are all here. . . . None of us are worried. Now if you're so worried, why don't you leave, and if they blow up the place, we'll build another Y."

In March, when the group began picketing Southwestern Bell Telephone, Stearns informed a *Houston Chronicle* reporter that ending "job discrimination" was now part of the PYA's agenda. "About 73,000 phones in the Houston area are used by Negroes," Stearns said, "but the company will not hire any Negroes except [as] sweepers and garagemen."

Neither the theaters nor Bell Telephone took kindly to the PYA's new tactics. Between February and June, when eight mass arrests took place, 176 charges were filed against members of the PYA. Of these charges, 93 were dropped; convictions were obtained in 62 of the remaining 83 cases, but almost all convictions were being appealed or pending motions for a new trial. Over the next two years, George Washington, Jr., and Hamah King handled hundreds of cases at great personal cost to their careers and families. Although the Harris County Council of Organizations raised over ten thousand dollars for the bonds and fines of student demonstrators, it refused to pay Washington and King for their legal work.

Mass arrests put the students back in the news and galvanized support in the African American community. Longtime activists such as Moses Leroy, Sid Hilliard, George T. Nelson, and Raymond Duncan came out publicly in support of the PYA and urged others to do so. Stearns's uncanny knack for publicity won him large audiences at community forums, black unions, churches, and professional groups. He took each opportunity to promote himself, to urge support for direct action, and to boost the PYA's revenues and membership. In early May, for example, he printed up an ingenious handbill to bring people out for a mass meeting at the Antioch Baptist Church on Robin Street: "ATTENTION," the leaflet fairly screamed, "PYA presents a Mother's Day MASS MEETING, A Tribute to Mothers of Sit-In Students. Come out, see and hear the youths who have made life better in Houston for Negroes. Principal Speaker ELDREWEY J. STEARNS."

By June, PYA promotional literature boasted of impressive achievements: sixty-nine lunch counters opened; thirty-six saleswomen, nine cashiers, and four managers hired in various businesses; and open seating in bus stations, Jeppersen Stadium, Busch Park, and Playland Park. So successful was the PYA campaign that longtime activist and publisher Carter Wesley wrote a provocative *Informer* editorial entitled "Will the NAACP Have to Move Over for the PYA?" "Within a scant year PYA, Progressive Youth Association, has brought a new dimension to Houston," wrote Wesley, " . . . it has been a few years since NAACP has been in the forefront of any significant efforts to bring first-class citizenship to Houston's quarter-million Negroes. How does it happen, for instance, that the Negro doctors of Houston, who are in better financial position individually than any other group, have moved much closer to the program and activities of PYA than to what the NAACP is doing?"

Wesley's question had a single answer: the leadership of Eldrewey Stearns. "I can't imagine anybody else who could have done what Eldrewey did to spark the movement," remembers Earl Allen. "Eldrewey was *the* leader. We all understood that. The inspiration behind the whole movement was Eldrewey. And people would listen to him, he could inspire people. And he loved to talk. He *loved* it. . . . He **did** something really tremendous." During the summer of 1960, Earl Allen and Charles Lee had both left Houston to complete their seminary education — Allen at Southern Methodist University in Dallas and Lee at Gammon Seminary in Atlanta. Perhaps, as Holly Hogrobrooks speculates, they were enticed by scholarships arranged to siphon off some of the movement's militant leadership.

In any case, their departure left Stearns as the movement's undisputed leader. "He was always smooth," remembers Judge Andrew Jefferson. "He had all this leadership skill about him. Courage that few people have . . . he had it all. He was as effective in our community as [Stokely] Carmichael or Julian Bond, probably not as smooth as Bond, but certainly as outspoken as Carmichael or John Lewis. . . . You were dealing with someone who knew he was right and you knew he was right and he was courageous enough to take the leadership and run the risk of being killed. And you just have to love him for doing those things."

Stearns had a knack for stirring up racial tension and capitalizing on the publicity or fundraising opportunity that followed. On Friday June 2 — a payday — he arranged a rally at the Union Hall of the segregated local 872 of the International Longshoremen's Association. Houston's black longshoremen made good money; they stood tall in the African American community, and they were grateful for new opportunities to find a lunch counter or restroom that would serve them downtown. The PYA rented a small truck with a public address system to play dancing music. Stearns ordered a plaque to give to union president Raymond Duncan.

When the music started playing that afternoon outside the union hall on Memphis Street off 75th over by the Houston ship channel, blacks and whites, students and stevedores, were dancing together — several hundred longshoremen and several dozen students. Stearns remembers this loud celebration and the ensuing police confrontation vividly.

> **And we had the music blasting, and the police, all dressed in blue, you know, coming through. . . . Because they resented the white girls dancing, you see. That's all it was. All of a sudden the race problem [be]came, was then and will always be, in my eyesight, a sex problem. . . . White girls dancing with black guys. . . . They were all together. Black, white, they were all together. . . . That didn't make no difference down on the waterfront.**

Suddenly, a caravan of paddy wagons and patrol cars with police dogs moved in and arrested four longshoremen and four PYA members — purportedly for disturbing the peace. Several longshoremen went to their cars and came back with shotguns. Stearns ran upstairs to get Raymond Duncan. Reverend King, who led the workers with a prayer and hymn at the start of every workday, began to sing. The police arrested him. Raymond Duncan came downstairs and told the men with their shotguns to back off. The police were badly outnumbered, remembers Jim Daniels. "They hauled ass — fast. . . . Nancy Smith grabbed the money we'd collected and ran upstairs with it. And as soon as the police left, donations increased. Nothing like a live demonstration to help."

After the police — who had nearly started a riot — were gone, the students and longshoremen assembled upstairs in a large meeting room. Reverend King began the meeting with a prayer. Stearns presented Raymond Duncan with a plaque of appreciation from the PYA. Then Duncan spoke: "You are our children," he told the students, "and we will protect you. Next Wednesday morning, we're going to City Hall to see the City Council about this. And I want five hundred of my men with me." (The following Wednesday morning at nine, somewhere around a thousand longshoremen, their wives, supporters, and PYA members packed the City Council chambers and hallways at City Hall. Raymond Duncan and Reverend King protested the incident. They also complained to Mayor Cutrer and the City Council about certain city policemen who were in the habit of arresting a few longshoremen late at night on payday and shaking them down for money. The unlawful assembly charges were dropped.)

After the award ceremony, Stearns turned on the jukebox again and people began dancing.

And they put a barrel up there, you know, and I'm telling you it rained money. Every nigger out there who was worth his salt was into his pocket, with dollar bills, and fives and tens, and twenties, you know, puttin' money into that barrel. Now I hated to profit by something like that you know . . . but, uh . . . that's the way it was.

As the Progressive Youth Association was reaching the peak of its influence in Houston, James Farmer launched CORE's new interstate bus campaign known as the Freedom Rides. On the morning of May 4, Farmer sent out thirteen Freedom Riders in two mixed-race groups from the Greyhound and Trailways bus terminals in Washington, D.C. Farmer was refurbishing a tactic which CORE had used unsuccessfully in 1947, when it tried to test a Supreme Court ruling that blacks could not be forced to sit in the back of the bus on interstate routes. Farmer expected that restaurants would refuse to serve blacks in bus stations along the way. He instructed Freedom Riders to inform managers that the Supreme Court decision in the *Boynton* case guaranteed their right to be served. Refusal of service would be followed by lawsuits.

After eleven days and 700 miles of journeying through Upper Dixie, the Freedom Riders met fierce white violence in Anniston, Alabama, where a mob smashed and firebombed the Greyhound bus and then severely beat the Freedom Riders, who barely made it to a local hospital. A photographer's picture of the flames and smoke escaping from the abandoned bus was sent out on the wire services and became an instant icon of the struggle. Undaunted, the Freedom Riders persisted, facing more violent attacks in Birmingham and Montgomery, followed by arrests in Jackson. By the end of May, Attorney General Robert Kennedy took up Martin Luther King's suggestion to seek a ruling from the Interstate Commerce Commission.

While an ICC ruling (eventually handed down in September) was pending, Freedom Rides continued throughout the summer of 1961. George Washington, Jr., and Hamah King saw Houston as a natural extension of CORE's campaign through the Deep South. They contacted Farmer, who agreed to send Freedom Riders to Houston. Stearns and other PYA activists objected to this tactic, concerned they would lose control over their own movement. Washington persisted. "You must realize now that sometimes you can't see for the light of day," he told them. "If you've got the attention of the community, the state, and the nation — and you have people you think are genuinely in league with you and your purposes — it would belittle your movement if you told them not to come."

In early July, radio and TV stations carried an announcement that CORE would be sending a group of Freedom Riders to Houston. Enraged, Stearns denounced CORE's decision in a radio interview at station KILT. "Stay out of Houston until you find out what the hell is going on and consult somebody," he advised James Farmer. Listening to this tirade on the radio, Dr. A. W. Beal hurried to the station and caught Stearns as he was leaving.

"Why in the hell did you do that?" asked Beal.

"Look, man, I know what I'm doing," Eldrewey responded.

"No! You should be welcoming them to come and help in our struggle."

Stearns rambled on about CORE stealing his movement. Beal paused. "You know, you're not yourself, Drew," he noted. "Something's wrong with you. Why don't you come around and let me talk with you."

"I knew it was going to surface to somebody," Stearns answered, acknowledging and denying his trouble almost in the same breath. "But I am as sane as God. You understand that? You just don't understand my actions. I'll be all right in the morning."

Not a single PYA member went to the airport to meet Freedom Riders Patricia Baskerville and Frank Johnson when they arrived in Houston in late July. Baskerville and Johnson, who had just been released from the Mississippi State Penitentiary, slept on the floor of George Washington's house at 3507 Wheeler. Stearns decided to join them. On July 21, all three purchased interstate tickets and requested food service at Union Station. James Burleson refused to serve them, waited long enough to see that they were not going to leave, and then called the police, who arrested all three on charges of unlawful assembly. Baskerville and Johnson each posted $500 bond. Stearns remained in jail to protest the arrests and to force the ICC to rule on a PYA complaint filed in June on behalf of two young women traveling from Texas to Louisiana.

Here George Washington, Jr., was at his strategic best. Though he was one of the first Texans to benefit from the Supreme Court's ruling in *Sweatt v. Painter*, Washington believed that local solutions worked better than federally imposed mandates. Unlike Stearns, who pushed for immediate and full integration, Washington took a long view of things: "I was trying to posture our public demands toward reasonably achievable goals. So that we could measure it without asking for pie in the sky, expecting all of a sudden for these people who had grown up with one hundred years of segregation to say: 'You have to get on your knees tonight and wake up a bawn-again Christian in the morning.'"

When the ICC failed to rule on the PYA's complaint, Washington filed a motion in federal court for a habeas corpus hearing requiring the city to show cause for holding Stearns. Washington knew that he would be on strong ground in arguing that the *Boynton* decision prohibited discrimination in interstate commerce facilities: Stearns had therefore been improperly arrested and should be released. On the day before the hearing, Washington sent a telegram to Mayor Cutrer asking him to prohibit "the unlawful arrests of persons seeking to enjoy their rights." He asked Cutrer to help find a "Southern solution to a Southern problem" in order to avoid future appeals to federal courts.

"I think there is a misconception that we as a minority group would like to run off to Washington and the Supreme Court to settle such things," he told the press. "We think there has been too much buck-passing to the federal courts. We have avoided that as long as we could. And we still feel we can solve our problems without going out of Houston."

Washington believed passionately in the rule of law, and he had always treated jury trials as a means of educating the local community. Although his partners sometimes thought he was asking the impossible, Washington knew that more lasting benefit would come to Houston if a local jury — rather than a federal judge — found demonstrators not guilty. "We al-l-ways went to the jury in each one of these cases," he remembers, "at great cost and time and expense to us because I had fixed upon it that we wanted Southern juries of *citizens* to say, 'We're going to find these people not guilty because we don't think they're doing the wrong thing.'"

On Thursday July 27, Judge Allen B. Hannay ruled that his court lacked jurisdiction and dismissed the habeas corpus motion. The next day, Mayor Cutrer announced that black travelers would be arrested only after warrants had been issued. Stearns then agreed to be released on $400 bond.

In early August 1961, a mixed-race group of Freedom Riders arrived from Los Angeles. On August 11, they joined seven Texas Southern students (Eddie Douglas Jones, Herbert Hamilton, John Hutchins, Robert Jones, Holly Hogrobrooks, Marion Moody, and Willie Handy) for a demonstration at the Union Station cafeteria. After warning the students and Freedom Riders not to enter the coffee shop, Burleson went to Justice Tom Maes's office, filed a complaint for unlawful assembly, and obtained eighteen arrest warrants.

Despite the summer heat, Holly Hogrobrooks wore three or four layers of clothing in anticipation of a long jailing. Holly and her brother Ted Hogrobrooks both worked vigorously in the student movement. Their father, Theodore Hogrobrooks, Sr., had been a staunch activist in the Houston NAACP chapter during its strongest days under Lula White in the 1940s and 1950s; he was a major financial backer for the student movement. "Turns out I needed those clothes," remembers Holly. "We were in jail for nine days, because we would not come out. If there was a time in my life that I thank God for segregation, it was in the jail setting." While several white male Freedom Riders were being beaten by prisoners in the "white" section of the Harris County jail, Holly and the other black female protesters found protection among the toughest women in their cell block. "They looked after us. Okay, you know, the things that we were very green about that happened in jails, they just said, 'Hey, ain't gonna be none of that. These chirren are in here, we gon' look out for them.' One old sister named Octavia came out of the Fourth Ward and walked with a limp. And Octavia did not take nothin' offa nobody, including matrons. . . . So, you know, if Octavia said it, we did it. She laid down the laws and everybody got along fine."

The young black men and women sang to each other from their separate cell blocks at the Harris County Jail at 301 San Jacinto. The "old Harris County Jail . . . had a very lousy ventilation system," remembers Holly Hogrobrooks, "but it's a great telegraph, 'cause we would sing and the guys would pick it up and would sing back and we would have the whole building rocking."

In September, these unlawful assembly cases went to trial in the courtroom of Judge George E. Miller. Hamah King asked for a motion to dismiss the charges, arguing that no laws were broken and that the case was merely a pretext to avoid integrating the Union Station cafeteria. Miller denied King's motion. The jury found the students guilty. Miller fined all eighteen Freedom Riders one hundred dollars each. Washington and King immediately gave notice of appeal, feeling that the verdict directly opposed federal law.

In April 1962, the Texas Court of Criminal Appeals reversed the lower court's decision on the unlawful assembly charges. This victory (in *Texas v. Eddie Douglas Jones*) meant that the city could no longer stop protests by arresting students and charging them with unlawful assembly. Previously, the municipal courts had become clogged with unsubstantiated loitering charges, and local judges began dismissing them. Now Washington had deprived district attorney Frank Briscoe (with whom he enjoyed a cordial relationship) of another legal weapon. "We beat 'em on loitering, we had beat 'em on unlawful assembly. And as long as the kids were peaceful, and there was no damage or destruction of property, and there were no assaults upon other individuals, he'd be pretty hard-pressed to stop a peaceful demonstration."

While the PYA and its lawyers were struggling against segregation in the streets and in the courts, Quentin Mease and other influential blacks were quietly enjoying the culmination of a long campaign to make Houston a major league baseball city with an integrated sports facility. Back in 1957, a group of thirty-five investors, promoters, and community leaders, led by George Kirksey and Craig Cullinan, Jr., had formed the Houston Sports Association (HSA) to spearhead the effort to bring a major league franchise to Houston. Within a few years, independent oil and real estate man R. E. "Bob" Smith and former Harris County judge and mayor Roy Hofheinz became the dominant figures in the HSA's mission.

At the time, there were no major league teams in the South. Only the Brooklyn Dodgers and the New York Giants, who moved to the West Coast in 1958, had altered the major league map, still centered in the Northeast. Although the Houston Sports Association provided the necessary money and the organizational support, the city still needed a new stadium to obtain a major league franchise. Hofheinz dreamed of building the world's first air-conditioned, domed stadium — a project he later touted as the "Eighth Wonder of the World." To build the proposed stadium, the HSA needed voters to approve a public bond issue. Smith and Hofheinz asked Quentin Mease to gather support among African American voters. Mease and other black leaders agreed to campaign for the bond issue — on the condition that the new stadium would be opened as an integrated facility. Hofheinz and Smith gave their word that the new stadium, soon to become the largest public venue in the city, would be entirely integrated in seating, bathroom facilities, and hiring policies. Houston's minor league team — the Buffs — had been integrated since 1954. In 1958, Harris County voters passed a twenty million dollar bond issue to construct a new stadium.

In August 1960, armed with public financing, a proposed building site, and plans for a lavish indoor stadium, Hofheinz and Smith flew to Chicago, where the National League expansion committee was meeting at the Conrad Hilton. When they arrived at the meeting to plead their case, chairman Walter O'Malley pulled out a letter he had received from Quentin Mease and others specifying that Houston's black community organizations supported the new franchise on the condition that employment, seating, and bathrooms in the new stadium would be integrated. Hofheinz and Smith — no doubt embarrassed that Mease's implicit leverage had been made public — agreed to this condition.

When Hofheinz returned from Chicago, he called Mease and asked why he had sent the letter.

"Well, Judge," Mease responded slyly, "we sent that letter up there *supporting* this."

"Yes, but some of those crackers didn't like your threats. Anyway, I gave you my word, didn't I?"

"Well, Judge," Mease retorted, "you gave us your assurance. But some of us felt we ought to have a little insurance because we didn't know."

On the eve of the final game of the 1960 World Series between the New York Yankees and the Pittsburgh Pirates, the National League announced that expansion franchises had been awarded to Houston and New York, to begin in the 1962 season.

In early 1961, the Houston Sports Association purchased and began refurbishing the Houston Buffs, soon to be known as the Colt .45s and later the Astros. But since construction of the domed stadium was plagued by huge cost overruns and construction delays, the Houston Sports Association had to go back to the voters of Harris County for another bond issue. Three years after passing the first bond issue, Harris County voters were increasingly divided over Hofheinz's fantastic scheme of the world's first indoor, air-conditioned stadium. Although Oveta Hobby's *Post* supported the bond issue, John T. Jones's *Houston Chronicle* came out against investing public tax dollars in a facility which benefited the stockholders of the Houston Sports Association.

Judge Hofheinz — a "grand huckster" if there ever was one — initiated an aggressive public relations campaign. Leon Jaworski agreed to co-chair a citizen's committee to generate support for the stadium. Hofheinz hired Stearns to lobby in the black community on behalf of the domed stadium. Stearns in turn paid PYA members to drive through the Third, Fourth, and Fifth wards with loudspeakers urging African Americans to vote for the bond issue. As Stearns tells it, Hofheinz was particularly concerned with Reverend L. H. Simpson, who vocally opposed the bond issue. Stearns recommended paying Simpson $5,000. "He sure changed his mind in a hurry," Stearns claims. " . . . what a little money won't do to put a man on the right side of God." Harris County voters narrowly approved a bond issue of $22 million.

Hofheinz's associate Gould Beach called Quentin Mease and asked him to attend a ground-breaking ceremony for the new domed stadium, scheduled for January 3, 1962. Hofheinz wanted Mease, A. E. Warner, and James Brooks — influential business-men in the African American community — to participate in the ceremony along with R. E. "Bob" Smith and members of the Har-ris County Commissioners' Court. Using Colt .45s rather than shovels to break ground, members of the Commissioners' Court fired their weapons as media photographers snapped their shut-ters. Then Hofheinz's public relations man gave Mease, Warner, and Brooks the guns and asked them to stage a second ground-breaking for photographers. "When he dropped his arm, we pulled the triggers," Mease remembers. "Nothing happened. And R. E. 'Bob' Smith just howled: 'You tenderfeet. You don't know what you're doin'. Those are single shot!' And then each of us cocked our guns and shot."

Mease knew that integrating the Colts' new stadium would set the stage for desegregating other facilities in Houston. Hofheinz, who as mayor had overseen the integration of city buses, munici-pal golf courses, and libraries, understood this too. During the planning stages of the new domed stadium, Hofheinz chartered a jet named "Rain or Shine" to take prominent Houstonians and journalists to see the new stadiums being built in Los Angeles and San Francisco. In each city, the host baseball club gave receptions that conspicuously included African American players. Attending one of these parties, Jack Harris, general manager of television and radio stations KPRC, went over to Hofheinz.

"And I said," Harris recalls, " 'Roy, have you thought about what will happen when the Giants come to Houston? They will want to stay at the Shamrock Hotel. And you can't have Willie Mays and other ball players staying at a segregated hotel. They won't stand for it.' And Judge Hofheinz said, 'Well, that's a prob-lem we're gonna have to face pretty quickly, aren't we?' "

On April 1, 1962, convention hotels in downtown Houston

dropped their policy of segregation — again, by prior agreement and without any local press coverage. As in August 1960, when Bob Dundas had spearheaded the silent and simultaneous integration of downtown lunch counters, John T. Jones played a central role. Jones — whose Houston Endowment then owned the posh Rice Hotel, along with the Lamar, the Texas State, and the McKinney hotels — was already sympathetic to Hofheinz's desire that downtown hotels accommodate African American baseball players. And he knew that segregation was chasing away national convention business. Jones called his hotel managers and informed them of the new policy. "To a man, they thought it was gonna be just absolutely disastrous," he remembers. "And they were very pleased when it didn't turn out to be that way."

Jones made sure that "it didn't turn out to be that way." After securing an agreement with owners of other hotels (including the Sheraton Lincoln, the Towers, the Hi Way House, and the Shamrock Hilton), he notified Hobart Taylor and Quentin Mease. Mease held a meeting at the YMCA, where he instructed well-heeled black individuals and couples to make reservations at each of these hotels. "If anybody attempts to deny you, let us know and then we'll get back with the proper people," Mease told them. The plan went into effect without a hitch.

On April 10, 1962, more than 25,000 fans watched the first official major league baseball game in Houston, between the Houston Colt .45s and the Chicago Cubs. Those who came through the turnstiles at Colt Stadium (a temporary structure used while the domed stadium was being built) entered a ballpark free of formal racial discrimination on the playing field and in seating, restrooms, press facilities, and employment — even upstairs at the exclusive Fast Draw Club for monied patrons. Hofheinz announced that the Houston Sports Association was proud to have integrated its facility without external pressure or white backlash. "We look forward to the continued support and patronage from all fans who are proud of first-class citizenship and major league recognition."

Actually, the issue of race seemed far away in the new Colt Stadium designed to look like a great Wild West theme park. Parking lot attendants wearing ten-gallon hats, blue handkerchiefs, and white overalls directed motorists to sections of asphalt labeled "Wyatt Earp Territory" and "Matt Dillon Territory." A Dixieland band paraded through the aisles, and 150 Triggerettes in gaudy baseball outfits ushered people to their seats. In Colt Stadium, soon to become nicknamed "Mosquito Heaven," seats were not labeled "white" or "colored." Instead, the seats themselves were colored — chartreuse, turquoise, burnt orange, and flamingo — and where you sat depended on how much money you paid.

I had to look back over the things
I didn't want to leave. I wanted to go
back to Amelia, I wanted to go back
to all the streets. Integration wasn't
coming fast enough for me, and they
were slipping away. I was becoming
history. . . . I had television people
to tell me, "You're history now,
Stearns. You don't need to say
anything. You've made history. Step
aside and let somebody else come on
through."

Eldrewey Stearns

When Eldrewey Stearns sparked a new stage of the Houston civil rights movement in 1960, no one could have known which elements in the white community would react more strongly — the race-baiting segregationists rooted in the East Texas piney woods or the West Texas frontiersmen and free enterprise elites bent on transforming Houston into a major league city and the country's center for manned space exploration. Stearns's seemingly fated role in this racial drama was to force these actors out from the wings and onto Houston's historical stage. For almost three years after policemen beat him up in August 1959, he enjoyed the spotlight as the most militant of Houston's young black leaders. Stearns was well suited for this role as racial catalyst. He was charismatic, decisive, full of emotional intensity, willing to take risks — and he had a theatrical sense of humor.

One day late in 1961, Stearns went down to the television station KHOU for an interview with news director Dan Rather. Ron Stone, then a cub reporter for the Houston CBS affiliate, opened the door and invited Stearns in.

"Where's Dan Rather?" Stearns asked aggressively.

"In the next room, putting on his makeup."

"If he gets makeup, so do I," demanded Stearns.

Flustered, Stone knocked on the door and asked Rather what to do. Rather opened the door and quietly motioned to the makeup jar sitting on a table. Stearns took a handful, smeared it on his face, and looked in the mirror at the large white streak across his cheek. The three men stood silently, until Stearns wiped his face and quipped, "I think I'll just do mine natural." They all burst out laughing and went into the studio for the interview.

"One thing you knew about Stearns," remembers Ron Stone, who later became news director at Houston's Channel 2, "is that he was smart as hell. His mind was always working, and he always had a good grip on the political situation. If he ever could have channeled all that energy and intelligence in one direction, there's no telling what he could have done. But as the years went by, he lost credibility. Much that he did began to seem like a fantasy."

Stearns was twenty-nine years old in 1961, ten years older than many of the students he led. Yet he still looked like a boyish college student and consistently told reporters that he was younger than his actual age. Behind this youthful mask, Stearns was turning into a kind of Dorian Gray, haunted and obsessed with three things: the movement, alcohol, and women. Away from television cameras and newspaper reporters, he was beginning to unravel.

Most evenings found him at the Groovey Grill. "I was drinking in there every night. Going down there with a different woman and it got to where I didn't even feel it. I didn't remember what sex I had. Girls had to remind me, 'Don't you remember me?' And I'd say, 'What?' I was embarrassed to have gone to bed. And I came to the conclusion that when you're drinking a lot of whiskey, you can't get drunk if you've got anything else on your mind. I had so much in my mind; I couldn't get drunk. I would drink myself sober."

In the midst of this growing turmoil, which he could neither acknowledge nor control, Stearns maintained a redemptive fantasy that he would marry his fiancee, Amelia Solay. Amelia was a quiet and attractive Louisiana Creole majoring in business administration at TSU. Several years younger and devoutly Catholic, Amelia represented the sexually pure and adored wife who could give his troubled story a happy ending. But after three years of waiting, this innocent young woman — whom Stearns had swept off her feet with his good looks, his intelligence, and his charm — ran out of patience with his nocturnal habits and unfulfilled promises.

In early April 1961, Amelia broke off their engagement. Losing her opened up cracks in Stearns's psyche, through which the molten lava of mental illness began to flow. His memories of that event reveal the confusion and delusions of grandeur that were becoming apparent to people around him.

I had been in jail. I was in flames. I was very into the papers. Every day I was in the newspaper headlines. Until then, I had been all over the country every day.

It was Amelia, too, was halting me then. Halted me. Amelia. I came to her one day during Lent.

I would never forget that day. I walked to her and I had just been out with one of the girls that night before in the movie. One of the PYA girls, with long, flat hair, looked

like an Indian girl from Amarillo. I took her to my apartment and she didn't want to have sex or nothing, but I said to myself, it was so prophetic, I said, "Well, I thought I had a girl, but I don't think I got one anymore anyway, thanks to you." I could see the handwriting just by being with her, and Amelia had found this thing out some kind of way and put the squeeze on me.

When I went to Amelia the next day, it was April 1. It was Lent—high Catholic Lent. And when I looked at her eyes she stepped aside and said, "No, it's all over." I said, "God, not really."

I was big. I was big as little James Farmer, whom I was going to see in the next two or three days in New York. Martin Luther King. They were no match for Eldrewey Stearns. Jesse Jackson. None of these people were no match whatsoever. I was going places, clear across Texas, clear across the plains of America.

Stearns refused to accept his fiancee's decision. "She had the audacity to quit me without my permission. Here I was a general almost and I got to put up with her?" On Easter Sunday, Stearns went to the Paladium Dance Hall, where he found Amelia dancing with someone else. "She got through dancing with the guy that night and then the music was storming and moving — and I didn't want the night to end because I didn't know how it was going to end. I said, 'Let me dance, this last dance.' And this was to be the last dance I would be able to dance with her too, in my life. She said, 'Well, come on if you're going to dance; stop twisting around.'"

The dance was a slow one. "I tried to talk and dance, but I couldn't. She didn't want to hear what I had to say. My mind was leaving me at that point — my faculties were going haywire. I couldn't control myself." Stearns tried to seduce Amelia and win her forgiveness. She pried herself loose, ran outside, and got into her car. Stearns followed her into the parking lot, got into the car, and tried to kiss her. She slapped him.

He tried to pull her out of the car. "I started pulling her and I struck her accidentally, but on purpose I suppose. I slapped her in the face and she grabbed my left arm and gnawed on it like a hungry dog gnawing on a bone, and she kept it in her mouth just like she delight in biting me. I pulled it out, but it was the kindest cut of all. Of all the scars I have on me today, this was the most important scar that I have. It was like a bite from God. I was so delighted that I got this bite from her."

Stearns followed Amelia to her home on Cavalcade Road. She bolted the door, forever. "She wouldn't talk. She would not communicate with me. She had learned from somebody who had schooled her: 'Don't let Eldrewey Stearns talk. Don't let him talk, because you're going to back up.' And I think that's what she got me on — 'don't let the man talk.'"

As he often did in a crisis, Stearns went to Quentin Mease: "Eldrewey, if she doesn't come back, it wasn't meant to be," he advised. "That's all and don't even fret about it." Otis King's response was characteristically direct: "What did you expect, Drew? After the way you treated that girl, what did you expect?" Stearns found no consolation in his friends' reactions. "I didn't want any advice. I wanted Amelia. I wanted her in the flesh. I got to where I wanted no appeasements. I could not be appeased."

Stearns's mind raced through the reasons why Amelia might have left him: his uncontrolled drinking and infidelity, their unconsummated sexual relationship . . . But deep down, he believed that he had lost Amelia because he tried to double-cross God, before whom he had promised to sacrifice everything in return for becoming a leader:

I tried to fool God. I had done it all in the name of leadership—all in the name of God. That I would forsake everything, Amelia. So now, here I was now wanting to go on my knees and swing from trees and go in the darkness and weep. When it was all coming to light, I said I'd give them up. Suddenly now, I don't want to give these things up, particularly Amelia. I had risen to where I really wanted to go. I had gotten there and it was trying to kind of level off—coming down the altitude somewhere, where I could land to be fitting to my station in Houston.

Throughout the spring and summer of 1961, Stearns still believed that he could win Amelia back. First he went to see Father Ball, Amelia's priest at the Mother of Mercy Church in "Frenchtown" — the area where most of Houston's Creoles lived. Stearns assumed that Father Ball would be pleased that he had respected Amelia's virginity; he asked the priest to intercede. Instead Ball offered a prayer and gave him a rosary.

Next, Stearns asked Amelia's brother Gabriel and sister Agnes to convince her that he deserved another chance. One night after a long talk with Agnes, Stearns drove down Chocolate Bayou Street and contemplated suicide. "I felt something in my head snap. . . . If I couldn't have her, I'd rather have death. That's the way it was." But actually, Stearns still thought he could win her back. So he took a six-week conversion class to become a Catholic. "I was actually prayerful every night, praying to God that Amelia would come back and I had not given her up one inch." Neither God nor Amelia relented.

Stearns threw himself back into the movement in the spring of 1961. "When you want to do a lot of things, don't sleep, that's the key," he says. "And without Amelia, the longer I worked the less I felt the pain." Several friends saw that Stearns had been thrown into a crisis. They advised him against flying to the New York office of the Congress of Racial Equality, where he was scheduled to negotiate with senior officials of the Loew's Theater. "I was getting weaker behind Amelia. It was taking a toll on me. Various things were taking its toll — sex, no sleeping. I couldn't think straight. My thinking started getting blurry."

Despite offers of help from Dr. A. W. Beal and others, Stearns drove himself harder than ever. When he arrived at CORE headquarters in New York, he met executive director James Farmer and Marvin Rich, who had agreed to set up negotiations over the Loew's Theater in Houston, where African Americans were only allowed to sit upstairs in the balcony. A native of Marshall, Texas, and graduate of Wiley College, Farmer was well known to Stearns and most veterans of the Texas civil rights movement. Farmer excused himself from the meeting in order to prepare a public announcement of CORE's new demonstration campaign, soon to be known as the Freedom Rides.

Stearns and Marvin Rich faced a Loew's executive named Charles E. Kurtzman and his team of lawyers. The PYA was aggressively picketing the Loew's Theater on Main Street; Stearns indicated that the picketing would continue until Loew's allowed open seating for blacks.

Kurtzman pointed out that if Loew's acted alone, white people would stay away. "You can get this theater open and then what you have is an all-black theater on Main Street — is that what you want?" Loew's had integrated simultaneously with other theaters in both Louisville and Lexington, Kentucky. Kurtzman proposed a similar plan to make sure that no single theater in Houston would risk losing its white clientele. Stearns acknowledged Kurtzman's point but refused to call off the PYA's picketing. "I was putting quite a bit of pressure on them and I was a very hard man to deal with, because I had nothing but pain on my mind and suffering and I had nobody's feelings to consider."

When Stearns returned from New York, Sam Nabrit tried to convince him that it was foolish to continue picketing the theaters. Nabrit had spoken with the manager of Houston's Loew's Theater, who told him that he would never voluntarily integrate the theater as long as Stearns continued picketing. Nabrit knew that Stearns was troubled and suspected that he was using the movement for personal gain. "You could never tell what he was gonna do," remembers Nabrit. "First of all, he didn't want the protests to stop. His excuse was that something happened to students when they protested, some kind of transformation that he wanted 4,000 students to have. Many of the merchants in the black community made contributions. And as a result, Stearns was sort of feeling his oats."

Stearns was indeed feeling his oats — and for good reason. The new sense of self-respect that grew from asserting one's rights as an American citizen was in fact central to the experience of the civil rights movement throughout the South. Stearns outlined the PYA's ambitious goals for a *Houston Chronicle* reporter: "Total integration, better job opportunities and equal use of public facilities." On April 30, police arrested twenty-four students he had sent to picket the Loew's and Metropolitan theaters. Twenty-two were convicted of unlawful assembly and fined $250 each. Yet as Nabrit and others recognized, Stearns often lost his balance. On May 3, he demanded that Louis Orlando, owner of a grocery store on 3317 Lyons, fire all white supervisory personnel and replace them with blacks. When Orlando refused, the PYA began picketing his store. Orlando filed an injunction against the picketing and a suit for $110,000 in damages, claiming a 75 percent drop in his business.

Meanwhile, Stearns was drifting in and out of the TSU law school. In April 1960, he had withdrawn to devote all his energies to the movement. He reenrolled in January 1961, but spotty attendance and poor performance put him on the brink of being expelled. In July 1961, he again withdrew in a letter signaling his desire to return. "If in the event I am not in jail or suffering under any other incapacitation," he wrote to Dean Kenneth Tollett, "I will be most grateful upon being re-enrolled in the school of law this coming fall."

During the summer of 1961, Stearns continued to lose control of himself and of the movement. As a leader, he was unable to formulate a set of measurable goals or a long-term program of action for the PYA. "It just all centered around him," remembers George Washington, Jr. "All the priorities, all of the programming just emanated completely from Eldrewey. There was nothing out there for everyone to look at and say, 'That's next for us all.'" When people who had obtained jobs with the help of the PYA refused to buy memberships, Stearns would fly into a rage. He thought that they owed it to him. Money passed out of his hands much more quickly than it came in. Whores picked his pockets in drunken back-seat encounters; thugs rolled him in dark bathrooms at all-night bars. He kept no records of how much money came in and what expenses were paid.

Ever since he quit his YMCA job with Quentin Mease, Stearns had lived without a steady source of income. Some people saw this as a sign of selflessness, of complete devotion to the movement. Others, like Holly Hogrobrooks, came to suspect that he was "out there *pimping* the movement." "There's just no other way to put it," she says. "Eldrewey did a lot of pimping the work that we were doing; that left a bad taste in the mouth of some people."

In addition to church assemblies, union fundraising, and door-to-door solicitation, Stearns received money from the Twentieth Century Men's Club through Dr. A. W. Beal; from the Houston Medical Forum through Dr. C. W. Thompson and Dr. L. Robie; and from the Business and Professional Men's Club through Quentin Mease. On the streets, people would stop him and hand him money in support of his efforts. "It was always a good feeling to have hundred dollar bills or fifty dollar bills or twenty dollar bills put in your pocket," he remembers.

"And money would also turn out to be evil to me because I didn't keep books. . . . And I said, 'Well, I'm no goddamn accountant, I'm a leader.' You understand? So I stopped worrying about that, but it catch me up and haunt me in my absence." PYA members began to object. "We were naive," Holly Hogrobrooks recalls. "We didn't understand how to finesse and maneuver. Eldrewey was older, slicker. . . . He was always scheming, a consummate con artist. Eldrewey took money off a lot of people. We never really understood how much money came in and how much just stopped with Eldrewey, 'cause while the rest of us were living with parents or working, Eldrewey was living off the movement."

By August, Stearns had lost considerable credibility in the black community. One former supporter canceled a bail bond, landing him briefly in jail. A rebellion was growing in the PYA ranks. Nancy Smith and John Hollie cornered him one afternoon in the PYA office. "We love you, Stearns," he remembers them saying, "but you are making bad decisions. You're not yourself. You need to take a break." Others were less sympathetic. "We sent him to Mexico because he had his hand in the cookie jar," recalls Holly Hogrobrooks, who prevailed on her father, Theodore Hogrobrooks, Sr., and other benefactors to withdraw their financial support from Stearns. Mr. Hogrobrooks (along with Mrs. Moses Leroy, John Butler, W. Bonner Berry, H. I. Garner, and Mrs. Daniel Clay) formed a Sit-in Foundation, which took control of the PYA's finances, thereby limiting its activities. At the end of September, Stearns resigned as executive director and was replaced by a new leadership built around Holly Hogrobrooks, John Hollie, Freddy Goodall, John Bland, and Prentice Moore.

Newspaper accounts looked at Stearns's resignation from various angles. The African American *Forward Times* paid tribute in an unsigned editorial: "It is bad news that Eldrewey Stearns has decided to leave the Progressive Youth Association. . . . Although radical in some ways in his approaches, his forwardness and his personal sacrifices are something to marvel. . . . No matter how moderate we may pretend to be or hope to be, we can't deny the fact that Eldrewey Stearns's radical approaches, his boldness, his fearlessness and sometimes senseless efforts have been effective."

The *Houston Post* noted that Stearns was going back to finish his law degree and that he was writing a book about race relations entitled "The Light of Freedom." (This was the first of at least five manuscripts he had been trying to write when I met him in 1984.) The *Post* story played down differences between Stearns's radicalism and the moderation of the new leadership. Saul Friedman's *Houston Chronicle* story — "Negro Youth's Ex-Leader Says Movement Is 'Dying'" — aired these differences, including Stearns's complaint that the PYA was becoming merely a "social club." Stearns told Friedman that the effectiveness of the PYA was being sabotaged by blacks no longer willing to support direct action and the costs of going to jail. None of the newspaper accounts indicated that Stearns was accused of mishandling PYA funds. "We did not . . . make a public announcement of it, because we were trying to keep unity and did not want all this known," Hogrobrooks remembers.

Wounded by the loss of Amelia, rejected by his former troops in the PYA, and increasingly incapacitated by alcohol and the onset of undiagnosed mental illness, Stearns sought refuge. Like many of his white male Texas counterparts, he saw Mexico as a place to drown his sorrows. His friend Dr. Walter Minor wrote a letter to the Almeda State Bank urging it to lend Stearns $500 so that he could take a vacation. Stearns's request was denied. Minor then gave him forty dollars but warned that no matter how far south of the border he went, he'd still have to sleep in a square room and face the same troubles. With forty dollars in his pocket, along with the engagement ring Amelia had returned, a rifle, and a camera, Stearns set out in his brown, wing-backed 1960 Chevrolet for Monterrey.

When he reached San Antonio, Stearns stopped and spent the night at Frank and Gloria Bryant's home on Pine Street. Dr. Frank Bryant had not forgotten the many crab gumbo dinners he enjoyed at the Stearns household in the mid-1950s, when he was a struggling medical student in Galveston. Andrew Jefferson, then assistant criminal district attorney in Bexar County and a close friend of the Bryants, was visiting. Jefferson told Stearns that he had a bright future ahead of him, that he needed to forget about Amelia and get on with his life. That night, Stearns drank most of the Bryants' liquor and poured out his heart to Gloria Bryant. "She thought I was more angry than hurt and more angry than in love," Stearns remembers. It would not be the last time that the Bryant family sheltered Stearns in time of trouble.

The next day, Stearns drove across the border into Mexico. At nightfall, on a narrow mountain road outside Monterrey, he half tried to drive over a cliff. "I really intended to kill myself," he says, "because I knew I didn't see . . . ever recovering and I just wanted to get it over with . . . and I was full of whiskey." When his car came to rest on a boulder by the roadside, Stearns got out and looked around. "Damn!" he said out loud with self-mocking relief, "Can't even commit suicide." Looking down into the city at nightfall, Stearns recalls seeing a bright light, which he afterward always referred to as the Light in Monterrey. He backed up and drove toward the light, which was perched on top of the Hotel Yamayel. When he reached the hotel, Stearns sat at the bar for a few hours before he checked in.

A few weeks later, after the hotel management realized that he had no money, Stearns went into hiding in another hotel on Madero Boulevard. Using a scrapbook of his civil rights accomplishments and the little bit of Spanish he had acquired at Michigan State University, he set out to establish a public persona. He recalls meeting a U.S.-educated Monterrey lawyer named Plutarco Guzmán Lunez, who invited him to a party and introduced him to a reporter for the newspaper *El Porvenir*. The reporter photographed and featured Stearns as a lawyer and one of the three leading integration leaders in the United States.

But as Walter Minor had predicted, Monterrey offered no cure for Stearns's troubles. "Here I was a grown man . . . crying over Amelia. I couldn't get over her," he remembers. "I couldn't get around it and kept on getting more drunk." His mother Devona and Amelia's sister Agnes wrote letters begging Stearns to pull himself together and come home. To pay for days spent drinking sixteen-cent bottles of Carta Blanca beer and nights spent with Mexican prostitutes, Stearns pawned Amelia's ring, his rifle, and his camera. He came down with a case of gonorrhea. Desperate phone calls to Dr. Frank Bryant and Reverend E. R. Boone of the Antioch Baptist Church produced money wired to him at the Hotel Madero. After about two months, Garfield Clarke, a wealthy Houston friend, came down and bailed him out of exile. They went to bullfights and dances. "He [Clarke] had the money now and I had nothing but time." In December, they drove back to Houston through San Antonio, where Frank Bryant gave Stearns a shot of penicillin to cure his gonorrhea.

Two days after Stearns returned to Houston, the Southern Motor Company repossessed his car. Then TSU Law School dean Kenneth Tollett notified him that officials from the South Main Bank were planning to issue a warrant for his arrest if he didn't turn himself in voluntarily. A bad check he had written to Nancy Smith was catching up with him. Stearns did turn himself in, but he refused to plead guilty. "I didn't *intend* to write that check on a bad account," he claims. "It was just that I was so upset that I didn't realize that I didn't have any money at the time. I wrote that check before I went to Mexico and the bank was malicious in bringing that action against me." Fortunately for Stearns, the president of the South Main Bank decided not to press criminal charges. District Attorney Frank Briscoe — elected with the support of the black community in 1960 and a respectful adversary of George Washington, Jr., in several sit-in cases — put an end to the matter by tearing up the check.

Meanwhile, the Sit-in Foundation attempted to restore support for the restructured PYA. On December 30, 1961, the *Forward Times* published an unsigned editorial praising the new look of the PYA under Prentice Moore, who was described — in implicit contrast to Stearns — as a "young man of high ideals and high moral standing . . . above seeking personal glory." Mrs. Daniel Clay, president of the foundation, aimed to continue raising money for the PYA while moderating the number of sit-in targets and demonstrators. "This is not a struggle in which only students have the duty to participate," Mrs. Clay announced to African American readers of the *Forward Times*. "It is your duty to participate. We do not ask you to take the battle field, we do ask you to man the supply line. Your contribution is needed desperately."

In early January 1962, Stearns again attempted to take control of the PYA, this time in an unannounced election for president held at a meeting where few members were present. Herbert Hamilton, who counted the votes, shocked Holly Hogrobrooks and the anti-Stearns faction by announcing Stearns's victory over John Hollie, who promptly resigned from the PYA. Actually, Hamilton now acknowledges, Stearns did not receive a majority of votes from the seventeen members present. Convinced that Stearns's contacts and charisma were central to the future success of the PYA, Hamilton simply declared him the winner.

But when Stearns attempted to take control of the organization and its finances, he was thwarted by Mrs. Clay and Theodore Hogrobrooks, who informed him that all funds would henceforth be released only through a vote of the foundation officers. Determined to stop paying for what it called "compulsive sit-ins," the foundation suspended all aid to the PYA but continued to help individual students whose cases were pending. Without financial backing or student unity, the PYA became an empty shell. Within a year it was dead.

By the spring of 1962, Houston's downtown lunch counters and convention hotels had opened their facilities to blacks. Yet the city's restaurants and movie theaters remained segregated. Although he had become a leader without many followers, Stearns sporadically continued his offensive against all forms of segregation.

In September 1962, some 53,000 Houstonians gathered at Rice University's football stadium to hear President John F. Kennedy, who announced in a historic speech that the United States planned to put a man on the moon by the end of the decade. Houston, which had already been named the center of America's manned space exploration program, was suddenly thrust into the national spotlight. Within a few years, the city's image makers would trade in its Victorian nickname, "The Bayou City," for "Space City, U.S.A." Likewise, the Colt .45s would be renamed the Astros, and the Harris County Domed Stadium would become known as the Astrodome.

Stearns's last hurrah as an effective leader came in the spring of 1963, when he took aim at the Achilles heel of Houston's shiny new image — nationally and internationally televised scenes of demonstrations or racial unrest. One hundred years after the Emancipation Proclamation, segregation still reigned in the city's downtown theaters and restaurants. Racial tension was rising throughout the entire country. In April, Martin Luther King joined veteran activist and minister Fred Shuttlesworth in a determined effort to end segregation in Birmingham, Alabama, where police commissioner Eugene "Bull" Connor vowed to incarcerate every black demonstrator. King was promptly placed in a cell with no mattress or linen, where he wrote his famous "Letter from a Birmingham Jail."

On May 2, a thousand African American children marched down the streets of Birmingham. Six hundred were arrested. The next day, demonstrators who marched out of the Sixteenth Street Baptist Church were attacked by police dogs and high-pressure firehoses designed to sweep them off the streets. Birmingham's jails bulged with 2,500 protesters. Although store owners agreed to desegregate all facilities on May 10, white extremists bombed the home of Martin Luther King's brother, A. D. King, as well as a black-owned motel that housed movement headquarters. Black neighborhoods exploded into rioting over several days. The city seemed to be on the verge of a race war.

Television and newspaper images of firehoses and police dogs unleashed on unarmed demonstrators galvanized national and international support for the fight against segregation. The principle of nonviolence began to lose its uncontested moral primacy in the black community. In a secret meeting in New York City, James Baldwin and other prominent African Americans told Attorney General Robert Kennedy that the Kennedy administration's race policy was "totally inadequate" and warned that race relations were about to explode in the North as well as the South.

When the president sent a message about the unity of the free world to a conference of independent African nations, the prime minister of Uganda sent a reply protesting the firehoses and police dogs used in Birmingham. Worried about racial violence breaking out in a dozen cities across the country, the Kennedy administration met privately with theater and hotel owners, restauranteurs, and other southern businessmen, urging that they voluntarily desegregate their facilities and open up employment opportunities. The president also began preparing a new civil rights bill.

On May 15, 1963, astronaut Gordon Cooper took off on the final flight of the Mercury series, aimed at demonstrating to the world that the United States could compete in space with the Soviet Union. Following the splashdown, an internationally televised tickertape parade was announced to welcome Cooper back to his hometown of Houston on May 23. Stearns, Otis King, and Reverend Bill Lawson (who had moved from TSU to become pastor of the Wheeler Avenue Baptist Church) seized this opportunity to attack the last bastion of Houston's all-white consumer economy — segregated theaters and restaurants. They leaked word that a major protest was planned for the day of the Cooper parade, when the eyes of television viewers around the world would be on Houston. For over two years, students had been demonstrating sporadically at downtown theaters. In the heat of the Birmingham crisis, many were eager to reenter the struggle.

As usual, Quentin Mease had his finger on the pulse of Houston. Mease, who had earned the trust of more players in the civil rights drama than anyone else in the city, devised a strategy to use the threatened demonstration as leverage in negotiations over desegregating the theaters and restaurants. He turned to the wealthy African American businessman Hobart Taylor, who had been on a first-name basis with Jesse Jones and had worked closely with John T. Jones for the United Negro College Fund. Taylor made a visit to John T., proposing that movie theaters and restaurants be desegregated in the same way that lunch counters and hotels had been. "I don't know how long it took Taylor to do this," Mease remembers, "but I recall distinctly when he called me and said, 'Well, I just left John T. Jones's office, and he's going to work with us.'"

Jones drafted Bob Dundas to work again as the point man in restaurant negotiations and handled the theaters himself. Although Stearns and King didn't specify exactly what kind of guerrilla protest they were planning, their ranks had long since been infiltrated by police informants. Jones and Dundas were undoubtedly aware that if they did not have an agreement in place by the morning of the Cooper parade, students, with picket signs hidden under their jackets, would rush out into the street and unfurl their antisegregation signs when the parade arrived.

Driven by fear of racial violence and "maybe a little charity in his soul" (as Jones puts it) Bob Dundas — who was dealing with many small family businesses and local fears rather than a few theater owners and national chains — had the harder of the two jobs. "He had to change a lot of people's minds . . . to convince them that it was a good idea to change customs," remembers

Jones. Ever the good businessman and lobbyist, Dundas went to work with Granny Harbor, president of the Houston Restaurant Association. Jones, whose Houston Endowment owned three of the four downtown buildings that were leased to theaters, was in a strong position with local operators. He traveled to Dallas and spoke with John Q. Adams of Interstate Theaters, which operated the Loew's State and seventy-five other theaters in Texas.

On the evening of May 22, there was no indication of an agreement. "We spent the whole night getting . . . signs ready and people lined up," Otis King recalls. The demonstration was planned like a military operation. Students were instructed to mingle unnoticed in the crowd until the parade reached the middle of Main Street, near the center of downtown. Then they would rush out into the street — both in front of and behind the parade — and raise picket signs protesting the persistence of Jim Crow in Space City, U.S.A.

"It became almost like a novel," remembers King, "because we were all over at Wheeler Avenue Church, and we were on the telephone with the local people who were on the telephone with the people in New York." He particularly remembers a conversation about black-Jewish relationships with a sympathetic local Jewish theater official. "And I told him that if he came into my neighborhood and someone tried to discriminate against him, that I would fight for him. . . . And I said, 'You have to fight for us on this.'" But King did not rely on moral suasion alone in dealing with theater representatives. "We told them that . . . we're gonna reach a fail-safe point . . . and we won't be able to call it off and it's gonna make national and international news and it's gonna really embarrass the city and you're gonna be responsible for it."

The next morning, over a hundred excited students from TSU and Rice went to their assigned places along the parade route on Main Street, where people were already lining the streets to welcome "Gordo" home on a clear, eighty-five-degree day. Eleven A.M. was the fail-safe point — the last time that designated students were to call in and ask if the demonstration would go forward. Around 10:30 that morning, Quentin Mease phoned Stearns. He had just received a call from Hobart Taylor, who relayed a promise from John T. Jones that the theaters and restaurants would be open within thirty days. Mease's strategy — and his credibility with Jones — required that the demonstration be called off at the last minute.

Yet Stearns's renewed credibility with an energized student movement required that he lead a dramatic demonstration that would garner worldwide publicity. Stearns balked at the idea of calling off the demonstration. He wanted to press for immediate desegregation and asked why they should trust Jones. "At least give them a try," Mease answered. "If the theaters aren't open within thirty days, you can always start picketing again."

Stearns was in a difficult position. If he went ahead with the demonstration, he would lose Mease's support and derail the agreement. If he called off the demonstration, he would lose the support of most students. With fifteen minutes to spare, he and Otis King decided to cancel the demonstration. The parade celebrating America's triumph in space rolled jubilantly down Main Street before a clamoring crowd of 300,000.

After the parade, deflated and angry students came by the South Central YMCA to drop off their unused picket signs. "You're an Uncle Tom — a sell-out artist, Stearns," yelled a white student. "That's what you are to your own people."

"We've waited four hundred years for these freedoms," Stearns answered (using the same argument that Bill Lawson had used against him in April 1960). "We can wait for thirty more days." Despite this act of sound political judgment, Stearns was deeply wounded. "I felt browbeaten and defeated. The students hurried on by and left me standing and bent over as an unwanted dog, an old dog." After almost four years of relentless campaigning, the last segregated public accommodations were about to fall. Again, a news blackout deprived Stearns of publicly savoring the moment. There was no interview with Dan Rather to acknowledge this historic accomplishment — no one to tell God that Eldrewey Stearns had lived up to his end of the bargain.

Within a month, the secret plan for simultaneously desegregating downtown restaurants and theaters was put into effect. Hobart Taylor had assured Jones that these facilities would be visited by very small numbers of well-dressed, quiet, and orderly blacks. Jones and Dundas again made sure that there would be no newspaper, radio, or TV coverage. At a meeting at the South Central YMCA, Quentin Mease distributed pairs of movie tickets to

YMCA board members, students, and other well-connected blacks. He and Stearns went to the Loew's Theater to see Steve McQueen in *The Great Escape*. Mease, Dundas, and Granny Harbor worked out a plan whereby well-heeled African Americans would be quietly served at key downtown restaurants. High school principal Arthur Gaines and his wife were told to dine at George Dentler's Pier 21 seafood restaurant, where they were met by white waiters eager to serve them. Each group was given a phone number to call in case of trouble. There was none. "There was a lot of looking and maybe some whispering," remembers John T. Jones, "but nothing happened."

As Jones's words imply, Houston developed the reputation of a place where "nothing happened" during the civil rights movement. Yet a great deal happened, thanks to the persistence, skills, and patience of many blacks and whites who worked to make it happen. At the end of June, Chicago-based *Jet* magazine ran a short piece crediting "grand old man Hobart Taylor" with spearheading the desegregation of Houston. A *Forward Times* editorial, "It Takes More Than One Bullet to Win a War," angrily replied that integration was the fruit of countless organizations and individuals over many years.

On June 19, 1963 — 101 years to the day after news of the Emancipation Proclamation arrived in Texas — a small group of black leaders met on the steps of Houston's City Hall to celebrate the almost forgotten holiday known as Juneteenth. Carter Wesley, in his regular column "Ram's Horn," argued that Houstonians had more to be proud of in 1963 than in any other year since emancipation. He urged that whites as well as "Negroes who fought for this emancipation" be given credit. "The truth is that Houston, mostly through its leadership," wrote Wesley, "has set the pace for equal accommodations of all the citizens in a quiet but effective and permanent way."

Peaceful desegregation occurred in Houston — as in many cities in Texas and throughout the South — because moderate white Southerners felt compelled to break with diehard segregationists to preserve social peace, a positive media image for their city, and a prosperous economy. Once it became clear to Houston's powerful blacks that white business interests would not unite to defend the color line in public accommodations, Eldrewey Stearns's role as militant integrationist lost its historic edge.

Writing in the liberal Austin-based periodical the *Texas Observer*, Saul Friedman penned Stearns's political epitaph late in 1963: "Stearns was not as steady a leader as the Negro students might have hoped for. But then what leader worth his salt doesn't have some faults? He was vulnerable because of them, and one day he found the bail money and financial backing had been withdrawn, and he was deposed as leader. The PYA died, and so did Negro militancy in Houston."

On June 15, 1963, Mississippi's NAACP chief, Medgar Evers, was murdered. That same month, Stearns graduated from Texas Southern University Law School and began a sporadic law practice. As the strategic core of Houston's civil rights struggle moved on to other venues, Stearns slipped bitterly into obscurity. On the public stage, his sporadic cameo appearances gradually came to appear farcical or pathetic. In the theater of his personal life, later acts followed the course of tragedy.

part TWO

A Boy from Galveston and San Augustine

Devona Trim and Rudolph Stearns standing on Seawall Boulevard in Galveston, ca. summer 1930. Courtesy of Devona Stearns.

Devona Trim standing by a Galveston wharf, ca. 1930. Photo by Rudolph Stearns.

Three-month-old Eldrewey and the Stearns's dog Beauty, on the front porch of 1712 Avenue M, Galveston, March 1932. Photo by Devona Stearns.

Eldrewey on a tricycle at age 4, 1936. Photo by Devona Stearns.

Devona Stearns and her first three children (Eldrewey, left; Earl, center; and Geraldine, right) at 1617 Avenue M ½, Galveston, ca. 1937. Photo courtesy of Devona Stearns.

Eldrewey at age 5, 1937. Photo by Devona Stearns.

Mollie Sterns, before her stroke, in the
Roberts Community section of San
Augustine, mid-1920s. Photo courtesy
of Devona Stearns.

Headstone marking the graves of Rudolph's parents, Corey
and Mollie Sterns, Roberts Community Cemetery, San
Augustine, 1990. Photo by Eric Avery.

Field and trees marking the place in Roberts Community where Eldrewey lived between 1939 and 1942 with his grandparents, Corey and Mollie Sterns. Photo by Eric Avery, 1990.

Roberts Community Church, which doubled as a schoolhouse when Eldrewey lived there. Photo by Eric Avery, 1990.

Eldrewey (right) and classmates in Mrs. Jones's English class at Central High School, 1949. Photo courtesy of Devona Stearns.

Eldrewey and his date, Doris Jones, before the Junior Prom at Central High School, 1948. Photo courtesy of Devona Stearns.

Eldrewey's graduation photo, Central High School, 1949. Photo courtesy of Devona Stearns.

Eldrewey (left) at Michigan State University, talking politics with Dr. Dickson, the first African American professor there, ca. 1955. Photo courtesy of Devona Stearns.

Devona and Rudolph Stearns moved to this Galveston house in 1949 and have lived there ever since. Photo by Eric Avery, 1988.

Eldrewey as a corporal at Fort Sill in Lawton, Oklahoma, 1951. Photo courtesy of Devona Stearns.

Right then and there I solemnly
swore to God that I would answer
a call to see that such inhumanity
would never be visible to my
eyes again.

Eldrewey Stearns

In the summer of 1935, Devona Stearns took her two small children, Eldrewey and Geraldine, on a bus trip from Galveston to San Augustine, Texas. She planned to spend a month with her husband's parents, who lived in a remote rural area known as Roberts Community. Devona had never met her in-laws, Mollie and Corey, and she didn't learn about Mollie's meanness and mule-driving ways until much later.

Devona, Eldrewey, and Geraldine got off the bus in San Augustine and stopped for lunch at the Garner funeral home, run by Mollie's sister's husband. After a while, Corey came down in a wagon to pick them up and take them out to Roberts settlement. "Just an old country man, you know," Devona remembers. "It was hilly. One side of the wagon would go up and the other side would be down. And it was up and down, up and down, you know, and I was kinda frightened goin' through the door."

On that first trip to San Augustine, four-year-old Eldrewey acquired his reputation as a "wise child." It took a week or so for the children's stomachs to adjust to the raw cow's milk but no time to fall in love with Grandpa Corey's horse and the meadows, fields, forests, and songbirds. One afternoon, while Devona was inside talking to Mollie, two-year-old Geraldine toddled over to the doorway of the outhouse Corey had just built. She was holding "one of those dolls that have a hole in the top of the head, to root the hair down in there, but it was bald." A snake had crawled inside and was coiling itself up. As Geraldine peered into the doll's head, Eldrewey happened to walk up. "He was a little bitty thing — never saw a snake in his life," Devona recalls. "And he shouted, 'Sister, throw down that doll, there's a snake in it!'"

Devona, who was inside talking with Mollie, heard the commotion and ran outside. "Sure enough, she was standing there holdin' this doll with a black moccasin inside its head! And I couldn't hardly get it out of her hand fast enough to throw it away!" Devona went back and told her mother-in-law; neither of them could figure out how Eldrewey knew what a snake was. "But he was always a wise person," Devona remembers, "and see, people did not understand wise children. They would abuse them, you know. He could notice things, he could give you answers. But we could not see it, you see. We couldn't see it. Because my husband was young at that time, my husband didn't spend very much time at home."

Eldrewey Joseph Stearns — whose oddly original first name forecast a life of odd originality — was born at Galveston's John Sealy Hospital for Negroes on December 21, 1931. The day before, Devona had sent her husband Rudolph down to the wharf with fifty cents to buy a rabbit for dinner. ("Rabbit" would later become Eldrewey's nickname — but for a different reason.) "So I cooked that rabbit that Sunday and made some cake and went to bed after dinner," Devona recalled. About twelve o'clock, she woke up with a pain. "I thought the rabbit had made me sick. And I kept sayin' 'O-o-o boy!' We were with my sister-in-law and brother at the time, and she say, 'Girl, you are in labor.'"

After Devona's family calmed her down, they took her to the delivery room at the Negro Hospital. "I told the nurses I'd rather have a girl, because I like to dress little girls and comb their hair and make them pretty and everything," Devona remembered. She gave birth to Eldrewey the next night around 10:45: "The nurse say, 'Devona, you don't have a girl but you got a pretty little boy.' And I say, 'A-a-aw.'"

One night several months earlier, Devona — who was then working in the John Sealy Hospital dining room for doctors and nurses — had fallen off a step stool while closing a transom window above the dining room door. When back pain finally forced her to go to the doctor, she was hospitalized for a month to avoid losing the baby. The John Sealy Hospital records indicate that the birth of six-pound "baby Stearnes [*sic*]" was normal and that the infant's condition was good.

At the age of fifty-three, however, Eldrewey's own assessment was not as optimistic. "The event of my birth was not as successful as that of Benito Cellini, which means 'welcome,'" he reflected in 1984. "My father had just been divorced from his first wife. *He* was the one who was welcome to my mother. . . . I was a bastard, really."

Following Eldrewey's birth, Rudolph (everyone called him Rufus) began gambling at night, staying out until five or six in the morning. Those were long nights for Devona, who sometimes waited up all night, sick with anger and worry. Other nights she cried herself to sleep, holding on tightly to her baby Eldrewey and dog Beauty. Shortly after his birth, Eldrewey began vomiting and crying immediately after nursing. In February, Devona took him to the hospital; perhaps fear and rage were seeping into her maternal milk. Doctors found no abnormality. For at least another month or so, Eldrewey was vomiting, though in smaller amounts, after each feeding. After March, the hospital records fall silent.

Devona had good reasons to worry about feeding her son. She had left her job at John Sealy Hospital, and there wasn't much work for Rufus cleaning ships at Galveston Dry Dock. Eventually, Devona got used to Rufus's night-time habits, which were common on the island, where organized gambling drained large sums from an already poor, largely black population. Like prostitution and alcohol consumption, gambling was illegal in Texas. Yet all three flourished in Galveston, where the Maceo family controlled lotteries, poker games, crap shooting, slot machines, policy tickets, keno, monte, bingo, and horse betting. By the time Eldrewey was seven years old, the family had moved to five different houses, often for lack of rent money, always looking for a better place. That summer he was taken "Uphome" — to San Augustine.

"Whatever President Roosevelt was doing with his New Deal," remembers Eldrewey, "he wasn't doing it for the Rudolph Stearns family in Galveston, Texas." By 1939, the family included Geraldine, "who we called the yellow girl"; dark-skinned Earl: "we called him the beautiful child"; and Shirley, the baby. The Stearnses lived in a three-room rent house at 29th and N. "I slept on the floor on a pallet made out of a quilt of colored cotton scraps, many colors like the rainbow Jesse Jackson talks about." Groceries came from "Shirley's," a little store on the corner. "We bought nickel lard and nickel oil from him. A nickel worth of lard, nickel worth of oil, nickel worth of salt pork, and then nickel worth of beans. That's how my mother Devona fed the family."

One evening Aunt Lena and cousin Little Wiley Roberts arrived in Galveston just after the family finished eating. Lena (Rufus's only sister) and her husband Frank were childless; they lived on the outskirts of San Augustine with Grandpa Corey and Grandmother Mollie, who had been paralyzed by a stroke. Lena had gotten Little Wiley to drive her from San Augustine in a Model A Ford — the only car in the Roberts Community section of San Augustine. "I was tickled to death to see a Negro man with an automobile and I wanted to ride in that automobile and I didn't care where it went."

For over three years, Lena had been feeding, bathing, lifting, and moving her mother between bed and wheelchair. She needed help, and she had come to get Eldrewey. "I remember my aunt asking my mother point blank—'Devona, let me take Eldrewey from here. We can take care of him. He can have plenty to eat, his own room, and he can go to school there, and you have three more children that you can hardly take care of now.'

"I pulled at my mother's dress tails. 'Mama, please let me go.' My mother told me later that she cried. 'All right,' my daddy said."

Little Wiley was a heavy drinker, and he was drunk that evening when he left Galveston with Lena and Eldrewey. "I remember them putting cold ice packs around his face to sober him up." With the Gulf breeze at their backs, Wiley headed north over the causeway that linked the island and the mainland. Past Houston, the gravel highway into East Texas veered to the right, shrinking under pine wood forests capped by the night sky. "We went down that dark road faster than a Texas jackrabbit. The country is dark at night. There are no lights anywhere. It's a long drive, two hundred miles into the interior. When we arrived, there was a fat pine torch burning in the house. It's amazing how bright that light shined. It's lighter than darkness for sure."

When Eldrewey arrived in San Augustine that summer night in 1939, he was moving against the tide of a great exodus from the rural South. He was returning, actually, to a setting of early Texas history and the site of his own half-buried multiracial origins—a site his father had fled with great relief. San Augustine sits on a narrow belt of rich redland soil that once supported hunting grounds and agricultural lands for thousands of Indians. In 1717, the Spanish established a mission there among the Aies Indian tribe. Following the footpaths that linked Indian villages, the Spanish gradually developed an overland wagon route, known as El Camino Real, which passed from the navigable waters of the Red and Mississippi rivers, through the redlands across to San Antonio, and down to Mexico.

Anglo-American settlers and their slaves followed this trail when they moved into the area during the 1820s. On either side of the old wagon route, near the ancient Indian village and Spanish mission sites, they set up large farms and began cultivating cotton. After the Texas War of Independence, landowners purchased large numbers of new slaves from traders who took them on riverboats from New Orleans up the Mississippi and Red rivers and moved them overland on foot or in wagons.

The Roberts Community area of San Augustine County derived its name — and many of its inhabitants — from Elisha Roberts, one of the earliest white settlers in East Texas. In 1822, Roberts first passed through the area while pursuing a runaway slave. This slave was himself following his wife, who had been taken from Washington Parish, Louisiana, to Central Texas by another master. Roberts was apparently so taken by the area's untapped natural beauty that he resolved to make a home there. He returned and found a squatter occupying the land he had picked out along the old wagon road.

Roberts traded a slave for this land and quickly built a house and tavern out by the road, which had become the principal artery of upland commerce in Texas. His home soon attracted important visitors like General Sam Houston. James Bowie and Davy Crockett also stopped to rest at the tavern, which served as a recruitment place for the Texas Army. Roberts was on the committee that selected the location of the town of San Augustine, helped incorporate the University of San Augustine, was elected *alcalde* in 1831, and put together a large plantation.

Elisha Roberts's sons — Isaiah, Elisha Jr., Tommy, Lige, and Dix — all had children by slave women. According to Joanna Phillips, who chronicled the centennial history of the Roberts Baptist Church in 1972, Elisha Jr. took over the plantation when his father died in 1844. "Elisha II was a very kind old man after the slaves were freed," wrote Phillips. "He told all those that wanted to stay on the place they could. It was more than one hundred fifty families on the plantation [and] some still have ownership of the old tract. . . . Here was a group of people wandering around in a community meeting from house to house singing and praising God that they are free at last. They didn't have to steal away to pray any more."

The matriarch of the "black" Roberts families was Liza Roberts, a slave woman born about 1845 of Indian and African descent. Among Liza's nine children was a daughter named Anna — born in October 1864 and begotten by Elisha's son, Tommy Roberts. As a young woman, Anna learned the skills of a country midwife and was often sought out by neighbors — including her half-brothers' families — when someone was sick or in labor.

After Anna's husband Jim Cook was killed in a gunfight, she had seven children by Frank Scott — a big, handsome, half-black, half-Irish man of legendary sexual prowess. Anna gave all Scott's children the surname Cook. According to Rudolph, when Anna died at the age of ninety-nine years, three hundred sixty-four days, and twenty-three hours, the Roberts boys wanted to bury "Aunt Anna" in the white cemetery. But her daughters prevailed and buried their mother in the "black" cemetery out on Farm-to-Market Road 2213, right by the church at the entrance to Roberts Community.

Mollie Cook, the first child of Anna Roberts and Frank Scott, was born September 13, 1885. She became a member of the Roberts Baptist Church in 1900, married Corey Sterne on December 26, 1901, and gave birth to Rudolph the following October at age seventeen. Mollie Cook and her husband Corey Sterne both came into a world where racially mixed children were seen through the binary prism of black and white, separate and unequal. In that world of sharecropping and segregation — built around the absolute prohibition of a black man impregnating a white woman — white landowners continued to take sexual privileges with women of color and publicly denied paternity of their children.

Corey was born in San Augustine on June 12, 1880, and never learned to write his own last name, which is spelled differently in various documents: Sterne, Sternes, Stearns, Stearnes. This confusion reflects the uncertain identity of Corey's parents. The 1880 census lists his parents as Joseph and Martha Stearns, both described as "mulatto" — a category dropped in later San Augustine censuses. Yet Rudolph remembers Corey saying that his father was a white man from Nacogdoches, whom he saw only once or twice in his life. According to Rudolph, Corey kept mostly to himself and nursed a lifelong grudge against his father. Like the mulatto Joe Christmas, who lived on the run in William Faulkner's *Light in August*, Corey may never have known who he really was.

Unlike Joe Christmas, Corey didn't run — from himself or anyone else. "He was a man that didn't run, and all the whites from up there knew that," says Rudolph. "He didn't bother nobody. But if you bothered him, you had to deal with him."

It is likely that Corey's father Joseph was a son or grandson of Adolphus Sterne, a German Jewish immigrant to Nacogdoches, friend of Sam Houston, and prominent supporter of the Texas movement for independence. This is what Eldrewey learned in later years from Joanna Phillips, the woman from Roberts Community who took special interest in the history of the place. And it is consistent with the family story that came down to Eldrewey's sister Shirley: "Daddy always told us that his daddy's dad was a German Jew and that was it. We never knew nothing else. At least two or three of his [Rudolph's] first cousins all look like little old Jewish guys. I'm not kidding."

Born October 11, 1902, in San Augustine, Rudolph Stearns was thus descended from a combination of the founding generation of white Texans, African American slaves, and American Indians. This fascinating ancestry, however, was of little use to a "colored" sharecropper's child born in a one-room, dirt floor sharecropper's house with a stick-and-dirt chimney. Growing up, Rufus heard plenty about lynchings in East Texas — especially the black man publicly hung without a trial at the San Augustine County Courthouse. At home, he was whipped routinely without a trial by his young mother Mollie.

When Rufus was a boy, the family sharecropped on the farm of R. N. Stripling, a druggist in town. Corey rented the land "third and four" — Stripling received every third bushel of the corn, every fourth bale of the cotton, and a share of the occasional peanut crop as well. After the harvest, Corey sold most of the food crop in town. He would take the cotton to be ginned, keep a sample of the seeds for the next year's planting, and sell the cotton to merchants at Clark and Downs dry goods or C. J. Childress hardware. The family lived on the cash received from its share of the crops, plus whatever Corey made working in the fall at Jones's Cotton Compress. For their own food, they raised sweet potatoes, watermelons, and all kinds of vegetables — as well as chickens, hogs, and cows. They were poor, but they never went hungry.

"I worked in the fields all my life till I got about seventeen years old," Rufus remembers. "Started as soon as I was big enough, say about eight or nine." Rufus went out to the fields with his father at seven in the morning. They worked until six or sundown with an hour out for lunch, six days a week. "We usually worked around thirty acres every year. Started long about March. Daddy had a pair of horses, one horse to a plow. Each of us had a horse. . . . One named Dan, a dark gray, and the other, Bob, was practically white. In a day, you could plow an acre and a half. . . . Every day, when I'd go to the fields, I'd wish there was some way out."

For eight years, Corey, Mollie, Rufus, and Lena all lived with Anna and her children in a house that Anna owned with her brother, Oliver Roberts. The house was divided by a long hallway that ran from front to back. The Stearnses lived in three rooms on one side of the house. Anna lived in five rooms on the other side with her five unmarried daughters and two sons—all of whom she raised herself.

In those years, it seemed to Rufus, Mollie beat him for almost anything he did. "She'd beat me within an inch of my life. Anywhere. All round." Mollie beat Rufus with a buggy whip, a rope—anything she could pick up. While she never hit him in the face, "she sure whupped the blood out of me," Rufus remembers. "Sometimes she started whipping me with my clothes on, and make me pull off my shirt. Then she'd make me pull off my pants before it was over with. Whip me, sometime, betcha twenty minutes. I'd be so sore I'd have to sit on one side at a time. That's the truth. . . . You know, it is bad to have to say those things, but sometime you just have to get them things off your chest. I feel better sometime when I can talk about it."

By the time Rufus got to be sixteen or seventeen, he began plotting his escape. He "wasn't gonna take no more of them whippin's . . . from nobody." One day, after Rufus stripped the buggy whip from Mollie's hand, Corey stepped in. "He tryin' to whip me with one hand and hold me back with the other. I just grabbed his arm and threw him against the wall, you know." By the time Corey got up, Rufus was gone. "I don't know how bad it hurt him. But when he got up, I was gone. Never did try to come and git me after that. Say he gonna send the sheriff after me."

Until the age of twenty-one, black runaways could be picked

up and returned to their parents by the white sheriff. Rufus figured he could "travel till I knowed they wasn't gonna find me." And he had saved enough money to live on until he could find a job and a new place to live. From a traveling bootlegger named Raymond Lee, Rufus learned to make moonshine whiskey, which sold for $10 a quart during Prohibition. For $25 a month, Judge Wilkerson, who believed that blacks as well as whites needed a way to make money during the Depression, protected the operation and notified Rufus when "the revenue was in town."

Rufus became an expert bootlegger. He raised corn for the mash or bought chopped corn from the local feed store. Mixing water and apples or peaches with the corn, he would blend these ingredients in a barrel "and let it set for three or four weeks." After it finished bubbling and the mash settled to the bottom of the barrel, Rufus cooked the liquid in his still — "a big copper kettle connected to a cooling drum with some copper pipe."

After half an hour or so, the liquid started to boil and produce steam enough to rise up into the pipe. "Then the drops flow down through the coils into the barrel of water. And after it cool down, you run it into a bucket, anything you want to catch it, you know." The clear white substance had the taste of alcohol, about 100 to 140 proof. Sometime Rufus had to "double run" it, cook it again. "And then you'd add a certain amount of water to where it wouldn't be too strong to drink or anything," Rufus explains. "Then you'd add charcoal or something to it and put it in a stone jug for a couple three months, what you call aging it." But if customers demanded the moonshine before it aged, "you give it to 'em right away. Called it White Lightnin' too. When the revenue come we close down, bury our still in the ground, everything."

After Mollie took most of the moonshine money and the sheriff got his share, Rufus usually had some left over. "What she didn't take, well then I'd keep it, put it aside. I guess she figured I was gonna do somethin' else with it, outside what I *did* do with it. She didn't know I was slavin' to leave on it. To get away. I saved around four or five hundred dollars. . . . Last me a long time." By 1926, Rufus had saved enough money to tide him over until he got to Galveston — "a young Heaven on earth outside of San Augustine."

Thirteen years later, Rudolph's seven-year-old son was thrust back into that largely unchanged life of white domination and half-acknowledged interracial families, great natural beauty and physical hardship, strong communal bonds and isolation. Eldrewey's memories of three and a half years in San Augustine are vivid — a mixture of freedom and pleasure, as well as violence, longing, and the struggle to fill up an empty self. Separated from his mother and family, required to care for his bedridden grandmother, Eldrewey the "wise child" spent a good deal of time by himself. In San Augustine, this lonely, precocious, and irrepressible boy took the first steps toward his career as an angry "raceman."

To get to the Roberts Community, a traveler had to journey three miles out of San Augustine on Farm-to-Market Road 2213 and take the third dirt road to the left, right next to the church and cemetery. Tall trees overhung that red dirt road, which curved to the right after half a mile and came to a dead end in front of Lorenzo Roberts's land. About six families still lived out in Roberts Community in those days. The Roberts church doubled as a one-room schoolhouse. "It was located right in the middle of the graveyard which provided enough ghost stories to make your hair stand on end. The 'haints' and white ghosts used to go up the road from the graveyard to Roberts Community, and we had to walk that road to get to school, a mile and a half each way."

Up a little footpath off that road, Eldrewey lived in a small house with his Aunt Lena, Uncle Frank, Grandmother Mollie, and Grandpa Corey. Frank's father, Grant Reed, had bought some land from Little Wiley's father, Lorenzo Roberts. "Except for the fields in front, the property was shrouded by piney woods and the thickets, which were smaller trees with underbrush that rabbits hid in and squirrels and armadillos."

Grant Reed's house sat a few hundred yards up the path from Grandmother Mollie and Grandpa Corey's gate. L. C. Reed, known as Coodlum, lived in that house and planned to die there. "Cousin Ophelia lived down the path in the other direction. Everyone was related to each other in some way," Eldrewey remembers. "A lot of people — white and black — worked at the sawmills, cotton gins, or cotton compressors in San Augustine. My Uncle Frank and the Reed brothers — Italy, A. K., and L. C. — sold their timber, cut and corded, and their harvested cotton in town."

Mollie and Corey's one-story house was about ten years old when Eldrewey arrived. It had never been painted and was turning gray. "It looked like a little colonial house, with a front porch and a back porch that ran the whole length of the building and pillars holding up the front porch roof. A little bit of Mississippi and a little bit of East Texas."

Frank and Lena's room overlooked the meadow. "That's where he kept his .45 and his shotgun." Eldrewey slept in a sturdy iron daybed in the living room, "except there was no living — no activity in it except for me and my friends and my cousins when they visited. My aunt was very particular about sewing heavy quilts that made the bed look very attractive during the day when no one was in it." Mollie and Corey had their beds in a room facing the road.

The kitchen also served as a dining room. "It had an ice box that was iced once a month from the city to make ice cream or something special. There was no refrigeration, no electricity at all." The outhouse seemed to be a mile away, "especially when you had to go in a hurry. It had two toilet holes in case of two emergencies occurring at the same time."

Behind the house was a big backyard that Eldrewey took to "like a newborn calf to its mother's tits." The yard had a cement well, a smokehouse where salted meats hung all year round, a crib where cotton was kept, a large hog pen, and a chicken yard in which stood a majestic mulberry tree. They also had a good-sized vegetable garden, well fenced in to keep the chickens and hogs out. "I loved [that garden] better than any other plot of land on earth," Eldrewey says. "I used to grow red, juicy tomatoes as big as cantaloupes. There is a glint of salvation in my mouth right now as I think back on many cool mornings when, as the chickens left their roost, I'd sneak into the garden armed with salt and pepper, pull one of those luscious ripe tomatoes, douse it, and then sink my teeth into it. I have often joked since that if given the choice between sex and a tomato, I'd take the tomato."

Water was very valuable in Roberts Community, since no one had indoor plumbing. Eldrewey's family hauled their water from a deep well with a square top, thick wooden shoulder, and red clay sides. "There was red land there too. Red dirt. Red clay. I had never seen red dirt before, but it was in all the ditches where I used to fish for crawdads. And there were hills, up hills and down hills to Steep Creek, where we swam and watered the horses. Steep Creek ran into the Toac River, an Indian name, and Mollie Branch, named after my grandmother, ran into the creek."

Lena and several other women washed their clothes on a rub board at Mollie Branch. Frank used to muddy the waters in Steep Creek to make the fish come to the top. "At Steep Creek ford, I've seen my grandfather let his horse drink first and then lie down on his belly and drink himself."

One night Eldrewey baited a fishhook and left it out overnight in Mollie Branch. Early the next morning before school, he raced "through the back yard, past the chicken house and the meadow, past the cattle that were still sleeping, to see how my hook was doing. When I got there, I couldn't see the hook in the shallow water." But when he pulled in the line, "it was the best pull of my life. There was a big catfish, and I loved that catfish; I put him in a water barrel next to the well and went to school, but I kept thinking all day about that fish." Eldrewey worried that somehow the fish might get out or that someone would find him. "I was just praying that nothing would happen to him. I didn't want to fatten that fish for someone else's supper. I left him there for three days to fatten and then I decided to go ahead and eat him."

Along with tomatoes, catfish, and boiled corn on the cob, Eldrewey loved hunting in San Augustine — something he learned from Uncle Frank, whose rifle put many kinds of wild game on the table. Hunting allowed him to channel a rage whose origins he could never acknowledge: the terrible hurt and loneliness of being separated from his mother. "But what could I kill with a BB gun? Birds, birds, and more birds. I was to birds on this land of bushes, tall grass, and trees what the boll weevil was to cotton. Death." Eldrewey slaughtered birds with a vengeance — "bluebirds, redbirds, yellow hammers, blackbirds, hummingbirds, doves, fealock, jaybirds, robins, woodpeckers, and sparrow. The bird I was afraid to kill for fear of being caught and made to pay a twenty-five dollar fine, was the mockingbird."

Eldrewey's idyllic descriptions of the Roberts Community

camouflage the isolation and emptiness he felt in San Augustine. But at least his love of the wild outdoors helped offset the grim life inside that small graying house. Mollie had mellowed little since Rufus left home in 1926. While she rarely beat Eldrewey, she made it clear that he must rise in the world, an ambition he powerfully internalized. And she gave no warmth to this "wise" grandson — only the cold, unyielding standards of a world she could not enter.

Grandmother Mollie spent most of the day in her hospital bed, raised almost to a sitting position. "She was bedridden, people said, because she had eaten too much salt. I was fascinated over her, and a bit nervous. I knew I was supposed to be waiting on her, not for my keep but because it would give me something to do, something honorable since she was my father's mother." Eldrewey's job was to bring Mollie her food, water, and black coffee. He would set the tray down on the bed next to her and retreat as quickly as possible. "I wouldn't watch her eat because she'd want me to help and I'd always spill something. I'd get the wrath from her when I'd spill coffee on her pretty white sheets."

In the winter, Eldrewey kept the kindling in the fire of a big cast iron, wood-burning stove, right by Mollie's bed. "My Grandpa Corey would spit tobacco juice on the hot stove to the disagreement of my grandmother and anyone else watching him." On cold mornings, Corey would warm his hands over that stove, before putting on his thick leather gloves and going out to cut wood. Grandmother Mollie would be sitting there, mad at every move he made.

"My Grandpa Corey couldn't read or write," remembers Eldrewey. "He was a meek, humble man, very silent, even when he was in the house. He kept his lips as tight as a drum. When he walked through the house, he tiptoed. My grandmother would curse him all the time, saying, 'You son of a bitch, you don't want me, you hate me! You hate me!'

"'I don't hate you, woman,' he'd say."

In Eldrewey's eyes, Mollie dominated Corey "and he felt like a kept man. He slept in her room in his own bed. If she got angry with me, she'd take it out on him. He had no hand at all in my upbringing. He was more a fixture around the place than a husband to anyone." In those days, Corey didn't have a steady job, "but now and then he'd give in . . . and work at the sawmill for a while."

If Mollie couldn't give Eldrewey the love he needed, she did give him the social ambitions she thought he needed. When he first arrived, Eldrewey was fascinated by the field workers — "and there is no such thing as sayin' you come from the country and you ain't picked nobody's cotton or stepped in some horse shit or looked up a mule's ass." He'd watch them drag their sacks down the long rows, plucking the cotton from the bolls for fifty cents a hundred pounds. He enjoyed their songs and paid close attention when someone would go into the woods for water "and a girl would go too and they wouldn't come back for an hour."

When he got a little older, Eldrewey wanted to work in the fields along with the other kids his age. "One of the worst scoldings and outright whippings I received from her . . . was when I came back one evening and announced that I had picked some cotton." She turned "hot as a Texas branding iron" and shouted: " 'Let me tell you one thing, youngun. . . . Your daddy didn't send you here to pick cotton, or chop nobody's cotton. I don't ever want to hear you talk about it. You came here to get an education and to help me and Lena.' " Mollie forbade Eldrewey to do any kind of farm work, nor would she allow him to wear "blue jeans like some field hand." And when Grandmother Mollie said something, "you listened until she got through talking. You didn't make any remarks. You didn't talk when grown people were talking."

Two years later, when Devona mailed Eldrewey a pair of overall blue jeans, she overestimated his height by half a foot. "I was glad I didn't have to wear them field-hand clothes," he recalls. "Even years later when young whites started wearing blue jeans, I still refused to wear them. Even though I love them on other people, I never bought any in my life."

One of Eldrewey's most dreaded chores was sitting at Mollie's bedside for hours, reading out loud from school books and old medical books she had acquired to diagnose her own condition. "Sometimes I nearly hated Grandmother Mollie and actually plotted once in my mind to do away with her."

Even when attempting to put the best face on things, Eldrewey acknowledged the frustrated ambitions, the anger and coldness that impinged on his young psyche. "Grandmother Mollie didn't show me any affection 'cause she didn't have any to give, really. I believe deep down inside, she thought she was doing the right thing by me." Mollie had long straight graying hair, heavy brown freckles, and white features. "That nagging old lady looked like she could have been the queen of some empire. My mother says to this day that when she visited Aunt Lena and Grandmother Mollie during her honeymooning days, they were the two whitest women in San Augustine."

At the same time, however, Mollie turned a friendly face toward the world she viewed from her porches. In a wheelchair that made into a sort of bed, she was often wheeled out for a morning or afternoon's entertainment. Eldrewey remembers that she liked the back porch best. There "she could watch the fowl run around and the hogs playing in the mud and the dirt, and the back of the other animal pens and the smokehouse and the crib and the muscadine vines and the mulberries. It was nature itself. She loved to sit back there with her legs propped up."

From her front porch, Mollie could see neighbors or strangers — "if there were any strangers in San Augustine" — approaching. "On Sundays, the old people coming back from church would stop and chat with Grandmother Mollie. They'd be talking and eating and drinking red soda water and a little blackberry wine my aunt made and some bootleg beer she fermented. They'd be laughing and you could hear them for miles."

For Eldrewey, however, life offered little reason to laugh. He had only two playmates in San Augustine — cousin Granville Roberts, "who used to fight me all the time," and Celestine Reed, "my kissin' cousin." Celestine was a year and a half older than Eldrewey, stood a full head taller, and was much wiser in the ways of country life. "She was literally my hunting rock, on whose strong, broad shoulders I stood when robbing a bird's nest for eggs or luring the adult birds within shooting range. . . . She seemed to love hunting birds, rabbits, squirrels, or armadillos, all of which I shot with my BB gun or with my slingshot, which we, just like the white people, called a 'nigger shooter.' With my nigger shooter, I could inflict as much damage as David did with his against the giant Goliath."

Life in San Augustine offered Eldrewey little opportunity for friendship. On many days, he'd walked to school alone; often, the only other person in that one-room school was the "principal" — his uncle, Oliver Roberts. Aunt Lena didn't want Eldrewey going beyond the land they lived on to play with other kids who lived down the road. So he spent many days playing by himself in an open meadow behind the chicken yard. "I learned to live alone and loved it," he claims. "People, even today," he remarked in 1983, "seem to suffocate me. Although I am gregarious by nature, I still court loneliness."

In this country setting, Eldrewey remembers, "I engaged in my first sex. . . . One day while resting calmly behind the chicken yard, right under the shade of a tall mulberry tree, a big three-hundred pound sow came close. I began rubbing her side like she was my dog, who loved for me to rub his back and sides. I suppose any dog does. The hog, whose name was Lucy Mae, gave off a grunt, almost like a woman when she is saying 'no,' and God in heaven knows she means 'yes.' I stroked the warm hairy flesh of this female hog until I got the 'swimmin' in the head,' the head of my penis, which had penetrated Lucy Mae and come to glade water."

Although sexual encounters with animals were not uncommon among country boys, they were considered especially sinful in the Roberts Baptist Church. "I am sure there is a well-kept secret in the hearts of everyone," Eldrewey confided. "I would not be telling this now except for the fact that nearly forty years later, this sinful act on my part was redeemed." In 1979, Eldrewey and a friend were browsing around Times Square in New York City. Out of curiosity, they went to a peep show. "I put in a quarter and got back a million dollars. Right before my eyes was a film of a white woman lying beneath a big black burro twice the size of Lucy Mae. 'Oh God, am I glad to see this,' I thought. 'What is good for the goose is good for the gander.'"

After her stroke, Mollie Stearns only occasionally made the trip in her wheelchair down the red dirt road to the Roberts Baptist Church. But she demanded her grandson attend every Sunday. "If my grandmother had had her way, I'd be preachin' from somebody's pulpit right today. Along with the many books I read by her bedside, I read the Ten Commandments over and over in a catechism she owned. I not only memorized them, I also had to discuss each commandment as though I was being prepared to be a Jewish rabbi or a Baptist preacher."

At the Roberts Baptist Church — just as at the Shiloh African Methodist Church that Devona attended in Galveston — young people were trained to stand up, recite, and speak. Reverend Corn gave lessons in elocution and drilled the children for Bible competition — reading, memorizing, reciting, and discussing scripture. Eldrewey remembers him as a short, barrel-chested, bald-headed, fire-and-brimstone preacher. "That man could cause some of the old black sisters to do somersaults when he'd sing and preach each week. 'Sinner, when the sun goes down . . .' They be shoutin' and standin' on top of their benches and rolling under them, pouring out their souls." One hot Sunday, cousin Ophelia really got going: " 'Oh, help me, Jesus, Lord Jesus, I is coming home. I know I ain't ready, but I am coming anyhow,' she chanted. It took four strong men to hold her down."

Every fourth Sunday ("Preacher's Day"), the Roberts Church program included a speaker other than the minister. Eight-year-old Eldrewey's first chance to preach came when his cousins Lillian and Mildred were visiting from Houston. He was to recite the commandment "Remember the Sabbath and keep it holy." He planned to embellish the commandment, adding, "It is a sin to tell a lie on a Sunday."

Sporting my blue suit with short pants, I hopped up to the pulpit like a young Bible scholar in front of all those people from the surrounding hills and hollows.

Reverend Corn told me to state my name and then said, "Now you g'wan boy. Say what comes to your mind." With that, the cows were already halfway out of the pasture. I began with, "Today is Sunday. It is a shame to tell a lie on a Sunday." Before I could recite the appropriate commandment, there was a resounding "Amen!"

Why not wade further into the water, I thought.

"It is a sin to tell a lie on a Monday!"

"Amen!"

"It is a sin to tell a lie on a Tuesday!"

"Amen!"

And so went Wednesday, Thursday, Friday, and Saturday.

All the while, my cousins from Houston were moving around in their seats like they were sitting on one of those wild bull nettles. When I reached Saturday, I got adventurous.

"And it is not only a sin to tell a lie on a Sunday, but it is a sin to tell a lie at any time or anywhere. . . ."

Before I could get back to the commandment I knew so well, Reverend Corn had acceded to my Cousin Lillian's motion to set me down.

This was my first and last sermon.

But it was not the last time he would speak before a church congregation.

Aunt Lena walked ahead of Eldrewey as they made their way along the gravel road into San Augustine. Once a month, they went to town to buy staples like salt, pepper, and flour. Otherwise, the family was largely self-sufficient. They raised vegetables, meats, and poultry and made their own butter, sugar, and molasses.

In Eldrewey's mind, what happened that day in the town square "was as common as road lizards in East Texas. That hot, hot, blistering hot summer Saturday is as fresh on my memory as Grandpa Corey's steaming black, bitter coffee. My friends and family had told me many times: 'There is two things that don't live long. One is a dog that chases cars. The other is a nigger that talks back to white folks!' I was rather playful, I admit. My horse-driving grandmother always told me I was too playful for my own good."

Lena and Eldrewey walked across the old courthouse square and passed a group of black men in overalls, chewing tobacco and trading yarns. As they approached the Brookshire Brothers General Store, an old white man in his late sixties was barely making it out the door. He was carrying "six 'number 8' tubs — the kind we used to bathe in every Saturday — on his shoulders. 'You're totin' too much there, Jess. Let me help you,' another white man cautioned. Old Jess just grunted something like 'Outa my way. I'm all right.'"

Then the old man slipped on something. His long, bony legs went out from under him and the tubs went rolling down the cobblestone streets. The startled horses tried to bolt with their wagons. A crowd of black men was looking from across the square. "God knows I was laughing like my insides was going to bust open," remembers Eldrewey. "I couldn't wait to tell my cousins."

When Jess finally landed on the bottom tub, he looked around. A big black washerwoman was giggling as she walked by. Old Jess jumped up and "smacked the smile off her fleshy face. He kept beatin' on the left side of her face. 'Somebody help me, please!' she kept crying. 'I'll teach you to laugh at a white man, you black bitch. Don't you know better than to laugh at a white man?'

"'Please, Mr. Jess, don't hit me no more. I'z sorry. I swear I is. So help me, Jesus, I ain't gonna laugh at no white man no mo. I swear I ain't.'"

Jess stopped beating the woman. Then he wheeled around to see who else was laughing. "This tall, blue-eyed, white-wrinkled-face son of a bitch — I've been waiting to say this for forty years — looked at me," Eldrewey recalls:

> **Like a Texas jackrabbit, I jumped behind my Aunt Lena's wide dress tail. She turned and slapped me full in the face. The day turned into a night full of stars.**
>
> **"I got that little scamp for you, Mr. Jess," she yelled. "He knows better than to be laughin' at white folks."**
>
> **Old Jess was almost tickled pink. "You better get him, or I sure as hell will." He looked all around for more black-faced laughter. No one made a sound.**
>
> **Right then and there I solemnly swore to God that I would answer a call to see that such inhumanity would never be visible to my eyes again.**

Looking back from his fifties, Eldrewey remembered this event in the San Augustine courthouse square as "my first summons" to fight against racial injustice. He did not, however, mention that there are *two* events described in this scene: old Jess beating the washerwoman and Lena slapping Eldrewey. This burning memory thus contains feelings of powerlessness and anger directed at Lena as well as Jess. Her slap, though intended to save him from a worse beating, may well have felt like a betrayal, another reason for this lonely "wise child" to feel that no one could really be trusted. The next year, when Eldrewey's mother finally came to take him back to Galveston, he didn't even recognize her face.

"One eye-squinting day in the summer of 1942, Aunt Lena called inside from the front porch, 'Eldrewey, there is your mama.'"

Eldrewey hadn't seen his mother for three and a half years. "We had corresponded, but I had forgot what she looked like." Two women about the same age and size got out of a blue car. "'Which one is she?' I asked Aunt Lena. I thought I was going to take one of those fainting spells like Celestine's mother Miss Murdy always had on Sundays in the Roberts' church."

Eldrewey recalls Lena pleading with Devona not to take him away:

> **"He is happy here," my Aunt said. "He loves the country and is doing so well in school. We treat him like a king, he doesn't want for anything." She was taking the words right out of my mouth.**
>
> **My mother stuck to her decision like a big tick on a country hound. But my Aunt was just as stubborn.**
>
> **My mother was shoutin' and prancin' around Aunt Lena like a stallion in a corral. "Eldrewey is *my* son, Lena. My flesh and blood. Rufus has plenty of work now, and the children want to see their brother."**

Devona, who missed her son terribly during those years, remembers how awkward their reunion was:

> **I looked at him and said, "Eldrewey, you ready to go home?" . . . He looked at me and he looked at his Daddy and he says, "Uh-uh."**
>
> **I says, "Eldrewey, why you lookin' at us so strange?"**
>
> **He says, "You my mother?"**
>
> **I said, "Yes, I'm your mother." Kind of knew his daddy, because he hadn't lost his features, you know. He said, "I**

know Daddy." But women people changes a whole lot, you know. So I hugged him and kissed him and said, "This is mother."

Eldrewey was sent to pack up his things, and before long they were on that red dirt road heading away. "I was so filled with tears and mixed emotions, I don't even remember if I said goodbye. But Grandpa Corey, Uncle Frank, Aunt Lena, and Grandmother Mollie—who was on the porch in her wheelchair—all waved to me."

On that long trip down home, Devona tearfully tried to reconnect with her firstborn child. "All the way goin' home that day," she remembers, "he was standin' up by me in the car . . . and he kept lookin' at me, lookin' at me. . . ." Something was irrevocably gone from their relationship. Eldrewey had become, he says, "as wild as a wildebeest and as distant as a falling star. So close and yet so far away."

Many times I've thought, especially
as I've grown older, about an eye for
an eye and a tooth for a tooth. And
I've said to myself: I do not believe in
an eye for an eye; I do not believe in a
tooth for a tooth. . . . I believe if you
borrow my tooth, I want your whole
set. I want your whole set.

Eldrewey Stearns

Eldrewey's long absence in the country left him with life-long feelings of isolation, powerlessness, and rage. Wrenched away from his parents, this impulsive "wise child" never recovered the sense of stability and nurture he needed to experience the world as a safe place. Father figures appeared distant and ineffectual. Mothers could never be trusted; they might exile you to the wilderness, slap you down rather than stand up for you. Eldrewey's encounter with old Jess and Aunt Lena generated a strong moral outrage at racial injustice. It also left him feeling betrayed by his own family and yearning for an all-powerful figure to protect him.

In San Augustine, Eldrewey had to adapt both to the brutality of whites and to his lonely, demanding life with Aunt Lena, Uncle Frank, Grandmother Mollie, and Grandpa Corey. He developed a cunning style of meeting the demands of authority figures while concealing and avoiding his real feelings. He learned to live in his own imaginary world, a world filled with his own inflated powers and devoid of stable, caring relationships.

For three long years, Devona worried, cried, and dreamt about her "lost" son. At ten years old, he was already a legend and a stranger to his brothers and sisters. One evening in the summer of 1942, a white woman selling homemade roses knocked on the door of the family's rent house. "Would you like me to tell your fortune?" the woman asked. Devona invited the woman in. She offered to read Devona's mind for fifty cents. "And I said okay," Devona remembers. "I was worried about Eldrewey. So I gave her fifty cents which I needed very badly at that time." They sat down across the kitchen table. The woman took Devona's hand and spoke: "I see where you have a child somewheres . . . it seems to me it's a male child. . . . you worry about this child all the time. And this child has been ill." Right then and there, Devona decided to bring Eldrewey home. She prevailed on Rudolph to borrow a neighbor's car. They made the journey to San Augustine and back in a single day. Again, Eldrewey was snatched without warning.

When the old black Model A Ford turned into the alley behind the corner of 32nd Street and Avenue M½, the neighborhood kids were waiting. Earl had been boasting to Joe Gayden that his *big* brother Eldrewey would be home soon. Joe was about thirteen years old then, living with his parents and four siblings in a one-bedroom apartment — in the same alley duplex that housed the Stearns family. "So when they drove in the alley," Joe remembers, "I thought he [Eldrewey] was gonna be a *great big dude*, you know." Instead, a nervous little kid with a BB gun got out of the car. "Where's your brother?" Joe asked Earl mockingly. "Oh please! Oh, no, no, that can't be your brother."

To Eldrewey, this didn't feel like a homecoming at all. "Joe Gayden, a rough-faced brown-skinned neighborhood bully, the son of a jackleg preacher, was an eyewitness to my homecoming and he laughed at my every move." Eldrewey felt suffocated by all the houses and people so close together. He asked Devona to take him back to San Augustine. "I didn't want to cry. I was too big to cry, but I was sorry I was coming into this jungle of people."

Eldrewey was barely out of the car when he started shooting his BB gun at city birds perched on the telephone wires. Devona told him never to shoot his gun like that again. She was ashamed, he recalls, of "how wild and country I had become. . . . Every time I heard a bird, I couldn't help but raise my gun. . . . 'Country' was written all over my face and shoeless feet." They unpacked the car and went inside the yellow rent house.

Geraldine, Earl, and Shirley swarmed around their lost brother. Eight-year-old Geraldine — known as "Sister" in the family — was pretty and well on her way, Eldrewey thought later, toward a "life-long successful career as somewhat bossy." Earl was six years old, the "best looking male child I have ever seen, black as he was." Shirley was two and a half, "brown sugar, sweet enough for any-one's coffee." Eldrewey's sisters and brother had expected "me to be much taller but I wasn't a big corn-fed nigger . . . I was a snake-chasin', rabbit-eatin' runt as countrified as a backyard well."

That evening, Eldrewey went out into the alley to explore his new surroundings. He started playing marbles with Joe Gayden and a few other kids. Gayden hustled all the kids out of their mar-bles in a game called "holey." Eldrewey, who never took kindly to being beaten or teased, got mad and threw a brick at Joe. "And then he took off runnin'," Gayden remembers. "I couldn't catch him because he hit between so many aisles and exits and ins and outs in them alleys." Joe's fame in the neighborhood was derived from hanging John Jones upside down on a telephone pole by his cuffs. When he eventually caught Eldrewey, Joe didn't do any real damage. "Just shake him up a little bit. . . . throw him on the ground. And laugh."

After that, Eldrewey made a habit of baiting and throwing things at Joe Gayden. "You know he talked all the time. And he just talked, you know, bad things. But he stay about ten or fifteen yards in front of you. Can't catch him. And he'd throw sumpin at you — and run! . . . I thought he was a little bitty runt, and a rabbit. . . . So that's where the rabbit come in!"

"Rabbit" was a nickname that clung to Eldrewey until high school. "One reason they called me Rabbit was because I could run so damn fast," he remembers. It was not, however, a glamorous title. "The name stuck to me like the rabbit stuck to the tar baby of the Uncle Remus tales. I thought my big white buck teeth made me look like a rabbit." This nickname fit Eldrewey for other reasons: it symbolized his country ways, his small stature, his cunning and elusiveness, his tendency to run for cover. But "Rabbit" did not capture other characteristics: his aggressiveness, hot temper, apparent fearlessness, and fondness for provoking people. He liked to hang around and provoke the bigger boys — who, unlike Joe Gayden, enjoyed beating him up. "He was always getting into confrontations with people," remembers Geraldine. "He'd say whatever he'd feel like saying and it got him beat up. He didn't hold back."

Eldrewey was also known for his gift of speech. "My lies were nothing short of legend in that family." At night, children would gather around, listening to his "preaching," mesmerized by ghost stories from the country. "I mean he would have us sitting . . . and preach whole sermons," recalls Geraldine. "I thought he knew what he was talking about. Oh, he had a bunch, the neighbors, the kids. He would have church. He would preach. . . . the kids loved him."

In Roberts Community, where six families lived on four square miles of redland soil, Eldrewey had gone to sleep for three years to the roar of cicadas in late summer and awakened to chirping songbirds, crowing roosters, grunting cattle and hogs. Galveston's "colored" neighborhood had its share of fierce cicadas and early morning roosters too. But here families were squeezed into tiny rent houses, narrowly spaced along alleyways built on a layer of beach sand, oyster shells, clay, and Mississippi Delta silt that had been pumped out of the Gulf of Mexico to raise and protect the island after the devastating hurricane of 1900.

In place of piney woods, pastures, and fields stood barbershops, small businesses, churches, beer and barbecue joints. The neighborhood's main strip was 29th Street (now Martin Luther King Boulevard) between Broadway and Seawall Boulevard. Local black businesses included Hebert's Funeral Home, Heard's and Honey Brown's barbecue joints, and Robinson's Drugstore. Central High School, the state's oldest high school for blacks, stood at 27th and M. The Shiloh African Methodist Episcopal Church — where Devona Stearns took her family — was within shouting distance of others like the Avenue L Baptist Church or the Macedonia Baptist Church.

In the fall of 1942, Eldrewey entered the fifth grade in Galveston. Instead of walking along the red dirt road to the Roberts church and schoolhouse, he walked down Avenue M½ to George W. Carver Elementary School. That year, the teacher, John Clouser, told Rudolph that Eldrewey was extremely bright but needed more discipline. Clouser thought that Eldrewey needed to be in a private school, where he might develop the habits necessary to harness his intelligence. Rudolph had a good painting contract with the railroad, but private school was never a real possibility.

Eldrewey quickly learned his way around. He liked to hang out with Joe Gayden and his brothers, Pappy Gamble, Loni Dedrick, Lorenzo Dent (whose father was then the only black lawyer in Galveston), and Edward Crockett, known as "Nubby" because he had recently been circumcised. In the alleyways, between houses, and on street fronts, the boys kept busy breaking out street lights, fighting, shooting marbles, playing softball or football, and playing hide-and-seek with the girls.

"Nigger baby" was an especially popular neighborhood game played between the houses. The players were each assigned to one of nine holes spaced about a foot apart on either side of a straight line. They took turns rolling a tennis ball and waiting to see if the ball fell into a hole, like a golf ball on a green. Each time the ball fell into someone's hole, a stone was placed in that hole. If the ball missed all the holes, a stone was put into the thrower's hole. When any hole reached nine stones, a "nigger baby" was born. The player who possessed that hole had to put his face against the wall of a house, and the other players would throw the ball at his back. Each player had nine chances to hit the "parent." "It was a cruel game, no doubt about it," Eldrewey remembers.

When it came to playing hide-and-seek with the girls, Miss Gali, an Italian girl whose father ran a corner grocery store, was especially obliging. "I had longed to see what a white girl was made of," Eldrewey recalls. "I didn't think they were made of the same thing as black girls." One evening that summer, behind a pink oleander tree, Miss Gali gave the boys her challenge: "If one of you shows your dick, I'll show my pussy." None of the boys jumped immediately at the opportunity, Eldrewey remembers, because "every boy wanted to see how big another guy's prick was without exposing his own." After a minute Odell, "a friend of mine with the biggest prick I knew, stepped forward. He pulled out his 'meat,' as we called it, and the crowd jeered, 'We want Miss Gali.' True to her word, the young white girl let down her pants, and bending over backwards as much as she could without falling, she said, 'You see! You see!' I saw enough."

Historically, Galveston had a reputation for being enlightened in matters of race relations. Unlike other areas in Texas where plantation slavery prevailed in the nineteenth century, Galveston boasted a more genteel form of the peculiar institution. Although the island hosted auctions for Texas slave markets, local slaves often received special privileges. Before the Civil War, wealthy Galvestonians considered it genteel to indulge their slaves' desires for conspicuous consumption. Certain slaveholders bought silks, satins, crinolines, and hats with feathers for their black slaves, who might be seen Sunday afternoons driving about in their masters' carriages or parading on horseback. This tradition of elite whites showering their "house niggers" with special privileges persisted well into the twentieth century. It would provide Eldrewey with unique opportunities during his high-school years.

But Eldrewey's childhood and teenaged years in the Oleander City were also filled with racial encounters that were anything but pleasant. Shortly after he joined the Boy Scouts at age eleven, Eldrewey found that a scout's offer of service was not always welcome. One afternoon in the fall of 1943, Mrs. Heron, grandmother of Eldrewey's friend Tootsie, called out to him from her front-porch swing, "Come here, son. I want you to do an errand for me." Mrs. Heron, the only white woman in the neighborhood, raised chickens, turkeys, ducks, and pecans in her backyard. She asked Eldrewey to deliver a bag with two freshly killed hens to Mr. Gali's store on 33rd Street, offering him a nickel and two handfuls of pecans.

Eldrewey stuffed the bag under his arm and ran down to the store. "'Boy,' Mr. Gali screamed, 'what the hell do you mean bringing me those fresh chickens under your musty colored arms?'" Eldrewey struggled to contain his reactions: "I wanted to cry, but the tears wouldn't come. I wanted to kick his white ass, but my feet weren't big enough. In a second he was dialing Mrs. Heron, telling her so that everyone in the store could hear him: 'I'm sending these damn chickens back to you. This little nigger has ruined them by carrying them under his musty black arms!'" Mr. Gali hung up the phone. "'Now get, boy!,' and he slammed the door behind me."

In the segregated Boy Scout troop, led by Scoutmaster Charles Moore, Eldrewey soon came to a jaded view of the Scouts' basic pledges. "'Be Prepared' was what was really taught," he remembers, "especially if you were going to live as a Negro in white society." When Eldrewey was thirteen, his troop took a week-long camping trip to League City, thirty miles north of Galveston Island. There they camped on the swampy acreage of a white philanthropist named Waters Davis. Eldrewey, who was then a senior patrol leader and almost a first-class scout, walked through the woods with Mr. Moore to visit Camp Mohawk, where the white scouts were located. At Camp Mohawk, he found the whites diving and splashing about in a large blue swimming pool, eating in a mess hall. "It was a small paradise isolated in the woods. I remember talking with Mr. Moore on the way back, wondering why we couldn't have something like that—the swimming pool and all the luxuries."

If Eldrewey learned about inequality in the Boy Scouts, he also learned to break the rules and avoid the consequences. To impress his friend Joe Carmen, he took ten dollars from the cigar box that held the proceeds from the troop's annual Scout Jamboree ticket sales. The two boys went to the movies, played the slot machines, and filled themselves with barbecued beef and soda. "I was ashamed and scared to tell Mr. Moore what happened to the ticket money," Eldrewey remembers. "I couldn't tell him a lie. So I quit the Boy Scouts."

Eldrewey's fondness for breaking rules and provoking people occasionally got him into serious trouble. One afternoon, he and some friends were sitting on a log across the street from Pappy Gamble's house. Pappy, an older teenager whom Eldrewey admired for his "awkward Louisiana ways," was whittling on his front porch, leaning back against a banister in a straw-bottomed chair. The younger boys began throwing chinaberries at him. Pappy looked up from his whittling and brandished his Texas Jack: "Throw another goddam chinaberry at me and one of you little motherfuckers is going to get this."

At the next volley of chinaberries, Pappy, who never allowed anyone to touch his chest, walked across the alley. Joe Gayden warned Eldrewey: "Man, don't touch him up there." Laughing, Eldrewey grabbed Pappy "by his titty" and then took off down the alley. Pappy pegged his switchblade, which hit Eldrewey in the back of the head. When Pappy went to pick up his silver weapon, he noticed that a piece was missing from the tip. "Everyone was all concerned that the broken-off piece was in my head. . . . Blood was trickling from the back of my head like water from a country spring. Pappy pleaded for me not to blab a word."

When he got home, Devona noticed blood trickling down the back of his head. "Eldrewey, come here," she said. "What happened?" She put his head under the faucet, stopped the bleeding, and cleaned the cut with rubbing alcohol. "Oh, it's nothin'. I just scratched it on a nail," he answered. He was out the door again before Devona had finished putting the alcohol away.

For weeks, Eldrewey and Joe had been scouting oranges, peaches, and plums in the neighborhood. They knew that Old Mrs. Simon patrolled her yard during the day with a .38 caliber pistol. Figuring that darkness would protect them from her wrath, they waited until night to collect their forbidden fruit. Standing on Joe's shoulders, Eldrewey bagged a dozen of Mrs. Simon's plums, eating a bellyful between the pickings. The plums were covered with a strange white substance, which the boys ignored in their excitement. Apparently, Mrs. Simon had climbed her own tree and covered the plums with white roach powder, which reached Eldrewey's stomach at school the next afternoon. "My little stomach was churning like we churned milk in the country and my head was threatening to leave my shoulders." He begged the teacher to let him leave school. Walking home, Eldrewey "threw up barrels of nothing but white foam." An old man they called "Doc" took him to the alley steps of his home.

By the time Rudolph got home from work, Eldrewey was limp as a dishrag and losing consciousness. Rudolph took him to the emergency room at the John Sealy Hospital. While they were at the hospital, James Mayes came to the door looking to trade comic books. "Where is Rabbit?" he asked. "Eldrewey's in the hospital," answered Devona. "Because of the knife Pappy Gamble stuck in his head?" asked James. "I say, *what!?*" remembers Devona. "I didn't know what to do with myself, and I jumps up and I ran over to this woman's house. And I said to her, 'Mrs. Gamble, did you know that your son has stuck a knife in my son's head?'"

Eldrewey was brought home from the hospital that night, still unconscious. The next day, he opened his eyes to a roomful of anxious family and friends, including a tearful Mrs. Gamble. Rudolph took him back to Dr. MacMurray the next day, armed with the story of Pappy Gamble's Texas Jack blade. Dr. MacMurray shaved Drew's head but couldn't see or feel anything. "I stayed my distance from Pappy and plums from then on," Eldrewey remembers. Forty-five years later, a CAT scan of his head done at John Sealy Hospital revealed a tiny piece of metal still lodged in his skull.

From the time he returned from San Augustine, Eldrewey was an ambitious, enterprising youngster. For a year, he walked up and down 29th Street after school, hawking black newspapers like the *Pittsburgh Courier, Black Dispatch,* or *Chicago Defender.* The papers sold for fifteen cents apiece, with four cents left in Eldrewey's pocket. Once he worked for an iceman, hauling fifty pounds of ice in a grass sack from the truck to the iceboxes of poor blacks. After one week, his boss paid him and let him go: "You're too small for this work, boy." His next job was at Fort Crockett, Galveston's military establishment on the Gulf of Mexico. For forty cents an hour, Eldrewey set up pins at the bowling alley where white American soldiers sent pins crashing and screamed at black kids to set them up again. Outside, he talked through a cyclone fence to German prisoners of war, who coaxed him to bring them cigarettes.

In the 1940s, summer crowds from all over Texas and the Deep South came to Galveston for the cool Gulf breezes and the beaches. At night they flocked to casinos, nightclubs, bars, and brothels. Entertainers like Sophie Tucker, Frank Sinatra, and Bing Crosby sang at the Balinese Room on Seawall Boulevard. Summers were always busy on the beachfront, where blacks were confined to a one block area along Seawall Boulevard between 28th and 29th streets. On the "white" beaches, there were always jobs for black shoeshine boys, dishwashers, waiters, and hotel custodians. One place called "Hit the Trigger and Dump the Nigger" needed help. The job paid seventy-five cents an hour. "They wanted a 'little nigger' to sit on a platform over water," Eldrewey remembers, while some "white brute" would throw a ball at a bell over "little nigger's head. If the white man hit the bell, the contraption would throw the nigger in the water. . . . they had no takers. Certainly not me."

The summer after eighth grade, Eldrewey went to work at the Watermelon Garden on Seawall Boulevard, hauling watermelons, slicing and selling them for twenty-five cents apiece, putting up umbrellas and waiting on tables. Every May, Walter Young and his wife came down from Dallas, rented an apartment, and ran this flourishing little business until Labor Day. Above the Watermelon Garden stood a large billboard, beckoning thirsty white tourists and bathers: "Sho' nuff, best in town," read the caption underneath a stereotypical black boy with thick red lips and kinky hair. Beside him stood a black girl with pigtails, saying "Yes, suh, sho' am good."

While he hated this sign, Eldrewey nevertheless won Mr. Young's confidence with his energy, intelligence, and hard work. Occasionally, Drew rode with Mr. Young down to the west end of the island and fed rinds to the hogs. Devona remembers getting a phone call from Mr. Young in 1944: "Are you Eldrewey Stearns's mother? I don't know what I'd do without him. . . . How many more do you have like him?" he asked. "I have two more boys," she answered proudly. "But there's not another one like him."

The following summer, Mr. Young gave Eldrewey the key to the cash register and told him to handle the business himself until noon. Late one morning, a car from Mississippi pulled over; two couples who had already had their share of booze got out and sat down at a table. Grinning, the red-headed man called Drew over to the table. "Hey, boy! I just bet my wife here five dollars that this is your picture up there," he said, pointing to the billboard. "Now don't say I'm wrong 'cause you'll be in trouble, you hear?"

The man's wife turned pink and looked away. The other couple snickered. "It's your mama's picture, motherfucker!" shouted Eldrewey. He pulled off his apron, raced across the street, down the cement seawall stairs, and across the sand toward the 28th Street beach. The two white men threw over their chairs and followed him down the beach. "Stop that nigger. He stole my wallet!" the red-head yelled to the white sunbathers. Eldrewey reached the black beach yelling, "Help! Stop those white men. They want to kill me." A black policeman met the whites at the color line and defused what might have been a racial brawl.

Next door to the Watermelon Garden stood a whites-only roller-skating rink. Especially when business was slow, Eldrewey took his time cleaning seeds and juice from the tables, watching the girls skate in circles around the wooden floor. He seemed to attract all kinds of trouble, especially from the men who came around looking for prostitutes. Often, he was approached by men from out of town: "Boy, where can I get some black tail? I know you know. You live here, damn it, don't you? I want some good pussy, Negro pussy. Steer me straight and there'll be something in it for you." Looking for a tip, he'd direct them to the red-light district on Church or Postoffice streets, where the price of sex was pegged to skin color: white women cost ten dollars, Mexican women seven dollars, and black women three. Gamblers received directions to the Turf, Lloyd's, or the Brass Rail on Market Street, where they could play pool, slot machines, crap tables, card games, and roulette.

One Friday night, after collecting his fourteen-dollar manager's salary, Drew bought himself a pair of new shoes and went to a late movie at the Booker T. Washington theater on Market Street. After the movie, he stood on the corner waiting to catch the last bus home. A car pulled over and a white man rolled down his window. "Do you know where the Star Motel is, boy? It's on Stewart

Beach or someplace like that." Thinking he saw a free ride home, Eldrewey offered to show the man where Stewart Beach was.

He got in the car, driven by a white man whose hands were black with automobile grease. The man was stocky, unshaven, and wore a crewcut. Eldrewey remembers the sound of belching and the smell of alcohol on his breath as they approached Stewart Beach on Galveston's East End. In the darkness, the man pulled off the street and parked his car in the sand. He pulled out a knife, unzipped his pants, and forced Eldrewey's head down over his penis. "I thought then it was bad enough for women to suck a man's prick, let alone a man or boy," he remembers. "Sick from sucking and about to vomit," Eldrewey thought of a way out. "You can try my ass," he suggested, trying to buy time. "Now that's better, you little sweet nigger, you. Let's get into the back seat."

When the man climbed over the front seat, Eldrewey hesitated—and lost his chance to run. "I thought he'd surely catch me in the sand and kill me to keep somebody from knowing what happened. What was worse, I didn't want to leave my new shoes behind." The drunken white mechanic finally gave up trying to penetrate Eldrewey. As they drove into the 32nd Street area, Eldrewey—trying to lure him back "so that I could kill him"—suggested that other neighborhood boys would accommodate him. The man declined the invitation and pulled out a ten-dollar bill. "I knew then that he was afraid and he was giving me some hush, hush money. There was no need to say I had pride and did not accept the money, because all my pride was out the window."

When the man let Eldrewey off in front of his house, a local gang known as the Ziglers was sitting on the corner. They asked Eldrewey why he was riding with a white man. Afraid of being humiliated, he said the white man had given him some trouble and told them to butt out. "When I got home, I cried all night, thinking about what I'd do if I ever saw him again and how I'd been humiliated by this man and I couldn't tell anybody. I almost grew to hate myself more than that white creature for not saying, 'fuck the shoes,' or 'run, nigger, run.'"

The finale to Eldrewey's career at the Watermelon Garden began one bright morning, when a chubby Italian cabdriver called him over to the curb. "Hey, boy, bring me a cold slice of that melon." Eldrewey brought him the melon. "Lean over here a minute," he said, pulling Drew's head into the car. "I'm going to gamble tonight and I need some luck." He rubbed Eldrewey's head and flipped him a dime. "I could not sleep that night and kept thinking of what I would do if I ever saw this cocksucker again."

The next day, the cabdriver pulled into the same place. "Hey, boy, I want to see you," he called out. "I don't want no watermelon. I won real good last night. I got a piece of change for you." Eldrewey talked the cabbie into taking a piece of watermelon. "In his mind he had done no wrong; in my mind he had done no right. Rubbing my head was like calling my mother a black whore to her face." The cabbie was grinning when Eldrewey took the melon to his car. He reached into his pocket and pulled out a few silver coins. "Here's yours," he said. "Here's yours, motherfucker," replied Eldrewey, pushing the ripe red watermelon into the driver's face. "I could see him brushing the black seeds from his big scroungy lap and face. We were both in a state of shock." Again, Eldrewey took off running, this time toward the Galvez hotel, where he disappeared among anonymous black waiters, busboys, and custodians. That was his last day at the Watermelon Garden.

Despite his barely contained rage and hair-trigger temper, Eldrewey seemed unable to defend himself physically or to inflict violence directly on others. But he remained on good terms with various gangs who patrolled their neighborhood turf or went looking for someone to pick on. The roughest of these gangs—the Paddy Hunters—was led by Garland Edwards, a legendary fighter with a long scar down the right side of his face. Garland's penchant for hunting "paddies" was apparently motivated by revenge against the whites who had killed his father in a car accident many years earlier. The Paddy Hunters sometimes used Eldrewey as an innocent-looking decoy to attract their white prey. He used them to get revenge against the man who had raped him.

In the 1940s, Galveston was still a walking city. Cars had not yet completely taken over the streets. After dark, people downtown or on the Seawall spilled out of nightclubs, bars, casinos, brothels, and beer joints. Fear of violence did not occupy much space in the city's public imagination. But in Eldrewey's experience and in his intense fantasy life, violence loomed large.

One night, he was walking down Broadway with Garland and

Paddy Hunters Odel Ellis, James Smith, and Robert Madison. They sized up a white man waiting for the bus. Jumping behind some bushes, Garland said to Eldrewey, "Ask the motherfucker for a quarter. If he says no, give us the signal and I'll get his white ass." Eldrewey walked up to the white man. "'Do you have a quarter, mister?' I asked in a polite young voice, hoping and praying he would say yes for his own benefit." "No, I don't," the man answered, "but I have enough for your bus fare." Despite the man's goodwill, Garland and the Paddy Hunters pounced on him. "They beat and kicked this guy without mercy," remembers Eldrewey. "I ran home by myself." This episode epitomizes a characteristically confusing and enduring ambivalence: Eldrewey identifies both with the innocent victim and with the vengeful anger of the Paddy Hunters. Caught between powerful feelings of both sympathy and rage, he runs home by himself.

A few weeks after Eldrewey stopped working at the Watermelon Garden, he was sitting at Heard's Barbecue on 29th Street. The man who had raped him walked in and ordered. Eldrewey slipped outside and found the Paddy Hunters hanging around the corner. "That's the man who beat me up on East Beach," he told them. A few minutes later, the man walked out of Heard's and started to get into his dirty old car. Four Paddy Hunters jumped him and began kicking him and pummeling his face. Eldrewey's memory of this incident is revealing: "He was screaming for mercy. They had been beating up white people without a reason; now they had a reason. I wanted them to kill him, and if they did, I'd call it an execution. [And yet] I ran the short distance home. I couldn't stand to hear his agony, the pain that I knew he was going through. I wasn't that kind of boy even though I wanted him dead."

There's nothing wrong with
prostitution except the prostitutes
themselves. Like jail, there's
nothing wrong with jail as there is
much wrong with people in jail.
Nothing wrong with medicine,
just some of the doctors. Nothing
wrong with law, just those left to
enforce it and interpret it. There's
nothing wrong with me, the writer
of my life and teller of my dreams,
but sometimes something is wrong
with the dreams.

Eldrewey Stearns

When Eldrewey entered Galveston's Central High School in the fall of 1945, he was drifting quickly toward a life of street corner gangs and underworld activities. "I don't know why it's called underworld," he says, "because everybody could see what everyone else was doing."

No longer working at Mr. Young's Watermelon Garden, Eldrewey spent more time at the black beachfront less than a mile away. Though largely confined to the block between 28th and 29th streets, blacks came from hundreds of miles around to splash in the Gulf of Mexico and patronize businesses lining the north side of that block on Seawall Boulevard. Buster Landrum, a huge and legendary policeman — and the first African American to arrest a white man in Galveston County — remembered this block as a "Mecca" for blacks, who also congregated in more isolated areas of the beach, west of the ten-mile Seawall.

Every summer, thousands of black customers flocked from Corpus Christi, New Orleans, Port Arthur, and Houston to businesses like the Black Cat, the Bathhouse, Manhattan Rose, and the Gulfview Pavilion. On holidays like July 4 or Juneteenth (June 19), these places drew especially large crowds.

Money to start black businesses was often provided by the Maceo family. John Ned Rose, for example, borrowed money in the 1940s from Sam Maceo to set up the Gulf View Pavilion, a place as big as a cotton shed that seated three hundred people at a time. Rose served chicken, fish, shrimp, potato salad, french fries, and "set ups" (ice in a glass — customers provided their own liquor). Slot machines, swallowing nickels, dimes, quarters, and silver dollars, lined the walls of the Gulf View. Rose split the cash from the slot machines with Maceo, paid off his debts with the earnings, and loaned money with what was left over. Odds on the slot machines ranged from two to one all the way up to the "Long Shot" on the Horse Racing Machine — thirty quarters to one. Count Basie, Duke Ellington, Ella Fitzgerald, and the Inkspots came through singing their numbers too.

Harold Stovall, who became a lifelong friend after meeting Eldrewey at a Boy Scout Jamboree, credits himself with pulling Drew away from this world of gambling and "corner delinquents," like the Ziglers or the Paddy Hunters. Harold and his twin brother, Harry, lived in a largely white section of the East

End known as the Silk Stocking District. During the summer, their mother didn't want them venturing beyond 21st Street toward the rougher "West End" neighborhood, north of Broadway, where the Stearns family lived. Mrs. Stovall's wishes, however, didn't stop the Stovall twins from scuffling with Eldrewey and establishing their right to walk the turf of the West Enders. They soon became regulars and joined a tight-knit class that graduated from Central High School in 1949.

In 1945, the Stovalls were working at Galveston's elite Artillery Club, which stood at the intersection of 18th Street and Avenue P½, where it merged with Seawall Boulevard. The club was next to the Galvez hotel and across the boulevard from the entrance to the Balinese Room, the Maceos' famous illegal gambling establishment that sat on stilts extending over four hundred feet into the Gulf of Mexico. The Stovalls had been hired by their shop teacher, Mosely Jackson, who worked evenings as a manager. Jackson gave the club keys to the twins, who went in every day after school and had the club up and running at four o'clock. They worked mixing drinks, serving snacks and dinner, and cleaning up until eleven o'clock or when the last member went home for the night. Sam Maceo, whose slot machines got plenty of use at the Artillery Club, was only allowed in through the back door.

In late 1946, Harold got Eldrewey a job at the Artillery Club through an interesting sequence of events. When the new model cars came out that fall, Mosely Jackson, flush with the income from two jobs, bought himself a 1947 Dodge. Knowing the unwritten code that new cars were reserved for whites (with a few exceptions like T. D. Armstrong or Gus Allen), Mr. Jackson parked his car a few blocks away from Central High and walked the rest of the way to school every day. But, remembers Harold, somebody on the Galveston School Board found out about Jackson's new car "and they said he was making too much money." Mr. Jackson quit his job at the Artillery Club to protect his (and his wife's) job teaching high school. At the Artillery Club, Abraham Lincoln Tims was promoted to steward. Harold became Tim's assistant and hired Eldrewey to fill his spot as a waiter.

Not long after he started at the Artillery Club, Eldrewey walked into the bathroom one night and almost tripped over Gus

Isadore Arnold, a wealthy real-estate man and notorious drinker. Arnold had passed out and was lying "on the piss-wet floor" dressed in spats, tails, black tie, and vest. Eldrewey went over to help him up. Arnold's bachelor friend Dan Kempner, taking "a good piss over Mr. Gus's head," warned Eldrewey: "You don't know what you're getting into, young fellow. That man is like this all the time. He's too heavy to be lifting." Eldrewey was surprised by Kempner's clear concern for his personal welfare, but he ignored the warning.

To Eldrewey, it seemed to take hours to lift up "Mr. Gus's body, which was mostly stomach. When a white man wore spats and tails and bow tie and had a vest on with his stomach sticking out, the others didn't call it fat, they called it a 'bay window.' You had to be rich to look like that." All the members left for the night. Sucking characteristically on his toothpick, Abraham Lincoln Tims told Drew to close up for the night: "Be sure and lock the door when you take that old gobbler out of here." Old Mr. Abraham told Eldrewey that Negroes were only interested in two things: five o'clock and payday. To Drew, Mr. Abraham was mostly an Uncle Tom, "scraping and bowing, and yes sir–ing and yes ma'm–ing to all the white people in the club." But he also watched Tims "talk down to Mr. Gus whenever he caught him drunk."

Eldrewey dragged Mr. Gus out to his black Cadillac LaSalle, which "looked beautiful in the moonlight." He managed to drive Arnold to his house on 24th Street near N. They were greeted at the door by one of his sisters, who (like Dan Kempner) thought that her incorrigible sixty-six-year-old bachelor brother was too much for a fifteen-year-old boy to handle. She thanked Eldrewey but warned him against bringing Gus home by himself again. "Mind your own damn business," the old man snapped. "Shorty can handle me."

Eldrewey dragged Gus up a long flight of stairs to his bedroom. "I had to play nurse and valet and pull off all his clothes. I even had to hold his swizzled peter while he pissed himself back to partial sobriety." Gus directed Eldrewey to the bottle of sleeping pills in the medicine cabinet. He swallowed two of the pills, took off his wire-rimmed glasses, put on a pair of colorful pajamas, and sat for a while in his overstuffed chair. When he was ready to stretch out in his iron double bed, Gus instructed Eldrewey to put him in the middle "because he wasn't expecting any female company." "The truth is," Eldrewey remembers, "it kept him from falling out of bed."

Now it was Eldrewey's turn to see how he could handle the old man. "Mister Gus," he lied, "I have no money for cab fare. The buses have stopped running and I don't know how I'm going to get home." Gus didn't ask for his pocket watch to see if the buses had really stopped running. He sat up in bed and pointed to the keys sitting on the chest of drawers. "Shorty, take the car. It'll get you home. Good night."

Elated by his apparent good fortune, Eldrewey raced over to the Stovalls' house and got the twins out of bed. The three drove all over town and down the beachfront, where they hit a big log partially covered by sand. The log damaged the steering mechanism, which kept pulling hard to the right. Eldrewey managed to steer the car by yanking the wheel strongly to the left. He dropped the Stovalls off and got an hour of sleep before school the next morning, when he parked directly in front of the principal's office.

Gus came to the club by cab that night. He walked in and announced: "Here is my new chauffeur. I raised him from a pup." He handed Eldrewey a twenty-dollar bill, parked himself in a soft green chair, and called for his regular drink, a Manhattan. Drew couldn't bring himself to talk about the accident while Gus was sober. Nor could he induce Gus—clothed in his Hickey Freeman suit and Stacy Adams shoes—to drink himself onto the bathroom floor again. At eleven o'clock, Gus asked for the keys and announced that he would drive himself home. Eldrewey remained silent as Gus left the club. Gus backed his car out of the driveway and turned toward the Galvez hotel. He proceeded to smash into several cars parked along Seawall Boulevard and wound up with a brief visit to the emergency room at John Sealy Hospital.

If Gus suspected Eldrewey of anything, he never mentioned it directly. Eldrewey came late to the Artillery Club the next night, fearing the worst. Gus met him at the door. "I was in a serious accident last night, Shorty. I hope you will drive more carefully." It took a moment for Eldrewey to realize that Gus thought his own drinking had caused the accident. "I am through driving a car," Gus went on. "You take over from now on. The car will be ready in a couple of days. Pick it up. All you have to do is bring me to the club and then take me home at night."

In those days, Eldrewey's father Rudolph was still riding a bicycle. He refused to sign the driver's license application for Drew to drive Gus's black LaSalle. Mr. Gus talked with Devona on the phone, and she reluctantly signed the application, knowing that trouble as well as money would be flowing into her household. With his Artillery Club salary, valet wages from Gus, and extra income from selling stolen Artillery Club liquor, Eldrewey soon kept more money in his pocket than Rudolph. He began driving Mr. Gus's LaSalle with virtually no constraints, buying himself tailor-made suits and ties at Ace Tailor shop, living the illusion that "everything was free." He signed Arnold's initials, "G.I.A.," at the gas station and at the liquor store. "I fed him; I drank him; he became totally dependent on me, and in a way I became his master," Eldrewey says.

By this time, Rudolph's gambling days were almost over and Eldrewey's were just beginning. In 1946, Rudolph's days were regulated by the loud Water Works whistle that blew at 30th Street and Avenue H. Every day but Sunday, it blew at 8 A.M. for work, 12 P.M. and 1 P.M. for the lunch hour, and 5 P.M. for quitting time. Eldrewey's days followed a different pattern: he went to school during the week and generally stayed until 3:30. After school, he headed straight for T. D. Armstrong's Shamrock Hotel and Coffee Shop at 31st and L. A black tycoon who owned rent property, sold insurance, and operated a nightclub upstairs from his coffee shop, Armstrong took a liking to Eldrewey and gave him advice about making his way in the world.

After ice cream, soda (high school kids were not allowed upstairs into the nightclub), and "shooting the shit," Eldrewey picked up Mr. Gus around five and worked at the Artillery Club until eleven. After dropping Gus off at his home, Drew and his friends drove around town drinking and looking for girls until the early morning hours. Occasionally, they would sneak back into the Artillery Club, play with the girls and the slot machines, drink, or take the liquor out to sell to their friends.

Drew's new patron, Gus Arnold, was one of Galveston's biggest landlords, then in a real-estate partnership with W. E. Rankin.

As Ted Langham remembers it, Arnold and Rankin owned most of the houses north of Broadway from 26th to 41st streets. From his black tenants, Arnold collected five, ten, or fifteen dollars monthly, "depending on what alley you were in and what hovel you had." Born in Galveston in 1881 and well-traveled, Arnold fit in comfortably at the Artillery Club, populated by men who controlled many of the legitimate features of Galveston's economy — including the Kempners, who owned Imperial Sugar and a large share of the Galvez hotel and controlled the U.S. National Bank; the intermarried Sealy and Hutchings families, involved in banking and philanthropy; the Moodys, who owned the American National Insurance Company and the Moody National Bank; and the Lykes brothers, who ran a large steamship company.

In 1946, the year Eldrewey began working at the Artillery Club, Robert Hutchings, a scion of the two old Galveston banking families, Sealy and Hutchings, was named president of the Artillery Club. Hutchings had just returned to Galveston after serving in World War II. Fresh from his own military experience, he obtained two nineteenth-century cannons and bolted them to the front stoop of the Artillery Club to symbolize the club's historic origins. During the Texas War of Independence, according to Hutchings, Sam Houston raised a special artillery company from the skilled mechanics in Galveston (the center of Texas commerce in those days). After Texas joined the Union and the U.S. Army took control of all fortifications in Galveston, the artillery company was disbanded and later reorganized as a social club.

Hutchings remembers well how much Gus Arnold drank and how little he liked to pay for it. At the end of his year as president, the Artillery Club was four hundred dollars in debt. Members habitually signed a chit for every drink they took and paid the club on a regular basis. Arnold's signed chits amounted to eight hundred dollars, but he refused to pay up. Hutchings went to Arnold: "Gus, you owe the club eight hundred dollars. And I got to have the money. I'm going to pay up all my bills. When I leave the club, I want it clean." Arnold stalled until Hutchings settled for four hundred; then he closed out the accounts for the year.

Arnold's favorite place in the Artillery Club was known as the "Dog House" — a men-only back room reserved for serious drinking and card-playing. In the summer of 1949, Eldrewey called Mr. Gus from the Dog House to watch a ball game on the club's first television set. "He had his first drink and then we watched a live ball game. He didn't believe it until he had his second drink. I decided then that I could believe anything, that anything was possible."

Eldrewey's high-flying, hobnobbing days at the Artillery Club introduced him to a world far removed from rural San Augustine or from the Stearns household less than a mile away. Highly educated, often cosmopolitan men, powerful in the worlds of business, finance, and international commerce, spoke freely with each other in Eldrewey's presence. More importantly, they spoke *to* him with genuine respect. At the Artillery Club, Eldrewey developed a finesse that would serve him well in the future. Working for Galveston's elite gave him a sense of pride and hopefulness about his own future. Yet his idealization of and dependence on Gus Arnold also gave him the illusion that enough money and alcohol could make anything happen.

Both were within easy reach. Eldrewey and Harold often came back to the club after hours. They discovered that a clock spring could operate the slot machines and figured out how to stop the magic moving hand at the payoff number. Eldrewey remembers "reinvesting" the profits in slot machines in nearby black businesses. "I felt like a Robin Hood." Some nights, the boys would sneak bottles of Old Crow or Old Grandad whiskey out of the club and sell it on the street for four dollars per hundred-proof quart. Other nights, "when the white rich were fast asleep, I would drive Negroes to the club and I would cook for them, serve them some of the best drinks in America."

When Eldrewey began driving Mr. Gus's car and spending Mr. Gus's money, he thought he had it made. Remembering those heady days, he gives the impression that he was a ladies' man: "I learned that with girls, rubber wheels outshone rubber heels ten to one. But the girls had to give something." Yet Ted Langham remembers Eldrewey (five feet four inches tall and tipping the scales at 124) as being more of a "little brother" than a lover in the "crowd of girls that we hung out with. . . . 'Cause he was so *little*."

Moreover, the girls at Central High School were not in the habit of giving up their virginity. "In the whole high school," Langham remembers, "maybe three girls broke down."

Retelling a joke about cars and sex that used to circulate among

This guy took a fine-looking girl five miles down the beach. He parked and leaned over to kiss her, saying, "Baby, you know the score . . . fuck or walk." The chick stared him in the face and said, "I'll walk."

The next night he nerved up and tried the same girl. This time, the fella didn't stop at the five mile post down the beach but drove on to the ten mile junction and parked on a lonely beach road. "You know my philosophy . . . fuck or walk. That's the way it goes." Undaunted, the girl got out and walked home.

A couple of days later, the two of them met again and he convinced her that he wanted to show her a good time with no strings attached. They drove down the beach until they reached the twenty mile mark. He felt her fine legs and popped the question: "Are you going to do it tonight?" "No," she answered, looking him in the eye. "Then walk!" he announced, pulling his arm away from her shoulder. Much to his surprise, the girl didn't move a muscle. "Look, man," she blurted out, pointing her finger at him. "I have walked five miles and I have walked ten miles, but I'll be damned if I am going to walk twenty miles to keep from giving you a dose of the clap. Go ahead!"

When Arnold was sober, Eldrewey would sometimes drive him down along the beachfront and then over to the red-light district on Postoffice Street. One night they were cruising past a two-story gray house of prostitution. "Mr. Gus pointed his finger at a window and said, 'In that room, Shorty, I paid for a woman I didn't want. She didn't keep her windshield clean.' He meant that she was a white woman who smelled like a black woman." In Eldrewey's mind, the message was clear: certain kinds of women were basically sexual objects for hire — the whiter the better.

Once they reached age sixteen, Eldrewey and Harold decided to check out the red-light district for themselves. After a Central High football game one night, decked out in their flashy blue-and-white band uniforms, the two headed for a house at 28th and Church streets. "This was a black whorehouse," Eldrewey remembers. "A Negro caught in a white whorehouse could start a race riot or get hanged quick. White men could screw any woman they chose, but . . . segregation cost money down there."

Two women met the boys at the door. "Harold took the tall one since he was a head taller than me. The one I was with was short, brown, and all smiles. She took me into her parlor, skinned back my rod and milked it to ascertain whether or not I had gonorrhea. It should have been her who was to be examined since she was the one fucking everybody. Her 'windshield' was clean as a whistle, but her radiator was cold as a refrigerator. I was finished almost before I started, but it was better than masturbation any day." Both boys left feeling distraught and disappointed. "That bitch had no feelings at all for me," confessed Harold. Neither of them returned to a whorehouse again.

Throughout his high school years, Eldrewey's closest relationships were with Gus Arnold and the Stovall twins. In retrospect, Eldrewey saw the benefits of his relation with Mr. Gus. But he did not see the costs — the deception, lack of accountability, and internalized self-hatred that grew out of his deep identification with and love for Arnold. "I was living a rich man's life from sixteen to nineteen, thanks to Mr. Gus, who could care less. . . . There was a master-servant relationship going on for sure, but who could tell who was the master and who was the servant and I am eternally grateful for knowing him. . . . Whatever he had was mine for the asking and sometimes for not asking, but for the taking."

Sunday noons sometimes found Eldrewey at the Arnolds' dinner table, seated, over the family's protests, next to Mr. Gus. On weekends, they would go fishing and crabbing off the Galveston jetties, walks of granite boulders extending out from the beach into the Gulf of Mexico. Eldrewey took the big blue-clawed crabs home to his mother, who made them into Louisiana style crab gumbo. She kept half and he took the other half back to the Artillery Club, where members paid $2.50 a bowl for this "genuine original Negro gourmet dish."

Eldrewey enjoyed Gus Arnold's real affection and fantastic wealth. He also endured Arnold's racist teasing. Arnold often sang him "That Old Pepper-Head Boy" and asked if curly Negro hair hurt the scalp as it grew out. "Why don't you shave your head like Abraham [Lincoln Tims]?" he teased. Riding home at night with Harold in the back seat, the drunken Arnold would break out into song: "Coon, coon, coon. Mornin', night, and noon. Coon, coon, coon. I'd like a different shade. Coon, coon, coon. I wished I was a white man instead of coon, coon, coon."

Eldrewey coped with Arnold's racism by denying it and later by describing Gus in physically demeaning ways. "That notorious racial song," he remembers, "was funny coming from him, who didn't have a prejudiced bone in his wretched looking body. . . . Nothing looks worse than an old white man like him with his clothes off." Harold Stovall, however, hated Arnold and decided to take advantage of him one night after a drunken rendition of "That Old Pepper-Head Boy." As the boys were helping the old man out of his car, Arnold's glasses slid off his face and into the street. "Fuck it, I'm going to teach Gus a lesson," said Harold, stomping the lenses into little bits of glass.

Caught between conflicting loyalties, Eldrewey felt "like the man who had a snake and a rat and he loved them both. But one gloomy day the hungry snake wanted to eat the fat rat." In an artful resolution of this dilemma, he found a way to maintain both relationships: he asked the fat rat Gus not to tell Harold racist jokes; and he banned the hungry snake Harold from driving home with them after work unless Gus was sober.

Eldrewey's academic record at Central High School indicates that his attention was rarely focused in the classroom. In his first three years (courses included English, history, mathematics, science, manual training, mechanical drawing, and physical education), his average annual grade ranged from 72 to 80. These grades reflect three things: his real interests were elsewhere; the academic level at Central was far below his abilities; and his capacity for sustained attention to book-learning was limited. On the other hand, Eldrewey, along with Ted Langham and the Stovall twins, was quite able to engage the attention of Frank "One-Armed" Windom, the school disciplinarian. Cutting classes or cutting up in class generally earned a trip to see the principal, Dr. L. A. Morgan, who sent the boys to Windom's room. One by one, this one-armed Mr. Windom placed each boy's head between the rungs of a stepladder and gave him a few good licks with a paddle they nicknamed "Ichabod."

Another of Central High School's disciplinarians was Mr. Coleman, the mechanical drawing teacher from Tuskegee Institute in Alabama. Coleman not only kept order in the classroom but also enforced the reigning social order of color within the black community. "Mr. Coleman's concept of race," Eldrewey remembers in the popular racial rhyme, "was that if you are white, you're all right; if you are brown, stick around; and if you are black, stay back."

In Coleman's class, Drew and the Stovall twins were constantly teasing a student named George Howard about his "lily-white-skinned young aunt Frederica," who also attended Central High. George, "a high-ranking student and yellow in color," was eventually reduced to tears by their relentless, envious "whorawing" of Aunt Frederica. When Mr. Coleman got wind of this harassment, he herded the three boys into the principal's office and disciplined them with one of his twelve-inch wooden rulers. "Don't you know that Miss Frederica is a white woman?" he demanded. "You don't curse or swear about her. You are black compared to her, don't you know that?"

Coleman's enforcement of color ranks within the African American community enraged Eldrewey, whose hot temper and quick wit rebelled in numerous ways. One night, sitting at Al's Bar with his diaper-mate Edward Crockett and Charles Spenser, Drew decided to tear down the "Sho' nuff, best in town" sign that still hung over the Watermelon Garden, little more than a block away from the Artillery Club. Emboldened by his friends and relaxed after several drinks, Eldrewey ripped the sign off its frame and tied it to the rear of Gus Arnold's car. "We dragged it to West Beach to reap the sands of time and then returned to the bar to celebrate."

Not long afterward, Drew's anger toward the gas station on 46th and Broadway boiled over. The station had three toilets with signs painted in blue and gold: "White Men," "White Women," and "Colored." "I was so incensed by the sexlessness of this designation that I wanted to close the service station down." Unable to get other blacks interested in changing this sign of their second-class citizenship, Eldrewey "put trash and black tar in the colored toilet so as to cause Negroes to have to use the white toilets."

During his senior year, Eldrewey also received encouragement from various members of the Artillery Club. Dr. John Otto, Congressman Clark W. Thompson, and others regularly took him aside. They told him he "had potential" and advised him to go to college. That year, Mr. Byrd's civics class spent two days in the

Galveston County courthouse, witnessing Thomas Dent defend "Humpty" Ross, a black hunchback whose family ran the Ross Funeral Home. Ross was on trial for the murder of a liquor-store owner and two policemen. He was convicted and later electrocuted. But Eldrewey was captivated by Dent, "the big black Clarence Darrow of Galveston," who vigorously defended his client in front of an all-white jury. Eldrewey still remembers Dent's phrases: "It's highly inflammatory; it's misleading; it's unfair; it's unjust." He had long idolized Dent, the father of his childhood marble-partner Lorenzo. He was beginning to realize that his gifts of wit and speech could be channeled toward more ambitious personal and racial purposes. Dent's performance inspired him: "my mind was cocked then for a law career."

In his last year at Central High School — September 1948 through May 1949 — Eldrewey's academic work improved dramatically. He attended school much more regularly and lifted his grades from Cs and Bs to Bs and As. Everyone around him took notice, especially Mary McCloud, C. L. Davis, Elmo Bell, and Freddy Frank, who ranked at the top of the class. Drew's able performance in A. W. MacDonald's class shocked his classmates, particularly when he *taught* the government section, lecturing on city government, state government, federal government. "And MacDonald," according to Ted Langham, would "just sit back and listen to him."

By the end of the year, Eldrewey was asked to deliver a graduation speech that he wrote with his physics teacher, James L. Sweatt. This formal address, spoken to me from memory thirty-six years later, concluded with a metaphorical charge to his classmates:

The launching of a ship is always attended by considerable ceremony and justly so for much has gone into her in care, work, hopes, and prayers. If her hull is not seaworthy regardless to what has gone into her she will waver or sink. But let us compare our ship, trimmed and balanced, well-equipped for the most vigorous voyage . . . and regardless to the odds we may encounter, we must always hold to our helms and keep our eyes ever on our objectives.

James L. Sweatt was the brother of Heman Sweatt, the Houston mail carrier who was then challenging segregation at the University of Texas Law School. Sweatt later helped integrate Galveston schools and served as an anchor in the stormy seas of Eldrewey's future. He "believed in me til the day he died, when my ship was wavering and threatening to sink."

When Eldrewey graduated from Central High, most students pursuing higher education went to Wiley College in Marshall or Prairie View A&M, northwest of Houston. Lorenzo, however, was attending Texas State University for Negroes and convinced Eldrewey to begin classes there. Texas State University for Negroes (since 1951 Texas Southern University) was then less than two years old and known to Eldrewey as "Separate But Equal U."

In the fall of 1949, Eldrewey and Lorenzo described themselves as pre-law. In Gus Arnold's car, they commuted fifty miles each way to "Separate But Equal U," then barely a half-block long. After the old LaSalle threw a rod, the two rented a room in Houston at the corner of Burkett and Tuam. Rudolph and Gus Arnold had both given Drew some money to start college with, but not enough to pay all his bills. "I was ashamed to go back to Mr. Gus to get enough money to buy my books and pay rent and buy food." He did the cooking in the apartment and took several courses that fall, but his heart wasn't in it. Nor was he willing to take a lower-paying job in Houston that would have required sacrifices in prestige and lifestyle. By the end of the semester, he had decided to return to Galveston to work for Gus Arnold. "Mr. Gus welcomed me back to the club as a prodigal son. I could have kissed his feet for being so kind to me after leaving him the way I did."

Eldrewey worked for one more year at the Artillery Club. In March 1951, he enrolled in the United States Army. Gus Arnold died a few weeks later. At Fort Sill, Oklahoma, Eldrewey worked in the Troop Information and Education School and was honorably discharged as a corporal in March 1953. That summer, he moved to East Lansing, Michigan, where he began college at Michigan State University. In August 1957, he graduated from MSU with a bachelor's degree in political science.

part THREE

Wandering and Return

Portrait by Roger Haile, December 1995.

Portrait of Rudolph Stearns, 1988, by
Eric Avery.

Portrait of Devona Stearns, 1988, by
Eric Avery.

Eldrewey at Market Street Baptist Church with Reverend James Thomas, who often comforted him during hospitalizations. Photo by Tom Cole, 1990.

Eldrewey with his old friend Ted Langham, owner of the Busy Bee Cab Company, 1988. Photo by Eric Avery.

On a visit back to San Augustine, Eldrewey and Rudolph sit on the steps of the abandoned Grant Reed house in Roberts Community, April 1990. Photo by Eric Avery.

Eldrewey Stearns on the road to Roberts Community, San Augustine, April 1990. Photo by Eric Avery.

In January 1996, Tom Cole and Eldrewey Stearns drove from Houston to Galveston for an afternoon photo session with Roger Haile at the Institute for the Medical Humanities. These four photos capture various moments from that afternoon's session.

Portrait by Roger Haile, December 1995.

Portrait by Roger Haile, December 1995.

There is nothing worse for mortal men than wandering.

Homer

I had nothin' to do but just roam around heaven all day, you might say, like the lucky old sun that has nothing to do but roll around heaven all day.

Eldrewey Stearns

On Thursday March 16, 1967, at 10:45 in the morning, the jury took its seats in Criminal District Court No. 5 of Harris County. Assistant District Attorney Donald M. Keith read the felony indictment in case #124,944 — the *State of Texas v. Eldrewey Stearns.* Stearns was accused of having written a worthless check for $67.32 to purchase two pairs of shoes at Standard Make Shoes, 408 Travis Street. After evading arrest warrants for over a month, he had been arrested in December 1966. His attorney, J. K. Chargois, posted one thousand dollars for bail and subsequently obtained several court postponements to give him time to pay off the hot check. It soon became clear that Stearns — who by then had no permanent address and was living on the run — would not be able to pull himself together or to raise the money. Theodore Hogrobrooks and Chargois advised him to enter an insanity plea and obtain psychiatric help. Stearns accepted this plan, and the DA's office agreed to cooperate.

But a few days before the insanity hearing, Stearns spoke to radio and newspaper reporters from his jail cell. He told them that he had done nothing wrong and that all his legal troubles were motivated by revenge for his challenges to the white power structure. Worried that the DA would renege on his promise, Chargois released a statement indicating that the DA's office (whose files contained roughly fifty of Stearns's worthless checks written over a two-year period) had gone out of its way to cooperate. Stearns, he emphasized, had been seriously ill for several years: "anything that he has done in the past was done without criminal or wrong intent. He simply did not understand or know what he was doing."

At the insanity hearing, Chargois's first witness was Dr. Benjamin Sher, a psychiatrist from Baylor College of Medicine and director of Psychiatric Services at Ben Taub Hospital. Sher, who had examined Stearns on March 1, testified that he was suffering from a serious mental illness which prevented him from understanding the consequences of his actions and from knowing the difference between right and wrong. He believed that Stearns had been "of unsound mind" at the time of the alleged offense and perhaps as far back as 1957, when he had sought psychiatric help as a student at Michigan State University. "So this is a chronic affair which has been going on for many years, and he would be considered to be of unsound mind over a period of time, not only now," Sher told the court.

"Let me ask one question," said the presiding judge, Sam Davis, a direct descendant of Jefferson Davis, president of the Confederate States during the Civil War. "Dr. Sher, do you consider the defendant to be dangerous to the peace and safety of the people?"

"Yes, sir," answered Sher. "I do, because of his feelings of persecution and being victimized. I believe he is to be considered to be dangerous."

"And that he should be committed to some jail or other suitable place?" asked Davis.

"That he should be committed to a mental institution, yes sir."

The next two witnesses, Dr. Alfred H. Vogt and Dr. George Stevens, corroborated Sher's testimony. Their examinations also led them to conclude that Stearns was suffering from a profound mental illness. Both Vogt and Stevens testified that Stearns's mental illness probably dated back to 1960 — a claim that seemed to imply that his civil rights activism resulted from his mental illness. "On the basis of my history with him," said Stevens, who had only examined Stearns on the morning of the trial, "he first developed symptoms . . . in 1960, at which time I feel like that he essentially lost contact with reality and since that time has periodically been out of touch with reality."

Chargois's last witness was Holly Hogrobrook's father, Theodore Hogrobrooks. He said that he had known Stearns since 1960 and that he had provided financial help to him and the PYA over several years. "I discovered that he was a bit irresponsible and extremely irrational at times and even suggested that he get some help back in the latter part of 1960." Hogrobrooks told the court that he himself played a significant role in the "Negro Community" and testified that the Harris County Council of Organizations had asked him to find psychiatric help for Stearns.

At 11:20 A.M., Judge Sam Davis excused the jury for a brief recess. At 11:58, he instructed them to answer three questions using the evidence at their disposal: Was Stearns insane at the present time? Was he insane at the time of the alleged offense? Did he require confinement in a mental hospital for his own welfare and the protection of others? Twenty minutes later, foreman Harry

Taylor announced that the jury answered "Yes" to all three questions. Judge Davis ordered that Stearns be committed to Rusk State Hospital as soon as possible.

The next day, *Forward Times* reporter Sonny Wells visited Stearns in his jail cell. Unshaven, unkempt, and wooly haired, Eldrewey was pacing the floor and seemed to be speaking to people who were not in the cell. He did not respond directly to Wells but spoke in sporadic outbursts. "It didn't take a psychiatrist to see that here was once a strong man, now broken," Wells wrote. "Eldrewey Stearns is a very sick man."

To Wells and other reporters covering his case, Stearns insisted that he was not guilty, that the police were out to get him in retaliation for his civil rights activities. "I have been deserted by those I tried to help and persecuted by those I opposed," he told Wells. "Well, they got me, but they can't forget me. They can't forget the man that was responsible for the Domed Stadium being built here."

After the interview in Stearns's jail cell, Sonny Wells rode the elevator back downstairs. Other reporters were chattering about their stories and beats, but Wells stood silently, shaken by Stearns's suffering: "The troubled face, the clouded memory, the sometimes shaky voice and the pleading eyes of Eldrewey Stearns . . . ," he wrote. "Perhaps somebody can help him and those once alert eyes will smile again."

* * *

No one was ever able to help Eldrewey enough to relieve his suffering or restore him to health. Not until 1981 did he receive consistent diagnosis and treatment for manic-depressive illness. A few years later, he received a secondary diagnosis of alcoholism. But by the 1980s, he was permanently disabled by the downward course of his untreated disease and the effects of chronic drinking.

I have waited until late in *No Color Is My Kind* to discuss manic-depressive illness and its effect on Stearns's life. There are several reasons for this. I want to avoid reducing Eldrewey's life of suffering, accomplishment, and endurance to the simplistic explanation that he is a "manic depressive." I also want to resist the use of psychiatric categories to marginalize and stigmatize social dissenters. In the American South before the Civil War, slaveowners often argued that blacks who ran away or agitated for their freedom were insane. And then there is the danger of underestimating the social pathology of racism, which is built into Eldrewey Stearns's life history and psyche. In 1990, for example, when I gave a Grand Rounds presentation on Stearns's life history to the Psychiatry Department at the University of Texas Medical Branch, the department chair responded: "Obviously, the story of a promising young man brought low by biological mental illness."

But biology cannot account for biography. Every case history exists within a life history and a social history of which it is largely ignorant. Hence, my research strategy (listening to Eldrewey retell every episode in his life many times over, listening to others speak about him and the Houston integration movement, checking every available printed and oral source) was designed to surround, flesh out, and overwhelm the standard case history that appears in his voluminous psychiatric records. My writing strategy has been to allow Eldrewey to speak in his own words — but in dialogue with other voices from his life's journey and in a context framed by my own biographical and historical analysis.

Yet there is another reason why I delayed a discussion of manic-depressive illness. Once I became personally committed to Eldrewey, I found it very difficult to accept the brutal and intractable reality of his medical condition. For many years, I wanted to believe that by listening to his story I could facilitate his recovery and that by publishing it I could bring him peace. I overestimated my own powers.

By now, I hope readers will have some appreciation for Eldrewey Stearns as a fellow human being, as a unique and flawed historical figure. With great sadness — and against his vehement objections — I summarize in the following pages what I have learned about manic-depressive illness and what I believe is its place in his life story.

Even in the 1990s manic-depressive illness — sometimes known as bipolar affective disorder — remains a severe and baffling disorder, which physicians often fail to recognize and patients generally deny. One in four or five individuals with the disease commits suicide and fewer than one-third receive adequate psychiatric treatment. Proper diagnosis and treatment — the effective drug lithium became available in the United States around 1970 — can substantially relieve suffering and prevent the terrible mental and physical deterioration caused by the natural course of the disease. African Americans with manic-depressive illness bear additional burdens: they are commonly misdiagnosed with schizophrenia; they are more likely than whites to be treated in public mental hospitals and to bear the lifelong stigma of mental illness.

Psychiatrists today do not fully understand manic-depressive illness. But they generally consider it to be a genetically based disease, in which an individual's biological makeup creates special vulnerability to traumatic psychological and social influences. Symptoms include exaggeration (ranging from moderate to bizarre) of "normal sadness and fatigue, joy and exuberance, sensuality and sexuality, irritability and rage, energy and productivity." The specific form and content of any particular person's psychopathology emerge from the interaction of biological predisposition, psychological makeup, and social environment. About 35 percent of individuals with manic-depressive illness are also alcoholics, though there is uncertainty about when alcohol abuse is related to manic depression and when it is an independent disorder.

Manic-depressive illness is characterized by constantly changing emotions, an oscillation into and out of various states of the disease. The basic and recurring pattern is movement between mania (periods of high energy, creativity, and productivity) and depression (periods of profound fatigue and apparent indifference). But even within one of these two polar states there are often overlapping symptoms, constant fluctuations and transitions in mood, thought processes, and behavior. Manic-depressive illness inflates ordinary human experiences to larger-than-life proportions. Observing an individual with manic-depressive illness over time is like sitting in a theater when the same movie is shown several times during the same day: No matter where one takes up the plot, the story tends to swing around again to the point where it started.

Though mood changes and energy swings are often apparent much earlier, the first full-blown episode of manic depression generally takes place when an individual is in his or her twenties — for Eldrewey, these were the years between 1951 and 1961. Individuals who develop full-blown manic depressive syndrome seem to have certain kinds of temperament before they become psychotic and during the relatively normal periods between psychotic episodes. Long before they receive clinical attention, parents, friends, and siblings are likely to describe them as hyperactive, sensitive, moody, high-strung, and explosive.

Eldrewey's puzzling personality is partly captured in Emil Kraeplin's classic description of "irritable temperament." In 1921, Kraeplin described such individuals as "brilliant but unevenly gifted."

> They charm us by their intellectual mobility, their versatility, their wealth of ideas, their ready accessibility and their delight in adventure. . . . But at the same time they put us in an uncomfortable state of surprise by a certain restlessness, talkativeness, desultoriness in conversation, excessive need for social life, capricious temper . . . lack of reliability, steadiness, and perseverance in work, a tendency to building castles in the air . . . periods of causeless depression or anxiety. . . . The patients display from youth up extraordinarily great fluctuations in emotional equilibrium and are greatly moved by all experiences, frequently in an unpleasant way. While on the one hand they appear sensitive and inclined to sentimentality and exuberance, they display on the other hand great irritability and sensitiveness. They are easily offended and hot-tempered; they flare up, and on the most trivial occasions fall into outbursts of boundless fury. . . . Their power of imagination is usually very much influenced by moods and feelings. . . . The patients think that they are tricked by the people round them, irritated on purpose and taken advantage of.

The first few episodes of psychotic mania or depression — when it becomes obvious to others that the individual has lost touch with ordinary definitions of reality — can usually be traced to specific sources of external stress, often the loss of a love object. In Eldrewey's case, it seems likely that the stress of the sit-in movement in 1960 and the loss of Amelia Solay in the spring of 1961 triggered the first undiagnosed and untreated episodes. Afterward, the disease seems to take on a confusing cyclic life of its own, sometimes ultimately burning itself out after as much as four decades.

Individuals with manic-depressive illness tend to exhibit certain behaviors—all of which characterize Eldrewey: angry outbursts that alienate friends, colleagues, and family; promiscuity and repeated romantic failure; frequent shifts in line of work, study, interests, or future plans; excessive use of alcohol as a means of slowing oneself down or of augmenting excitement; financial extravagances. Manic-depressive patients are rarely able to acknowledge their illness and consistently deny the destructive aspects of their behavior. Even after Eldrewey began receiving psychiatric disability income from Social Security in 1991, he continued to alternate between acknowledging his illness and denying it.

Manic-depressive illness involves cyclic changes in mood, cognition, and perception, as well as behavior. The first stage of an upward mood swing—known as hypomania—is not always easy to distinguish from normal exuberance. Individuals feel ebullient, self-confident, or exalted, though with an irritable underpinning. They genuinely experience feelings of mental and physical exhilaration, which soon lead to a perception of unlimited ideas and possibilities. When opposed, however, hypomanic individuals are intolerant and subject to violent outbursts of rage.

In hypomania, an individual's cognition and perception become altered; ideas are profuse, and thinking jumps from one subject to another. In mild form, this rapid flow of thinking and the falling away of inhibitions facilitates creativity. The hypomanic is seemingly indefatigable, opinionated, and aggressive. Increased sociability, intensified sexuality, and heightened productivity are all characteristic behaviors of these individuals, who seem possessed by an inner drive that will not allow them to rest.

In the standard cycle of the disease, hypomania gives way to acute mania. Feelings of euphoria begin to evaporate and personal distress is heightened. But the major changes take place in the areas of cognition and perception, behavior and activity. Thinking becomes fragmented and often psychotic, that is, disconnected from awareness of how most people view reality. Individuals with acute mania often have delusions of grandeur or of persecution; they cannot carry on an ordinary conversation. They apparently understand empathic speech but are continuously distracted by internal and external influences. They seem to respond to voices not present and ramble on in endless detail. In acute mania, behavior is increasingly frenetic, seemingly aimless, and occasionally violent. People in this condition may engage in bizarre or grossly inappropriate activity, such as running down the street without clothes, starting an argument with the police, or preaching the Gospel. When manic individuals are interfered with, they are likely to become abusive, destructive, or homicidal. Suicide is a very real danger. In a manic episode, thoughts race ahead and ideas jump the tracks of logic; delusions of power or persecution are common.

Although individuals with manic-depressive illness rarely acknowledge their disease, various patients have written about their experiences of hypomania and acute mania. Some describe both a heightened sense of reality, similar to the beatific and mystical experiences of saints, and an increased sexual drive. Descriptions of an uninhibited quest for sexual release along with a sense of communion with God and all humankind correspond closely to Eldrewey's genuine belief that he was a "Playboy Messiah." Stearns's streaks of impulsive buying and his firm conviction that someone else would cover hot checks or unpaid bills correspond closely to the self-descriptions of other individuals experiencing a manic episode.

The depressive phase of manic-depressive illness is characterized by a slowing down of almost all aspects of feeling and behavior — the pace of thought and speech, sexuality, activity, and the ability to experience pleasure. Bleakness and despair cast a pall over patients' perception of the world. Whereas manic delusions are expansive and grandiose, depressive delusions tend to focus on ideas of guilt, sinfulness, poverty, physical symptoms and bodily concerns, and persecution.

Depressive episodes seem to involve a general dulling of emotional response, which makes it difficult to grasp the depth of a person's gloom. Sometimes, a patient "will mock at himself and at his complaints with a grim and sardonic but surprising humor or call himself a fraud or a fool; in another a sudden smile or expression of gaiety will deceive the physician about the severity of the underlying emotion." In twelve years of our work together, I have never heard Eldrewey say that he felt sad. But sitting over coffee or a meal, I have watched tears slip silently down his expressionless cheeks. On these rare occasions, if I asked quietly whether he felt sad, Eldrewey nodded ever so slightly in agreement.

Researchers are still far from understanding the subtle and complex relationships between personality and manic-depressive illness. An individual's personality may be an expression of manic-depressive illness, it may modify or be altered by manic depression, or it may predispose one to the illness. Psychoanalytic observers, usually writing in the days before psychopharmacological treatment, have described the interpersonal lives of manic-depressive patients as unstable, chaotic, narcissistically based, filled with rage, and motivated by gaining the approval of powerful figures. In 1949, O. S. English observed that manic-depressive patients ignored the feelings of others in order to avoid being hurt, thereby isolating themselves from the strengthening influence of friendship. Others have noted the illusion of normal relationships created by the exuberance, talkativeness, and wittiness characteristic of hypomania. This illusion tends to disguise a lack of genuine communication in relationships, which stems in part from the manic depressive's strong desire to avoid his or her own real feelings or those of others.

Although explanations vary, clinical observations and studies of behavior agree that people with manic-depressive illness are often capable of subtle yet powerful behavior that may confuse, manipulate, and enrage people around them. They can be extraordinarily perceptive and skillful in evoking and utilizing the feelings (especially guilt) and vulnerabilities of others. Their ability to increase or lower others' self-esteem functions as a way of exerting interpersonal leverage—though it is not clear how much conscious control manics exert and how much they are driven by the forces beyond their control. Manic individuals commonly exhibit three other basic interpersonal behaviors: (1) they try to shift responsibility so that others appear to be responsible for their actions; (2) they progressively "up the ante" by trying to extend any limits imposed on them; and (3) they consistently distance themselves from family members by alienating them.

Manic-depressive illness—for all the suffering it causes the individual and others—can also be a source of creativity and accomplishment. While there are no systematic studies of manic-depressive illness and leadership, hypomania and impassioned leadership share certain characteristics: a high energy level, a charismatic ability to inspire, intensity of emotion, increased belief in one's ideas and abilities, heightened alertness, willingness to take risks that others judge too dangerous, an early sense of destiny and decisiveness. These qualities are especially valuable (and also dangerous) for leadership in times of war or political crisis. Nevertheless, the productive and creative possibilities of this disease must not be exaggerated; most people with manic-depressive illness are not unusually creative and do not find ways to channel their prodigious energies into some form of accomplishment, artistic achievement, or leadership.

Manic-depressive illness, then, is a central and now dominating feature of Stearns's life. But it is still only one factor in understanding his life history. Even with the same genetic predisposition, the course of his life would have been considerably different under altered circumstances — for example, if his early childhood experiences had been less disruptive, if he had not suffered the psychic and physical wounds of racism, if his temperament had been different, if he had developed a keener sense of responsibility for his own actions, if he had been accurately diagnosed and treated while in his twenties. Many alternate routes might have been taken that built on the positive aspects of manic-depressive illness and moderated the wild swings between mania and depression.

Yet none of this came to pass. Given the actual circumstances of Eldrewey's life, I believe that his predisposition to manic-depressive illness both *made possible* his accomplishments as an integration leader and *made almost inevitable* his disintegration.

* * *

Though Eldrewey graduated from law school and passed the bar in 1963, he never consistently practiced law. For a brief time in late 1963 and 1964, he shared a law office with his TSU friend J. K. Chargois on Dowling Street next to the Satellite Club. He dressed himself up to look the part but could never really concentrate on the work itself. "I was really decked out," he remembers. "I had my mohair suit . . . and I had almost like alligator shoes . . .

and a beautiful briefcase, you know, with my initials in gold. . . . So, if I didn't have anything in my mind, I had something on my body that looked like a lawyer, you know." In July 1964, he moved around the corner into a lavishly decorated office at 2401 Wentworth — which he promptly lost for failure to pay rent. In August, he filed a futile law suit against Eddie Douglas Jones and the Progressive Youth Association, on behalf of George Washington, Jr., who was attempting to collect $6,500 for his earlier civil rights defense work. Several other efforts ended in disaster. By 1966, Eldrewey's office was his briefcase.

Nor did he have a permanent place of residence. He would move into an apartment and be evicted for not paying rent, live with one of his sisters for a while, then find some other place to stay until he was put out or left in a huff. During the day he could usually be found at a bar — the Sportsman, the Skyroom, Pandora's Box, the Ritz Lounge, the El Dorado Club, or the Falcon Club. He could no longer hang out at the Groovey Grill with his friends Faurice and Jessie Prince, since they had lent him more than five hundred dollars that he failed to repay. Gradually, he became estranged from virtually all his family and friends. Not only did they tire of giving Eldrewey money or a place to stay, but they often felt confused and angry at his self-absorbed monologues, his claims to have written books that never materialized, his insatiable needs for alcohol, women, and attention.

Even as he was deteriorating badly, Stearns still managed to create fleeting images of a publicly successful self. In February 1966, the *Chronicle* and the *Post* carried stories announcing that he planned to run for the Texas State Legislature from District 22 in Houston. Although some supporters contributed money to his campaign, Eldrewey missed the filing deadline for the Democratic Primary and later failed to get enough signatures to run as an independent.

During this aborted run for the state legislature, Eldrewey remembers a nasty encounter with Barbara Jordan, who had returned to her native Houston after finishing law school in Boston. "Stearns," he remembers Jordan saying at a party, "the trouble with you is that you think the world owes you a living. Far from it."

"Barbara," came the retort, "if I did have anything coming to me, you'd collect it." Actually, he admits, most of the time "I was so drunk I didn't feel I deserved to run for dogcatcher."

Jordan's cutting remarks left Eldrewey with a lifelong hatred of Houston's most famous African American woman — the more so since she spoke the truth about him without compassion. She eventually won the race and later achieved national prominence in the U.S. Congress as a powerful member of the House Judiciary Committee that held hearings to impeach Richard Nixon.

Describing his underground days before being arrested in 1966, Eldrewey both denies and acknowledges his suffering: "I had no worries. I got up sometimes at 11 o'clock in the daytime, sometime at 4 o'clock in the evening, and I'd go drink my whiskey. . . . I'd go to the back alleys, joints, go out in the Fifth Ward. . . . I'd stay out late at night, with the prostitutes and pimps. I bought an old Cadillac. . . . And I knew I couldn't pay for it when I bought it, but I was just buying it to feel good . . . at least to get me out of my misery for a few days, you know."

On March 29, 1967, Stearns was committed not to Rusk (a state hospital for the "criminally insane") but to Austin State Hospital, a psychiatric facility. Ninety days later, hospital superintendent C. R. Miller pronounced Stearns sane. He was returned to the custody of the Harris County sheriff. Judge Sam Davis, notorious for his blatantly racist treatment of blacks, allowed Eldrewey to languish in jail for several months before scheduling a jury hearing.

Marty McVey, then a young law clerk working for Richard "Racehorse" Haynes, remembers the Confederate flag and pictures of Jefferson Davis that decorated Judge Davis's office in the late 1960s. According to McVey, Davis, who was an old man then, made no attempt to disguise the dual standard of justice he applied to the "Niggers" and "Boys" in his courtroom. "I knew him to be an evil, prejudiced peckerwood," remembers Eldrewey. "He wasn't fit to judge nobody. And I'm sure he's somewhere burning in hell." On October 18, a jury agreed that Stearns was sane, and Davis ordered his release.

After his release from Austin State Hospital and then from the Harris County Jail in October 1967, Eldrewey embarked on a heartbreaking fifteen-year odyssey in search of his lost political career and peace of mind. First he went to British Honduras and stayed at several hotels in Belize City for a few months. "Put me where there's no race problems. . . . that would be my therapy," he hoped.

In Belize City, Stearns thought he had arrived in a tropical paradise. Each evening as the workday ended, he stood near the Post Office rapturously watching people cross the Queen Street iron bridge going home to their townships.

There would be thousands of people comin' across from work, and they'd be all colors, all classes, looking, and they would be so friendly, and their faces bore joy and lightness. . . . Like one of the boys told me when I first arrived. He said, "You're a stranger no more." And I felt that I was a stranger no more to the people that I thought were strangers to me, particularly if they were of a different race.

Stearns had been drawn to British Honduras because he thought he could be genuinely happy in a multiracial society which accepted various skin colors. But his drinking habit, his mental illness, and the FBI all followed him to the Caribbean. The Palace Hotel proprietor told an FBI informant that Stearns departed without paying his bill and "engaged in much loud, racist agitation" while staying at his establishment.

After Belize, Eldrewey's wanderings took him to Miami, New York, Washington, D.C., Baltimore, Philadelphia, Chicago, San Francisco, Phoenix, and Austin, among other places. FBI memos regarding him circulated between Mexico City, the American Consulate in the Yucatán, Houston, New York, and Washington. The memos describe Stearns as a "black power enthusiast" previously adjudicated insane and advised caution in contacting him. For a while in 1968, Eldrewey lived in dormitory rooms of white women studying at Columbia University; he later claimed that he had earned a doctor of jurisprudence from Columbia.

For several years, Eldrewey worked off and on to establish organizations alternately known as the New Center Movement and Black Emergence Day, in New York, Philadelphia, and Boston. He was left with hundreds of unused buttons. He also envisioned a Wall Street Convergence and says he contacted the president of the New York Stock Exchange. Nothing came of it. To further advance the cause of integration, he called the Nixon White House several times and proposed marriage to Tricia Nixon.

In 1970, the *Philadelphia Inquirer* covered Stearns's demand that Elizabeth Taylor turn over the 2.5 carat diamond she received from Richard Burton because it was mined in apartheid South Africa. In the late 1960s and 1970s, Eldrewey attempted to write his memoirs, variously titled "Black Rebel," "Playboy Messiah," "The Book of Eldrewey," "Paths of a Raceman," and "No Color Is My Kind." He lived in the streets, in apartments, with various women or friends. Wandering from coast to coast, he shuttled between women, jails, mental hospitals, and political organizing.

In June 1973, a newspaper headline covering Eldrewey's brief return to his hometown read: "Doctor Stearns Plans New Push to Bring Races Together." He told *Galveston Daily News* reporter Margaret Bott that he had been living underground in New York for the past five years "getting things together." Describing him as "a small but sophisticated and articulate man" who seemed "to be in constant motion," Bott outlined Eldrewey's long-planned "Black Emergence Day" — a mass rally to be held in Lebanon, Kansas, geographic center of the United States — to symbolize the "total emergence" of blacks from the wounds and stigmas of slavery and second-class citizenship. "One cannot free others until he frees himself," Eldrewey told Bott, who wrote: "Then with a tone of pride he pounded the table and said, 'I have freed myself and I have no animosity toward anyone. I will deal with people rationally because that is the only way.'"

In December 1974, Stearns told reporters in the lobby of a Chicago hotel that motor caravans of blacks from around the country would converge on Lebanon, Kansas, on October 1, 1975. "We don't have to go to Harlem to have a movement," Eldrewey told *Chicago Tribune* reporter Emmett George. "We are going to emerge from the center."

After the collapse of his hopes for Black Emergence Day, Stearns began leading sporadic boycotts against Arab, Chinese, and Korean merchants in New York and San Francisco. What is striking about his efforts in the 1970s is the way they give disguised expression to his deep yearning for relief. The search for a "new center" movement that would emerge from Lebanon, Kansas, the geographic center of the United States, symbolically represents Eldrewey's desperate and displaced search for a personal center of gravity. Emerging from a "center" would symbolically free him from wild internal oscillations where no solid ground could be found. The photographs accompanying newspaper articles in this period often capture what *Forward Times* reporter Sonny Wells had called "the pleading eyes of Eldrewey Stearns."

As the decade wore on and his despair deepened, Eldrewey's fantasized racial solutions became darker and more violent. In May 1979, he told a reporter for the *San Francisco Courier* that immigrant merchants were conspiring to take over America. His National Action Council Boycott, Stearns claimed, was "the last chance for the American white man and woman to unite with the Black man and woman in a common cause." In 1980, he announced plans to organize an international black militia to defeat the apartheid regime in South Africa. His "South African Vendetta" is a deeply disturbed, misogynistic poem of vengeance:

We'll Terrorize Your "Nazi-White"
Asses Till You Scream From Fright
We'll slay you one by one to
Our Heart's Delight,
We'll Take Back Our Diamonds
And Bullion in Gold,
We'll Ravage Your Women And
Tear Out Their Hole . . .

Texas Department of Public Safety records show that between 1970 and 1981 Eldrewey was arrested on charges ranging from forgery and theft of service to battery, resisting arrest, robbery, disorderly conduct with a firearm, and assault with intent to commit rape. (Eldrewey says he was never convicted.) These arrests seem clearly linked to exacerbations of his mental illness. In June 1970, for example, Eldrewey was arrested for failure to pay his hotel bill at the Sheraton Carlton in Washington, D.C. Judge Edgerton sent him for evaluation and treatment to St. Elizabeth's Hospital.

In his initial interview with psychiatrist Dr. John C. Chatel, Eldrewey claimed that he had been a practicing lawyer for ten years and had never lost a case. He said he had no idea why the Sheraton Carlton was suspicious of him, since he fully intended to pay his bill. He told Chatel that he was a candidate for United States president and wanted George Wallace to be his running mate. At one point in the interview, Eldrewey calmed down when asked to relax and said that he didn't mind being in the hospital, because it gave him an opportunity to think. Chatel made a diagnosis of "Schizophrenia, Paranoid Type" and treated him with the antipsychotic drug thorazine.

While he was in St. Elizabeth's, Eldrewey gave the social services division the names of two old friends who lived in the District of Columbia area—Sam Harris from undergraduate days at Michigan State and Julius Haley from his years in the army at Fort Sill, Oklahoma. In phone conversations, both men expressed a strong interest in his well-being. Harris told representative Lela Wortham that Stearns was one of the brightest people he had ever known, that he had received a law degree from the University of Texas and had a very successful law practice, that he came from a well-to-do southern family that owned a lot of land in Texas. After a month of treatment, Eldrewey's psychotic symptoms had abated and he was released.

Eldrewey's hospitalization in St. Elizabeth's followed a pattern that became sadly familiar. He would be brought to a hospital — usually after several days of agitated pacing and sleeplessness — in a highly anxious and psychotic condition, convinced that he was being persecuted. He'd insist on his importance as a public figure and present an extremely confusing story with just enough obvious truth to keep hospital staff guessing about its blend of fact and fiction. Though Eldrewey was often committed against his will — and sometimes refused to take antipsychotic medication — when he finally got to a hospital, he eventually welcomed the opportunity to rest and restore his mind to some fragile equilibrium. Then he would set out again on his mad and solitary odyssey, searching for the white Dulcinea of his dreams, drinking himself into oblivion, tilting at windmills of racial injustice.

In short, Eldrewey fell into the ranks of the homeless mentally ill. Between the spring of 1960, when he quit his job with Quentin Mease at the YMCA, and April 1991, when he began to receive disability benefits from Social Security, he had no steady source of income. During most of those years, he lived in a state of permanent psychic and financial emergency. "He is a tragic figure," concludes Andrew Jefferson. "He had it all and then something went click. . . . He knows that he was short-changed, that he gave to this community and didn't get fair return. He will probably always feel that way, that he was a great man in the making and didn't get made."

Eldrewey's mad odyssey came to a sad end when he returned to Texas after more than a decade of wandering. More accurately, the quest for a heroic return to public life came to an end, but the madness did not. One day in early June 1980, Dr. Frank Bryant received a call from Eldrewey, who had just arrived in San Antonio by bus. He asked if Bryant would come and get him. Since he was busy seeing patients in his family medicine office, Frank asked his wife Gloria to pick up Eldrewey, who was standing in the midday sun outside the Pigstand Drive-in Restaurant, dressed in a full-length tuxedo, floridly psychotic, carrying only his characteristic briefcase filled with newspaper clippings, leaflets, and other printed evidence of his career as an integration leader.

Frank Bryant had remained a loyal friend of Eldrewey's ever since his medical student days at UTMB in Galveston. And his medical background made him more able than most people to understand Eldrewey's confusing, frightening, and sometimes repulsive behavior. "He was in a manic type phase of his illness, 'cause he couldn't sleep. He was talking incessantly," remembers Bryant. "He was talking about things that . . . if you hadn't known him before you might have believed him, 'cause he would have made an excellent con man . . . he was very, very persuasive."

Eldrewey stayed with Frank and Gloria Bryant for five days, draining their liquor cabinet as well as their patience. Gloria had only met Eldrewey once before — when he stayed at their home en route to Mexico after his breakup with Amelia in 1961. Although she still had two young children at home, Gloria spent many hours listening to Eldrewey, trying to comfort him.

One morning, Eldrewey walked outside and recited a poem to the many pecan trees that surrounded the pool in the Bryants' backyard. Gloria asked him to repeat this poem, which he often carried in his briefcase. It conveys both the profound isolation he was feeling and the comforting, mystical sense of communion experienced in his psychosis:

One by one, like leaves from a tree,
all my friends have forsaken me,
but the stars above my head
that burn in delicate red;
and beneath my feet the earth,
that brings this sturdy grass to birth;
for I who was content to be
a silken singing tree,
in the mistful of the night,
and in the blissfulness of delight;
I have lost those leaves that knew
a touch of rain and weight of dew,
though I am covered by this earthly crown,
I shall look neither up nor down,
and those leaves that fall and die,
have left me room to see the sky;
and now for the first time I know,
there are stars above and earth below.

Gloria Bryant remembers how much Eldrewey appreciated her concern. "You are my last resort," he told her. "I came here because you were the last people that I could turn to." One late afternoon, after a long day listening to Eldrewey while Frank was at work, Gloria took off her shoes and lay down on a little cot to watch television. Eldrewey sat down beside her. "To show you how much I appreciate you, Gloria, I'm gonna kiss the bottom of your foot."

"Oh no, that's unsanitary," she protested. "And before I could . . . he had picked up and kissed the bottom of my foot . . . trying to say 'thank you.'"

On the other hand, Eldrewey's relentless movement and conversation exhausted the Bryant family. "He would never shut up," Gloria says. "I would tell him *please* sit over there and be quiet while I take a nap. . . . And he'd sit there and be quiet for about five minutes and then he would get on the telephone and start calling long distance all over the place."

After four days, even the loyal and kindhearted Bryants could no longer tolerate the disruption of their family life. Frank Bryant called the Houston Veterans' Administration Hospital and asked them to admit Eldrewey. Realizing that he had probably gotten to San Antonio because someone bought him a bus ticket to get rid of him, Gloria told Drew that she would personally drive him to Houston if he agreed to go into the hospital. "I stopped and bought him a bottle," she says, "because I wanted to make *sure* that he was happy all the way back to Houston."

Eldrewey was treated for two and a half months at the Houston VA Hospital. When he was released in mid-August, his sister Shirley Survance agreed to take him in and tried to nurse him back to health. Shirley had always admired and believed in her prominent older brother. From childhood, she remembered his jokes and energetic style — the way he had mesmerized all the neighborhood children after returning from three years in San Augustine. She also remembered the letters he wrote home from Michigan State University, saying he had been seeing a psychologist who told him that his emotional problems stemmed from spending three years away from his family. "The doctor told him that ages seven to ten were three of the most important years of his life."

Back in late 1966, when Eldrewey was staying with Shirley and her husband Billy, two detectives came to the house and asked to search the room upstairs where he was staying. At the time, Shirley thought that the police were harassing Eldrewey for his civil rights activities. "I didn't feel as though he had a real problem, except he seemed nervous," she recalls. The following March, Shirley was back in Galveston watching the evening news on Channel 2 with her parents. A newsman, showing earlier civil rights interviews with Ron Stone, announced: "Eldrewey Stearns has been ruled insane."

"The reporter's words rang out like a siren in my ears," Shirley remembers. "My Mom started screaming: 'Oh God, my son has lost his mind!' over and over again." Even then, Shirley didn't grasp that her brother had a severe mental illness. She figured that the police were out to get him and that Eldrewey had pleaded insanity only to avoid going to prison on a felony charge — a view he still holds today.

Eldrewey stayed with Shirley off and on over the years. After his first incarceration at Austin State Hospital, he spent long hours in the back yard writing a book about himself. Then he took off for New York and wasn't heard from for months. Once he returned "so high in spirits he could fly. He was calling himself the 'Playboy Messiah.' He was so convincing I almost believed it. . . ."

As the years went by, Eldrewey's presence took an increasing toll on Shirley's difficult marriage and her six children. After he was released from the Houston VA Hospital in 1980, she spent an entire year trying to help him get back on his feet—only to watch him spin out of control again. "We had to call the Mental Health Office to pick him up. . . . It was so sad to see them lead him out of the house, as he was yelling, 'Why did you do this to me Shirley?'"

After a month-long hospitalization at Austin State Hospital in the summer of 1981, the discharge planners called Shirley. She refused to take Eldrewey back. "I had to call my Mom and ask her if she could take him. I hated it because they were old and didn't need any additional problems."

In November 1981, Eldrewey returned to his hometown of Galveston to live with his parents. It was a humiliating defeat for him. For his parents, Devona and Rudolph (then in their seventies and eighties, and raising two grandchildren, Andre and Roderick), it became a terrible ordeal. For the next decade, he slept on a couch in their living room, scribbling his autobiography on thousands of pages of yellow legal pads. Devona took care of his meals and his clothes, kept up with his medication, and tried to keep him out of trouble. But Eldrewey's manic episodes, his outbursts of rage, and his endless talking and need for care took their toll. Exhausted and in despair, Devona often had to ask the Mental Health Deputies to hospitalize Eldrewey to get some relief.

In the summer of 1990, when Eldrewey had been walking around Galveston Island for several days in the midsummer heat with no food and no place to sleep, I called his mother and taped the phone conversation to use as an affidavit in his Social Security disability appeal. "Dr. Cole," she said,

Eldrewey is crazy as a road lizard and don't have no medication. . . . He sleep on our couch and he has slept it out. He's been on that couch for nine years. . . . He has not worked any since he's been here. He has not done any-

thing here. **No income. See, Eldrewey mainly likes to talk. That's why he talks to himself a lot because he's used to talking to people about law and stuff.** . . .

Sometimes I say, "Eldrewey, if you don't want to help yourself, I've got to give you up." And he tells me that I'm not his Mama. Now that's the hurtin' thing. . . . And what he want me to do, I don't know. I say, well, I wish to God I wasn't his Mama because I wouldn't have to take all this, and I wouldn't have to suffer.

We tell stories because ultimately
human lives need and deserve to be
told. This remark finds its strength
when we evoke the need to rescue
the story of the vanquished and the
losers. A whole story of suffering
cries to be told.

Paul Ricoeur

It's terrible . . . to think that all I've
suffered, and all the suffering I've
caused, might have arisen from the
lack of a little salt in my brain.

Robert Lowell

In August 1985, Eldrewey and I began meeting three times a week to tape his life story, which we then envisioned as an autobiography. For the next year, he relived his experiences in the sit-in movement and the integration of public accommodations. The taping was an endless struggle. Eldrewey often wandered inexplicably from topic to topic; I kept pushing him to narrate coherent episodes. Stress, mutual disappointment, and recrimination threatened the project every step of the way. Eldrewey insisted that I did not care enough about him, that I was not devoting enough time to the project. Overcommitted and resentful at his lack of gratitude, I half wished that I had never met him. Sometimes late at night, I would get out of bed and try to exorcise his voice by writing down a description of that day's encounter.

Several clinical colleagues suggested that I had fallen into a situation I did not really understand: I had stimulated the kind of intense transference that takes place between a patient and a therapist. They urged me to realize that Eldrewey both loved and hated me in deeply disturbed ways and that my own psychological responses were woven into the relationship. Richard Mollica, a Harvard psychiatrist visiting our campus, suggested that Eldrewey did not really want to finish the book, that he wanted me. If his whole life were organized around writing the impossible book, what would happen when he no longer had the one thing that gave his life meaning?

I refused to yield to these complexities, which I did not yet really understand. I resisted my own impulse to abandon the project. We continued to meet three times a week taping Eldrewey's reminiscences. He poured himself out hour after hour. His feelings ranged from intense pride and inspiration all the way to guilt and suicidal despair. Mostly, he felt angry and bitter, persecuted and left behind. His memories ranged from leading the picket line against segregated lunch counters to drinking himself into oblivion and waking up with his pocket picked by the unknown woman he had slept with. Some tapes were filled with poetic beauty and others with incoherent ramblings.

By the spring of 1986, the tapes reflected a new ability to remain on a single subject for more than a few moments. When I asked if he noticed the difference, Eldrewey said that he was about 75 percent himself and that he almost trusted me. Jaron

Winston, a senior psychiatry resident who was managing Eldrewey's drug treatment and providing a supportive space to ease the strain of our relationship, remarked that the clearer the narrative became, the clearer and more focused Eldrewey became. My hopes that the narrative work might enhance his personal integration were buoyed. In April, we drove to Rice University, where Eldrewey talked to historian John Boles's class on southern autobiography.

But each step forward seemed to result in another step backward. The birth of my daughter in late July 1986 precipitated another crisis. Although I canceled all other appointments in order to be home with my wife and new baby, I told Eldrewey that I would meet him twice a week during August. He was enraged. For a while, he contained his anger to the loud grinding of his teeth. Our sessions focused on the early 1970s, when he was living in New York subways, parks, and back alleys. He remembered the loneliness, hunger, and drunkenness, the frantic pursuit of women, and the increasingly fantastic efforts to regain political prominence: the scheme to organize an International Black Militia to overthrow apartheid and proclaim himself "the Playboy Messiah."

Most of the time, Eldrewey genuinely believed that these episodes were legitimate steps in "my path as a raceman," as he sometimes called his story. But one day he turned to me and said that he had achieved only one real success in life: the sit-in movement. "And this book will be another," I replied.

Shortly after my daughter was born, I received a call from the vice-chairman of microbiology; several women in his department claimed that Stearns was harassing them. He wanted me to control Eldrewey and took the case to the Office of Affirmative Action, which threatened to ban him from the medical school campus.

Again, I was torn between my allegiance to Eldrewey and my allegiance to the university. By now, my protests that he was not dangerous were wearing thin. I referred the Affirmative Action Office to Dr. Stephen Mitchell (who had taken over Eldrewey's outpatient care from Dr. Winston) and convinced them to let me warn Eldrewey before the university took legal action.

I called and told Eldrewey that his behavior jeopardized the whole project. His unbidden and persistent advances toward women violated their privacy.

"All I need is some money and some pussy," he replied.

"I don't believe that," I said. "They never made you happy before."

This confrontation marked another turning point in our relationship. For weeks he would not look at me when I came to the sessions. He was all business, presenting a dark and withdrawn countenance. The vertical lines between his eyebrows seemed to grow deeper. His glasses tilted to the left and slipped down to the middle of his nose; red eyes flashed with anger and the effects of booze.

In mid-August, Eldrewey exploded at me during a session with Dr. Mitchell. I was a "witness for the prosecution," he said. Not only was I taking the side of white women and a racist university establishment, but I was betraying him by cutting back my hours.

"It's because you're a Jew and you're rigid," he shouted at me. "If my parents die before this book is finished, I'll kill you."

My nerves already frayed from sleepless nights of diapers and bottles, I was shaken by this threat. Feelings of parental vulnerability and protectiveness led me to draw my boundaries more clearly: "My family comes first. If you can find someone else to do a better job with your book, be my guest."

The next few months were sobering. A new distance allowed me to see things more clearly. I saw how much more would have to go into this book than could ever come out of it. And I realized that if I didn't put a limit on the taping, which had already taken almost two years, it could go on forever.

Eldrewey read the transcripts of our early taping sessions, which were fragmentary and incoherent. He didn't seem to notice. Others kept asking me: who will want to read the suffering fragments of an unsuccessful life? My hopes for his recovery were slowly crashing on the rocks of reality.

I told Eldrewey that he had to distinguish between the things he needed to tell me and the things he wanted to publish. His whole life could not possibly be put between the covers of a book; it could not all be reclaimed. I decided to end the taping in December 1986 and said that beginning in January 1987 I would meet with him only once a week. Whatever reminiscences

Eldrewey wanted to include would have to be recorded by then.
We planned a celebration for his fifty-sixth birthday, which would
also initiate the book's next phase — shaping the raw materials of
early transcripts into chapters.

In October, I suggested that it was time to put a pen in his
hand. Soon afterward, he appeared in a three-piece suit; he had
spent the morning writing in Sandy's Room (named in honor of
Harris and Ruth Kempner's son, who died in Vietnam) at the
public library.

Despite valiant efforts, Eldrewey began to fall apart again. We
argued about a party to celebrate completion of the taping. He
insisted on a large public gathering to promote the book; I held
out for a small dinner with Dr. Mitchell and Eldrewey's parents.
In December, after I'd been away for two weeks, he lost interest.
He had fallen in love with a blonde woman who worked in the
Ambulatory Care Center, where we now met for our sessions.

"I love her more than you," he said. "If I had a million dollars,
I'd marry her tomorrow and live happily ever after."

"You look like you haven't been sleeping," I said. "Why don't
you call Dr. Mitchell?" He walked out of the room without
a word.

The next day his mother called. "Eldrewey has changed again,
Dr. Cole. He walks around the house talking to himself. Gets
worse every day. He's going to crack up again, and at Christmas
time." She asked if I knew what was wrong.

"No," I said, disingenuously.

"Well, there's no need of whippin' the devil around the stump.
He needs a lady friend. . . . But there's nothing we can do but put
him in the hands of God to make him stronger."

I knew he needed to be hospitalized then, but it took another
week. After waiting almost an hour one day for a taping session, I
went out to look for him. I found him in the Clinical Sciences
Building, walking around talking to himself, carrying a Coke can
wrapped in a brown paper bag. It was rainy and gray; seeing
Eldrewey's heavy-lidded, bloodshot eyes and greasy, unshaven
face did not raise my spirits any.

"Can I talk to you?" I asked.

"Sure."

"I think you need help. Can I take you to the Crisis Clinic?"

"No," he said, walking off. I followed him down the hallway.

"I'm through with you," he said, walking away again. "I'll pay you for two and a half years."

That night, the phone rang at home. "Dr. Cole, this is Officer Singleton. We have Eldrewey Stearns here. He's all mixed up; been wandering around the campus in the cold rain. We called his mother. She says she can't handle him at home and wants him admitted to the hospital. She gave us your number. Can you come down and take care of him?"

"No, I'm not a physician. But I just talked to Dr. Mitchell, his psychiatrist. Call and he will arrange Eldrewey's admission. If you have any trouble, call me back and we'll find another way." The next time the phone rang, it was Mrs. Stearns. We talked for a long time. She said she hated to see him suffer like this, especially when we were planning a celebration.

Later, when Steve Mitchell and I visited Eldrewey in the hospital, he greeted us warmly: "When's the party?" After a moment of silence, he realized that it would have to be called off. Then he turned to me — "You're the reason I'm here. It's because you're abandoning the project." I tried to reassure him that we were only entering a new phase, in which I'd be less available and he'd carry more of the weight. On the way out of the building that winter night, Steve told me that during this psychotic episode Eldrewey thought I was a spy sent to destroy his book.

When Eldrewey finally put pen to paper, we had reached the point from which I had assumed we would start more than two years earlier. If he was not producing great literature, the process of writing was itself a great accomplishment. A new feeling came over me, a kind of detached love and commitment, not so much to any ultimate product as to the process of self-recreation that emerged (I thought) from the narration. Still, I was not surprised when that process broke down again after Eldrewey had written several hundred manuscript pages. His handwriting was illegible; we were forced to return to the slow, expensive process of taping and transcribing. This time, Eldrewey dictated from the pages he had written, but a large gap emerged between how much he was writing and how much we could tape, meeting only once a week. Despite continual pressure, I refused to meet more often.

In late April 1987, Eldrewey announced that he would finish

the book on July 7 and begin a boycott of Arab, Chinese, and Vietnamese merchants in Galveston. He came to our next session smelling of alcohol; his eyelids had a yellow, fluttering, sleepless quality; his speech was slurred, thoughts trailed off into himself. I said I thought he needed a break from our work and suggested that he call Dr. Mitchell. By mid-June, we were back at it.

Again, we were in a continual tug of war. I tried to get him to sharpen his focus and select key episodes in his life rather than ramble interminably. I still hadn't realized how different our narrative agendas really were: I wanted the coherence and closure of a printed narrative with a beginning, middle, and end. Eldrewey needed the endless openness of oral storytelling. As the psychoanalyst Doug Ingram later pointed out in a letter to me, Eldrewey was a bit like Scheherazade in *Arabian Nights*, who told enchanted stories to King Shahriyar for a thousand and one nights to keep him from killing her. The only thing Eldrewey really possessed was his story. He felt compelled to keep telling it over and over and over again. If he ever stopped, he would be as good as dead.

Eldrewey insisted that if he had to wait a whole week to read his writing to me he couldn't maintain the enthusiasm to work. "If I don't get to tell the whole thing," he said, "I'm still an unfinished person." I relented. We began meeting twice weekly again in March 1988, and the story of his Houston civil rights activities emerged more clearly than in previous attempts. (He called the sections he wrote "Leader at Last.")

Throughout 1988, Eldrewey and I tried to fashion his memories into chapters. He hounded me relentlessly to spend more time on the book and raise money. I felt confused about what I was doing, uncertain whether anything worthwhile would come of it. Often, I felt angry and guilty at the same time. Colleagues and friends had told me for years that my northern white liberal guilt was wreaking havoc with my judgment. Maybe they were right. And yet I had promised to help Eldrewey publish his autobiography and already had invested several years of work. I refused to accept failure and felt obligated to continue. I knew that my persistence was obsessive as well as altruistic. But I couldn't distinguish, let alone untangle, these motivations and their implications for the shape of the work.

In 1988, Pat Jakobi, then a graduate student at the institute, helped me edit hundreds of pages of tape transcriptions into four prospective book chapters, which I began to circulate. But by the end of the year, we were running out of patience and ideas. As always, Eldrewey was out of money. In December, I went to Ruth Kempner to ask her to support him for one more year. Ruth, who had supported Eldrewey for eight months after her husband's death, was an avid reader and a woman of strong opinions. I got to her house around 5 P.M., not knowing what to expect. She showed me in and opened a bottle of white wine. We had a few drinks, munched on crackers and caviar. "Well, what is it that you want?" she asked. I said that one more year of support would enable us to complete a draft of the manuscript. She said she had read the four chapters I had sent and found them wanting. She asked if Stearns was still drinking. Yes, I replied.

Ruth had decided against any further support for Eldrewey. She said she was finished being a bleeding heart liberal: Stearns should stop drinking and pull himself together. Furthermore, she didn't think the book would ever be published — it was too rambling and self-centered. And she had some advice for me: she thought that I was a naive young man who had let Stearns pull the wool over my eyes. It was time for me to see what Stearns really was — a con man.

The next week, I took Eldrewey out to celebrate his fifty-seventh birthday with a lunch at Hill's Restaurant, nestled behind pier 19 in the Galveston harbor. Looking out over the shrimp boats, I broke this news to him as calmly and supportively as I could, never mentioning Ruth's brutal assessment, which I half-agreed with. He immediately became agitated and started scheming about sources of funding. We walked out on the pier. I tried to empathize with his frustration and anger without agreeing to his fantastic new schemes. He began calling old political friends and allies in Houston, dreaming up ways of raising money to finish the book. He drafted a letter to former Houston mayor Louie Welch, appealing for help in raising money; his letter included a long list of old allies and accolades. He asked me to have my secretary type the letter. I read the letter and told him it was incoherent, that I would not send it. His countenance fell.

I saw another break coming. His eyes had that angry, red look from sleepless nights of pacing and talking out loud. He asked me what I thought about his idea for a sit-in reunion. I said it was premature, that we ought to wait until his book was published. "I don't give a shit what you think," he screamed. "You don't understand. I need money now! I live this book. You only come twice a week and think you can understand it." He jumped out of his chair to leave the room.

"If you don't give a shit what I think," I said, "then don't ask me. Just go ahead and do this by yourself."

"Goddamn you," he shot back. "I don't need you. You never really cared about me. Sitting over there in your office, with your secretary and all those girls. To hell with you."

"Find someone else then," I snapped back. "I'm here to work on this book in ways I think are reasonable. I'm not your sugar daddy or your secretary. Now let's see if we can use our time productively."

He sat down again.

In effect, I had refused to go along with what I thought was an irrational scheme but affirmed my commitment to the book. I had come up empty trying to find money for him within the limits I found appropriate.

I told Eldrewey that I thought he needed to take care of himself, that I was worried that he would have another psychotic break if he didn't get enough sleep and get some help from Dr. Mitchell. As we went down the elevator after a session in mid-February, I struggled with feelings of guilt and sadness. "Take care of yourself," I said as we went our separate ways.

"You take care of me," he replied.

In the spring of 1989, I circulated four chapters of Eldrewey's autobiography, then entitled "Paths of a Raceman," to several commercial and university presses. I wrote to sympathetic literary agents, hoping one would agree to take on the project. Every response was negative: agents and commercial presses immediately decided that the book would have at best a regional market; the university presses doubted Stearns's credibility and significance.

I did have one lead, however. Shannon Davies of the University of Texas Press had taken a strong interest in the project after reading an essay describing my relationship to Stearns. She encouraged me to submit our autobiographical proposal and remained supportive when the press rejected it.

In her letter conveying the rejection, Shannon suggested that we move toward a biography. She knew that I was committed to protecting the integrity of Eldrewey's own voice and that he would be insulted by the idea of a biography. Her letter anticipated these objections: "Our intention is certainly not to silence this man once again," she wrote. "Just the opposite. We want his story to come through loud and clear. There will no doubt be many instances where Stearns's words will speak most directly to an episode or issue. . . . But, overall, . . . we think it needs the attention and commitment of a writer." If we decided to pursue a biography, Shannon indicated that the press would be willing to offer a contract.

Eldrewey and I were both disappointed by the resoundingly negative reactions to almost five years of work. But it had become obvious to me the autobiography would never be viable in the world of book publishing, and I had ruled out the possibility of ghostwriting it. Eldrewey, however, kept telling his family and friends that the book was almost finished. I told Shannon, who had become a much-needed source of encouragement, that I doubted Eldrewey would accept the biography proposal. Writing his life as a biography implied transferring power and authority from him to me. I was frightened by the responsibility and intimidated by the idea of writing in a new genre and by all the additional research involved. Nor did I have the emotional distance needed to handle the dilemma faced by all biographers: "To be cold as ice in appraisal," as Leon Edel puts it, "yet warm and understanding." I lacked the ice.

I copied Shannon's letter and mailed it to Eldrewey. He said no. I agreed to continue the autobiographical route, knowing that it meant at best an unpublishable manuscript. During the summer, Eldrewey changed his mind. He was desperate for money. I spoke with Shannon, who said that UT Press would agree to a $2,500 advance but would have no contractual relationship with Stearns. Eldrewey agreed to a biography if I gave him 70 percent of the advance.

By November 1989, I had a book contract and a huge lump in my throat. I faced several daunting tasks: finding and interviewing scores of friends, family, and former colleagues; doing additional background reading as well as primary research in printed sources on Houston's civil rights movement; assessing Eldrewey's role in that movement; crafting an interpretation of his life that I knew would never please him. And there was another task that I didn't yet grasp: achieving a deeper understanding of myself and my relationship to Eldrewey.

When the advance arrived in the spring of 1990, I called Eldrewey and asked how he wanted his share. He wanted the entire $1,750 in cash. I suggested that we put it in a bank account, so he could draw it out little by little. He brushed aside my doubts and demanded that I pay him his money. I drove to Houston, where he was staying with a friend named Nelson Fanner. His speech was rapid and pressured, eyes fluttering yellow and red. He looked awful to me, and I hesitated to put all that money in his hands. I asked if he was getting enough sleep and taking his medication. "I'm fine," he replied. "Just give me the money and stay out of my business." I gave Eldrewey the money and drove back down the Gulf Freeway to Galveston, wondering if I'd done the right thing. I was still trying to believe in Eldrewey's ability to make autonomous decisions, in which case whatever he did with the money *was* his business. But my guts told me that he was nearing a breakdown and could not handle the money.

The following day, Fanner called: the money was gone and Eldrewey was out wandering the streets. He had gotten drunk and slept with a prostitute who rolled him. Fanner was furious: Eldrewey had blown all that cash without paying enough for room and board. The next thing I knew, he had been admitted to the Veterans' Administration Hospital in Houston.

After six years, I faced the fact that Eldrewey would never be able to handle his own affairs. We might yet be able to recover his life story, but *he* would never recover. I decided to intervene as his advocate with the Social Security system. After he was released from the hospital, I told him yet again that it was time to apply for a disability income. He sheepishly admitted that he had already applied and that his application had been rejected. I convinced him to appoint me as his legal representative for purposes of appeal. (At this point, I had a lot more confidence in my ability to pursue his disability appeal than in my ability to write his biography.)

In April 1990, we decided to take a research trip to San Augustine with his father. My friend Eric Avery, a psychiatrist and artist who had already taken an interest in the project, agreed to come and take photographs. I was excited about this trip, which I imagined as a kind of *Trip to Bountiful*, the Horton Foote film where the elderly Carrie Watts makes her way back to her childhood Texas town of Bountiful — only to find that it has become extinct. I hoped that like Carrie Watts, who found peace by reconnecting with the land and mourning the loss of Bountiful, Rudolph and Eldrewey might find healing and resolution by revisiting their ancestral home.

Many unanswered questions led back to this rural East Texas town, from which Rudolph had fled with great relief as a young man in the 1920s and where Eldrewey lived for over three years looking after his invalid grandmother. As we drove northeast out of the coastal plain and into the piney woods, Rudolph recalled his decision to flee from his mother Mollie's relentless beatings and a life of sharecropping and timber cutting. He remembered Raymond Lee, who taught him to make corn mash whiskey during Prohibition, and Sheriff Wilkerson, who took twenty-five dollars per month to warn him when federal agents were coming to bust moonshiners.

Rudolph — or Rufus as he was sometimes called — looked forward to this homecoming, but with trepidation. Almost all of his contemporaries were dead or long since gone. Memories of living with his mother were almost entirely bitter, and we were also going to look into the identity of his grandfather, whom his father Corey had seen only once or twice in his life. Corey once told Rufus that his father was a German named Joe who sent him from Nacogdoches to be raised in San Augustine. This story matched the one that Eldrewey heard in the 1970s from Joanna Phillips, the unofficial historian of Roberts Community.

I hoped our trip would turn up some oral, genealogical, or documentary evidence regarding the identity of Corey's father. Eldrewey believed he was Joseph Sterne, son of the famous Adolphus Sterne, a German Jewish immigrant and founding father of Texas. Rudolph was tight-lipped about it, perhaps out of anxiety at breaking the taboo against mixed racial origins or embarrassment at having Jewish blood in his veins. The very uncertainty of it all seemed to unsettle him. Eldrewey resented the idea that I wanted to verify the story — he insisted that I was trying to rob him of his Texas blue-blood ancestry. He was drinking heavily and hit me up every few hours for beer money.

We stopped in Nacogdoches, where I consulted with Carolyn Ericson, a prolific local genealogist, and Mrs. Richard Holbrook, a descendant of Adolphus Sterne through marriage. Between 1850 and 1900, Nacogdoches and San Augustine counties contained a large number of white, black, and mulatto households listed under the names Stern, Sterne, Sternes, or Sterns. I could find no information at all regarding Adolphus's son Joseph, who was born around 1832. In Nacogdoches, we visited the original home of Adolphus Sterne, now preserved as a historical museum, but found no evidence of Joseph or his descendants.

We drove over to San Augustine, where I hoped we could talk with Joanna Phillips. When we pulled into the Garner and Son Mortuary, run by Rudolph's cousin Lon L. Garner, Joanna Phillips' newly cut headstone was sitting there in the parking lot, announcing that she had died in January. I learned that Lon L. had been the first black mayor of San Augustine and that his mother, Bessie Roberts, Mollie's sister, had died insane. Rudolph also remembered that one of the white Robertses had "cracked up just like Eldrewey" as a young man. Lon L. did not offer any reaction to my questions about the identity of Corey's father, but he did put me in touch with Joanna's son, James Phillips, who was kind enough to send me a copy of his mother's history of the Roberts Baptist Church.

Three miles out from the San Augustine town square, we turned onto that dirt road which leads into Roberts Community. At the entrance, we stopped at the cemetery and Roberts Baptist Church that used to double as a schoolhouse. Rufus hadn't been back since his sister Lena's death. That "day they brought my sister's body out of that church. . . . And comes a whirlwind that followed her casket from right there till it got to that tree. Raisin' up dust, just like that. And it got to that tree and went straight up. Kind of a mystery. Everybody was wonderin' about it." We found the headstones of Corey, Mollie, and Mollie's mother, Anna Roberts, who had almost been buried in town with the "white" Robertses.

None of the houses from fifty years earlier were still standing.

We found the plot of land that Eldrewey lived on with Mollie, Corey, Lena, and her husband Frank. A giant mulberry tree still marked the place where the house had stood. Eldrewey remembered the sights and smells of chitlins and cracklings cooking whenever hogs were killed. In those days, when one family killed a hog, it was quickly dispersed into the smokehouses of several families. We climbed through old dipping vats and cotton cribs, talking with the few people who still lived there. No one recognized Rudolph or Eldrewey.

Where the dirt road ended, we stopped beside the abandoned farmhouse of Wiley Roberts, the man with the first automobile in Roberts Community, who had taken Eldrewey from Galveston to San Augustine almost fifty years earlier. Rufus spoke lovingly of the land, the lilies and sweet williams, the wild roses, the cherry, peach, and plum trees. We stumbled across a rusty old "bull's tongue," a cast-iron plowing blade that he had used as a boy. It saddened him to see the once well-tilled cotton fields overgrown and untended.

Across from Wiley Roberts's farmhouse, a woman waved to us; it was Betty Savoy, who used to walk down that road to school with Eldrewey and Granville Roberts in the late 1930s. She recognized Eldrewey and motioned for us to cross the cattle guard. She invited us in and reminisced with Eldrewey. Betty's blind mother, sitting quietly in a back room, remembered Rudolph, whose whole countenance brightened during their conversation.

With a little prodding, Rudolph agreed to walk past the end of the dirt road into the woods, looking for the site of the last house he had lived in with Mollie and Corey. All that remained was a slight clearing, surrounded by cedar trees, whose branches Mollie had used to "smooth out" church clothes when she was ironing them. In front of Wiley Roberts's abandoned farmhouse, we cut wild rose blooms to bring back to Devona. As we drove back down the red dirt road, Eldrewey started humming the tune to the "Green, Green Grass of Home." Our trip to San Augustine did not produce the wonderful healing and resolution of *Trip to Bountiful*. But it was a good trip nevertheless.

During the summer of 1990, I began planning Eldrewey's appeal to the Social Security system. I drove to the Texas Southern University Law School with Eleanor Porter, who had begun transcribing Eldrewey's tapes and was fascinated by the story. Sandy Ogilvy, a law professor specializing in disability, directed us to the section of the Code of Federal Regulations regulating mental disability determinations. He suggested that I amass all the medical evidence, including letters from Eldrewey's physicians and parents; that I document precisely how he met the criteria for mental disability and write a strong cover letter to the administrative law judge Bennett Engleman.

Meanwhile, Eldrewey was taking another nose dive. He couldn't tolerate the idea that he had granted me authority over his income and life story. He began accusing me of conspiring to "commit legal murder" and threatened a $10 million lawsuit for damages. One afternoon in early summer, I went to see him in the backyard of his parents' house, where Rudolph still grew vegetables and my children chewed on their first stalks of sugarcane. Several empty lots of uncut grass swayed in the cool salt breezes from the Gulf. "You caused me irreparable damages and insults," Eldrewey began shouting. "You cannot repair me. I'm going to federal court to subpoena the materials and get James Michener to write this book."

The following week, Eldrewey left home after a fight with one of his nephews. His mother called and asked if I could do something. I said no. Eldrewey had started walking toward Houston but stopped short of the causeway bridge at Luke's, a little convenience store and gas station. About midnight, when I returned to Galveston from an Astros game in Houston, he was sitting alone at a table outside Luke's—silver speckled, matted hair lit by a street light, talking to no one with great gestures and enthusiasm. My heart sank, but I went on home, got into bed, and talked to my wife about it. After trying, yet again, to acknowledge that I was powerless to fix or control him, I decided to simply go out and talk to him.

I got dressed again, put some food in a paper lunch bag, and drove back down Port Industrial Boulevard. By the time I got to Luke's, he was nowhere to be found. The next morning I phoned his mother and taped the conversation to use as evidence in our SSI appeal. After Eleanor Porter transcribed the conversation and we transformed it into an affidavit, I took it out for Devona's and Rudolph's signatures. Devona hesitated to sign, knowing that her son would feel betrayed and not knowing what might come of it. I read the transcript out loud to them — slowly and with wry humor. Rudolph smiled and nodded his assent: "Yes, that's it all right, Doctor." They both signed the affidavit. Eldrewey was subsequently incarcerated again for ninety days at Austin State Hospital, and I completed his disability appeal to administrative law judge Bennett Engleman.

While we awaited the decision, Eldrewey — who was back home from Austin State Hospital — and I met with some of his old friends on Galveston Island and ate lunch often at a Church's Fried Chicken joint on Broadway near his house. "I feel like the spook that sits behind the door," he said one afternoon, munching on his usual two drumsticks and a large jalapeño pepper. Most of his teeth were gone, the others soon to be pulled and replaced with a complete set of false teeth. The previous night he had dreamed that we were sitting around a table and he came up with a new title for the book: "Another Little God That Failed." His despair was palpable. "My life is nothing . . . ill spent," he mused. We sat mostly in silence on December 21, the day marking his fifty-ninth birthday.

A few days later, he received the letter we'd been waiting for: Judge Engleman had ruled in his favor and recommended that I serve as the payee to handle his finances. Ironically, Eldrewey felt let down by the decision. The earlier rejection of his disability application had allowed him to preserve the fiction that he could still recover. The judge's ruling served as official public recognition that he was incurably ill.

I told Eldrewey that I would not serve as his payee and arranged for the local Mental Health and Mental Retardation facility to serve in that capacity. When we learned that he would receive four thousand dollars in back pay plus four hundred per month, he brushed it aside: "What good is money? I can't eat, can't talk, can't drink, and can't fuck."

Eldrewey's disability benefits were scheduled to arrive in April. A difficult decision had to be made about dividing the money between his parents, pocket money for him to spend, and savings. It was clear to me that Eldrewey did not understand the letters he was receiving from the Social Security Administration. I offered to serve as a broker with his parents and tell the payee what had been decided. I took him to lunch at the Original Mexican Restaurant, trying to soften what he perceived as yet another humiliating admission of his incompetence.

Wearing a colorful new madras shirt and seersucker pants, Eldrewey got into my car at a snail's pace. The combination of depression, beer, and medication brought his movements to a virtual halt. At the restaurant, I took out a pencil and paper to figure out an allocation scheme, but he refused to answer any of my questions. He began spooning hot salsa slowly into his mouth. Each spoonful would shake for several seconds in midair before reaching his mouth. Chips followed suit. I noticed thin tears dropping from the inside of his eyes down to his cheeks, following the deep lines that ran down either side of his moustache. We sat silently. I drank coffee. He asked for a beer. I said we had to go.

Back in his parents' living room, Eldrewey showed me the Social Security letter indicating his payments. Again, I offered to help them decide how to divide the income. "No," he said. "I don't want to. That's my business." I folded the letter, handed it to him, and sat back silently for a minute.

"Eldrewey, we've got to settle this now," said his mother.

"Yes," I answered. "I know you want to be fair to your parents. They've taken care of you here for ten years."

I looked at the SSI letter again. "How about $150 per month to your parents? That's what Social Security estimates for food, rent, and incidentals." Indignant, Devona said that her time was worth a lot more than that. In the 1970s, she used to make $75 a week taking care of Mrs. Louise Sawyer until she died.

"Yes," I said. "But only a mother would do what you've done for your son." I asked Rudolph what he thought.

"How much is it every month?" he asked.

"$406," I said. Rudolph's silence indicated that he didn't like the $150 figure. "OK, Eldrewey," I said. "How about two hundred to your parents, forty per week to you through the payee, and ten per week savings? Half and half." Rudolph nodded his agreement. Eldrewey looked away.

"Seems fair to me," said Devona. That settled it.

"I'm glad that's over," Rudolph muttered quietly as I got up to leave.

Eldrewey and I walked out onto the front porch. "So, you're giving away all my money," he said with a wry smile.

"No," I said. "Only half. And you know that's fair."

He went inside to get some cigarette money. I drove him back to Broadway and dropped him at a grocery store on my way home. "Thanks for everything," he said dejectedly.

Getting Eldrewey his disability income (and, later, income from the Veterans' Administration) deprived me of what I thought was the last obstacle to writing his life. I was wrong. The last obstacle was myself and my difficulty in sorting through the multiple layers of my relationship with him. After two years of gathering oral history interviews and newspaper accounts and checking medical, criminal, school, census, and vital statistics records, I began to write in 1991.

For months, I struggled with anxiety, confusion, lack of confidence, depression. I hit bottom in late 1991 and sought help from a Houston psychoanalyst. Gradually, I began to face my own problem. I could not write because the evidence of Stearns's life did not conform to the unconscious needs and mythological frameworks I initially brought to the work. For years I had led him to believe that I would write about him as a fallen hero redeemed from obscurity. I wanted to please him. Meanwhile, the actual shape of his life had emerged from my research. Despite mounting evidence to the contrary, I clung to a sentimental image of Eldrewey as a morally pure victim, destroyed by racism and mental illness. I resisted the obvious: that he was a complicated, ambiguous figure, personally flawed and partly responsible for his own failures.

In *Writing Lives*, Leon Edel suggests that a biographer must identify and analyze the private mythology of his or her subject, the hidden self-concept motivating the public figure. To write Stearns's life as honestly as I could, I had to discern not only *his* mythological self-construction, but my own as well. Identifying, acknowledging, and analyzing these intertwined self mythologies has been a long, arduous task.

When I met Eldrewey in 1984, I was an ambitious young professor, filled with dreams, wishes, and assumptions that I only half understood. Stearns became the unwitting recipient of these dreams. He came to stand for my beliefs and feelings about the vulnerable and mentally ill, the forgotten or unknown heroes of the civil rights movement. He became the brilliant, fearless leader whose recovered life would make us both happy and famous. At the same time, I became the recipient of Stearns's re-kindled wishes, fears, and dreams. I instantiated the white medical establishment (which would make him well), connections to the world of publishing (which would make him famous), and a loving father who could finally take care of — or betray — him.

Stearns and I both labored strenuously to force each other into the dream molds we had fashioned for each other, in the process often failing to perceive the boundaries between us. In the jargon of psychoanalysis, we were "merged" — each perceiving the other as an extension of ourselves. A decade later, we are both changed. After falling in love with Eldrewey the way a small child loves his parents, I have struggled to achieve a more mature form of love that allows me to see Eldrewey as he is, rather than as I dreamed him to be. And despite his continuing rage at me, I think he understands this.

There are still times when Eldrewey threatens to kill or sue me, insisting that I have done him irreparable damage. There are times when he seeks me out for consolation or to tell me that I'm his best friend — as, for example, when he called me from Austin State Hospital after the death of his old friend Dr. John B. Coleman in early March 1994.

As this book neared completion, our complex relationship heated up again. In the summer of 1995, when he was hospitalized at the Houston VA, I gave him a draft of the manuscript and asked for his reactions. The next time I talked to him on the phone, he said he had read parts of it and cried. After he moved back with his brother-in-law, Eldrewey launched a final attempt to make me rewrite the book according to his liking. He made clear what he disliked about the manuscript — sometimes with angry threats of lawsuits, or personal attacks on me, or harassing phone calls to UT Press or my university's administration.

In five or six visits, I listened carefully and took notes on his objections. These revolved around how much material I had left out, how revealing I had been about his mental illness, and how little I appreciated that he was an exceptional and gifted national figure. I told him that I respected his views and would accommodate them wherever possible. But I reminded him that he had given me permission to write his life story and that issues of selection, structure, and interpretation were now my responsibility.

I offered Eldrewey the chance to have the last word by writing his own epilogue replying to my version of his story. He refused — I think because "the last word" is precisely what he wants to avoid. I have assured Eldrewey that I will continue to look out for him long past the publication of this book, but we both know that I will never again lavish so much time and attention on him.

On a gray Sunday in January 1996, I picked Eldrewey up in Houston and drove down to Galveston for a photo session with photographer and artist Roger Haile. Although bruised by the continual stream of attacks he'd been leveling at me for months, I was excited about this penultimate moment. Roger had transformed the seminar room of the Institute for the Medical Humanities into a cocoonlike studio to help Eldrewey feel embraced and relaxed for the session.

We walked up the stairs of the Ashbel Smith Building, into the seminar room where reflectors and gray cloth backdrops welcomed the afternoon light which was filtering into the second-story arched windows that faced south. Roger began taking pictures. I tried to keep Eldrewey focused on the visual images of his life which I pulled from chronologically arranged folders. He was by turns sullen, angry, jovial, talkative, withdrawn, and pleasant.

The high point that afternoon came when we were looking at a 1961 photograph of Bobby Beasely leading a crowd of student demonstrators, lawyers, and community leaders on the steps of the Reisner Street jail. Eldrewey remembered that they were singing "Mine eyes have seen the glory of the coming of the Lord." Roger and I chimed in. After a moment of relaxed laughter, Eldrewey suddenly sat back in his chair. "It was all downhill after that," he said looking away. For the rest of the afternoon, Roger turned himself inside out trying to keep enough energy flowing to shoot the last rolls of film. Exhausted, we went to Mario's on the Seawall for dinner. On the way home to Houston, Eldrewey didn't speak a word during the entire hour-long trip — except for singing along with one popular song on the oldies radio station: "You don't have to say you love me, just be close at hand. You don't have to stay forever, I will understand."

I have come to see Eldrewey as a morally complex man whose life cannot be fully fathomed but can be appreciated both for its uniqueness and for its historical significance. Stearns played a singular and important role (though he and I see that role differently) in the integration of Houston, Texas — home to the largest African American community in the South. For at least thirty-five years, he has suffered from mental illness of varying severity. In the past, his illness could have been significantly ameliorated with better treatment; today he cannot be restored to anything resembling normal functioning. Stearns's illness cannot be understood by reducing it to any single factor, whether biological (manic-depressive illness), social (racism and the stressful fight for integration), or psychological (personality disturbances rooted in early family experiences).

The development of individual lives and selves is indelibly shaped by sociohistorical conditions and experiences. Eldrewey's lack of a cohesive self structure is not only a matter of psychopathology and biological vulnerability; it is also directly related to his experience as a "black" man in a "white" society. It reflects (in exaggerated form) a fragmentation common to minority populations who internalize the dominant culture's devaluation of their racial or ethnic group. In adapting to the values and practices of white middle-class culture, individuals from minority groups — including those who have successfully made their way into the mainstream — often carry with them a secret sense of shame, as Marc Kaminsky puts it, a kind of internal exile, an unnameable sense that somehow they aren't all there.

The greatest surprise in my work with Stearns came from realizing that such personal fragmentation affected me as well as Eldrewey. It directly influenced our relationship and blocked or distorted my writing efforts. Cognitively, I knew how complicated his life was, how various forces and motivations shaped the story. Emotionally, I couldn't free myself from the simplistic story line of a heroic figure brought low by evil forces. Why did I need to maintain the illusion of his purity and goodness? Why did I believe that I could cure him? — that I had to write a story with a happy ending?

Months of my psychoanalysis were spent trying to untangle the frustration, cloudiness, and anxiety I encountered in trying to write. Gradually I came to know a despised, unconscious, and exiled part of my self — the dirty Jew, the slob, the loser, the mo-ron. Idealizing Eldrewey was a way of avoiding my own ambivalence about being Jewish, my own inner experience of being inferior.

Like most psychoanalytic insights, this piece of self-knowledge was both paradoxical and costly. I was raised in an assimilated Reform Jewish family that placed great value on success, as defined by Connecticut's Anglo-Saxon Protestant elites. By all external measures — in my academic career and family life — I was certainly successful. And I remained a practicing Jew. So where was the problem?

No one likes to feel bad or anxious: I spent many hours of body tension, anger, and cloudiness resisting the tears and pain that accompanied the homecoming of my bad little Jew boy self. But it wasn't until I received help from yet another analyst that I came to realize what I hated about myself and why I attached it to being a Jew.

When I was four years old, my father left home one morning and never came back. All I remember is the scary phone call that got my mother out of bed that morning and the colorful Wonder Bread — "helps build strong bodies twelve ways" — bag sitting on the kitchen table. Five days later, my father died of injuries sustained in a car accident. My mother moved in with her parents for a while and later took a vacation to raise her spirits. I felt angry and yet guilty, utterly lost, alone, and helpless. At least my younger brother and sister, twins who slept in the next room, had each other. Even after she returned, my mother seemed distant and unavailable, preoccupied with her own suffering.

After my father died, there was no one to help me cope with or even name these overwhelming feelings of loss, rage, and guilt. I drove them underground; they took the form of a bad little boy who felt potent enough to kill his father yet helpless and abandoned at the same time. This bad little boy — so helpless and yet so powerful — lurked in the shadows of my psyche for almost forty years.

My father came from an Orthodox Jewish family. As a young man, he was extremely loyal to his parents, who were closely tied to their own Polish- and Russian-born parents. After his death, my mother spoke often and harshly of "losers" or "slobs" or "morons." In my four-year-old mind, she was talking about people like my dead father's family — people who looked like they just

stepped off the boat at Ellis Island, with dirt under their finger-
nails, fear of God in their hearts, and the intensely communal,
emotionally overflowing style of Yiddishkeit in their souls. My
mother's second husband also came from parents who were Eastern European Jews. In the 1930s, Bertram Cohen changed his
name to Bertram Cole to get a job reserved for non-Jews. It didn't
work. Over the years, my mother seemed to viscerally revolt
against spending much time with his extended family of siblings
and cousins.

The less my mother had to give me, the more I felt that *I* must
be a Jewish loser and a slob and the harder I worked to be a
"good" (not obviously Jewish) boy to win her attention. Afraid of
retribution and terrified of dying young myself, I did everything
possible to avoid being perceived as a loser — including denying
lifelong feelings of need, abandonment, and vulnerability. What
better way of trying to solve these problems than to find someone
else who was vulnerable, angry, and in need of continuous care?
If I could give Eldrewey the love and attention *he* needed, if I
could help him with the distorted ethnic self-hatred which tor-
tured him, then (so my unconscious reasoning went) I could
solve my own form of mental illness without having to face it
directly.

This reflexive process (of exploring my own life and my relationship to Eldrewey) has led me to believe that every human
life is finally too deep to fathom. The knowledge illuminating
any particular life is always limited, both by that subject's self-
knowledge *and* by the self-knowledge achieved by interpreters.
Yet according to Jewish mysticism, there is a holy spark trapped
in every soul; we are all in need of healing, which aims to raise
up that spark so that it can reunite with the divine light. Although
knowledge is always limited, it works in the service of healing,
which is endless.

Eldrewey and I are neither the same nor intractably alien. We
are separate, unequal, and related. When we met, we had certain
feelings in common: terror at being alone; rage at feeling abandoned; ambition to write/right the world's wrongs. He took refuge
in madness. I took refuge in writing truth. Yet looking relentlessly
at the facts of his life and mine, old truths failed me. No cure
emerged for either of us, but real healing continues.

Stearns's story and my relationship to it are specific and personal. Yet they also reflect broader confusions of identity and responsibility in American culture. Since the 1980s, a strong multicultural emphasis on diversity has tended to locate individuals exclusively within one or another protected ethnic or racial group. At its worst, this tendency in multiculturalism leads to a polarized politics of identity, in which racial and ethnic groups (among others) demand rights to their own exclusive truths and destinies. My work with Eldrewey has taught me that this is crazy-making and impossible. The story of our relationship is a reminder that individual lives cannot be understood as mere instantiations of group identities, whether singular or plural. Our story reveals the difficulty and the necessity of accepting our separate and related selves, maintaining relationships, sharing responsibilities, and negotiating differences.

Identity, loosely defined as a sense of who one is, is not a unitary thing that one simply finds and wears — like overalls, a dashiki, or a pin-striped suit. Identity is rather an unstable, relational process, a story always in flux, negotiated in difference and relationship. Identities, as Joan Scott points out in her seminal essay "Multiculturalism and the Politics of Identity," are historically conferred, subject to redefinition, resistance, and change. They are ambiguous, produced through multiple identifications, some of which are salient in certain contexts and hidden in others. These insights are crucial to the future of a democratic culture and to the creation of new cognitive maps of identity which will allow individuals to form selves that are not mutilated by cultural domination of the powerful or by exclusive claims of any group. "I've concluded that mixed race is probably the best way to recognize many people in the United States," Stearns says. "You can't call a child black who has a white parent, and you can't call a child white who has a black parent."

Eldrewey Stearns grew up under a regime of racial segregation and binary identity whose social practices he fought and whose psychological injuries he protested but could not overcome. The United States is the only country in the world where a single drop of "black blood" constitutes the cultural definition of black. This definition — rooted in slavery and segregation but accepted today by African American leaders and affirmative action officers as well as Ku Klux Klansmen — forces a wide range of racial intermingling into the binary categories of "white" versus "black." Stearns's refusal to live within these rigidly policed borders of racial identity is a sign both of his intelligence and of his illness.

"I've lived in the white world of images all my life," Eldrewey told me in 1985. "I'm beginning to get out of it, but I've lived all my life by images . . . through the looking glass of the white mind." The Algerian psychiatrist Frantz Fanon would immediately have grasped the *social* sources of Eldrewey's madness. Practicing in French colonial Algeria, Fanon recognized the impossibility of curing mental illness among Arabs who lived as permanent aliens in their own land.

Writing from within the struggle of divided psychic representation and racist social reality, Fanon described the crazy-making, depersonalizing "facts" of blackness, which so deeply wounded Stearns:

I had to meet the white man's eyes. An unfamiliar weight burdened me. . . . In the white world the man of color encounters difficulties in the development of his bodily schema. . . . I was battered down by tom-toms, cannibalism, intellectual deficiency, racial defects, . . . and above all else, above all: "Sho' good eatin." . . . I took myself far off from my own presence.

No Color Is My Kind, the title which Eldrewey and I have chosen together, expresses his ill-fated effort to find a color-free self, by fleeing from a culturally despised racial identity in an era that allowed no alternatives. It is true that Eldrewey's skin color is only an incidental feature of his unique and individual life. It is also true that being considered Negro, black, or African American is a social convention and not a fact of nature. Descended from African slaves, African Americans, American Indians, a German Jew, and an Irish plantation owner, Eldrewey insists that he is a "true American," a racial hybrid. This is a powerful human insight, but also a recipe for madness in the United States, still ruled by the notion, as Gary Nash puts it, "that each person has a race, but only one."

Yet much has changed since the 1960s, when the civil rights movement challenged white racism and the United States opened its borders to nonwhites from Third World nations as an alternative to communism. In the last thirty years, millions of Asian, Latino, and (to a lesser extent) African immigrants have transformed American demography. Today only one in five Americans is of British descent. Black-white marriages have tripled since 1970, and many of these interracial couples are refusing to categorize their children as white or black. A "multiracial baby boom" is building support for the cosmopolitan idea of affiliation by voluntary consent rather than by prescribed descent.

Eldrewey Stearns is a man whose soul is still not rested. Although his life story has been saved from oblivion, recovering his story has not redeemed his life. We must acknowledge that painful histories inscribe themselves deeply on the psyches of many Americans who are not mentally ill. These must be remembered, and their pain acknowledged, if we hope to build a democratic culture which can bear the disturbing truths of its own racist heritage. When Stearns began his civil rights career in front of the Houston City Council in 1959, he pointed to the words "Freedom," "Justice," and "Equality" stamped over the doors to the council chambers. The words await their fulfillment.

Archival Information

The original tapes and transcripts of audiotaping sessions with Eldrewey Stearns can be found in the Eldrewey Stearns files in the historical archives of Rosenberg Library, Galveston, Texas.

The first taping sessions, entirely spontaneous, between ES and the author, numbered 1 through 105, are dated from October 1984 through December 1986. In a second series, ES reads several autobiographical sections of his own composition and then goes over his life story again. These tapes and transcriptions are dated from March 31, 1987, through June 22, 1989. A third group comprises tapes and transcriptions of interviews with other key figures, from 1988 through 1996. A fourth group contains transcripts of video interviews made for a documentary script. These are dated from 1993 to 1996. Rosenberg Library also has most of the photographs and newspaper clippings connected with this book.

Persons Interviewed

The Reverend Earl Allen
Leonard Banks
Gertrude Barnstone
Leonard Bell
John Bland
Jack Blanton
Frank and Gloria Bryant
Deanna Lott Burrell
J. K. Chargois, Jr.
Sally Coleman
Corine Cook
Edward Crockett
Jim Daniels
George Dentler
Bob Dundas
Saul Friedman
John Frenchwood
Arthur and Jeannie Gaines
Joe Gayden
Curtis Graves
Herbert E. Hamilton
Jack Harris
Joe Hickey

Governor William P. Hobby, Jr.
Holly Hogrobrooks
Robert Hoskins
Robert Hutchings
Judge Andrew Jefferson
Marguerite Johnston
John T. Jones
Benny Joseph
Ester King
Hamah King
Otis King
Buster Landrum
Ted Langham II
The Reverend William Lawson
The Reverend and Mrs.
   Charles Lee
Lowell Lockett
Roderick Locks
Eddie Marx
Marty McVey
Quentin Mease
John D. Miller
Louis Mills

Dr. Samuel Nabrit
Faurice and Jessie Prince
Geraldine Saunders
Morris Smith
Andre Stearns
Devona Stearns
Rudolph Stearns
Shirley Stearns
Ron Stone
Harold and Harry Stovall

The Reverend James Thomas
Kenneth Tollett
B. A. Turner
Judge Carl Walker, Jr.
George Washington, Jr.
Louie Welch
Lloyd Wells
Hattie Mae White
Aloysius W. Wickliff
Francis Williams

Abbreviations

AJ	Judge Andrew Jefferson, interview, June 18, 1992.
AWW	Aloysius W. Wickliff, interview, March 11, 1993.
BD	Bob Dundas, interview, January 22, 1993.
BL	Buster Landrum, interview, July 19, 1988.
CG-a	Curtis Graves, audio interviews, March 3 and March 27, 1992.
CG-v	Curtis Graves, video interview, December 27, 1993.
CL	Rev. and Mrs. Charles Lee, interview, July 6, 1992.
D	*Defender*, 1959–1965.
DLB	Deanna Lott Burrell, interview, June 17, 1992.
DS	Devona Stearnes, interviews, July 1 and July 7, 1988; August 11, 1990; and November 18, 1991 [Note: Devona and her husband Rudolph spell their last name Stearnes. Eldrewey dropped the final *e* from Stearnes. To avoid confusing readers, Eldrewey's spelling — Stearns — is used for Devona and Rudolph in the text.]
DT	*Daily Texan*, University of Texas, Austin.
EA-a	Rev. Earl Allen, audio interview, April 22, 1992.
EA-v	Rev. Earl Allen, video interview, April 29, 1994.
EC	Edward Crockett, interview, February 27, 1991.
EK	Ester King, interview, August 14, 1992.
EM	Eddie Marx, interview, April 14, 1993.
ES	Eldrewey Stearns taping sessions with Thomas R. Cole.
ESFS	"My First Summons," unpublished autobiographical manuscript about San Augustine by Eldrewey Stearns, probably written in 1983 and transcribed sometime before ES and TC met in September 1984.
ESH	"Hobnobbing," unpublished autobiographical chapter composed from edited taping sessions, about Eldrewey Stearns's high-school years in Galveston. Also "Hobnobbing, Revised."
ESLL	"Leader at Last," unpublished autobiographical chapter; fifteen sections about the integration movement in Houston. Composed from edited taping sessions, in March and April 1988.
ESPR	"Path of a Raceman," unpublished autobiographical fragments composed from edited taping sessions, in March 1988.
ESSP	Unpublished autobiographical chapter composed from edited taping sessions, describing episodes in Galveston, Texas, after ES's return from San Augustine. ES called these sections "Spawning." The episodes are incorporated in Chapter 6, "Rabbit Returns."
FGB	Dr. Frank and Gloria Bryant, interview, May 7, 1991.
FJP	Faurice and Jessie Prince, interview, May 8, 1992.
FT	*Forward Times*
GB-a	Garvin Berry, audio interviews, August 8, 1990, and May 18, 1991.
GB-v	Garvin Berry, video interview, September 28, 1993.

GISD	Galveston Independent School District record of Eldrewey Stearns's attendance, grading, and promotion.
GS	Geraldine Saunders, interview, October 30, 1991.
GW-a	George Washington, Jr., audio interview, February 21, 1990.
GW-v	George Washington, Jr., video interview, September 17, 1993.
HC	*Houston Chronicle.*
HeH-a	Herbert Hamilton, audio interview, March 8, 1990.
HeH-v	Herbert Hamilton, video interview, October 8, 1993.
HH-a	Holly Hogrobrooks, audio interview, February 21, 1990.
HH-v	Holly Hogrobrooks, video interview, December 28, 1993.
HHS	Harold and Harry Stovall (twin brothers), interview, September 9, 1991.
HK-a	Hamah King, audio interview, April 3, 1992.
HK-v	Hamah King, video interview, September 17, 1993.
HP	*Houston Post.*
HPr	*Houston Press.*
I	*Informer.*
JD	Jim Daniels, interview, February 9, 1994.
JF	John Frenchwood, interview, February 27, 1991.
JG	Joe Gayden, interview, February 13, 1991.
JH-v	Jack Harris, video interview, September 17, 1993.
JKC	J. K. Chargois, Jr., interview, March 2, 1992.
JM	John "Doc" Miller, interview, March 17, 1990.
JSHR	John Sealy Hospital Records, Galveston, Texas. On microfilm. Eldrewey Stearns, Patient Number 177488.
JT	Rev. James Thomas, interview, January 9, 1991.
JTJ-a	John T. Jones, audio interview, March 31, 1993.
JTJ-v	John T. Jones, video interview, July 21, 1993.
LB	Leonard Bell, interview, May 28, 1991.
LW-a	Louie Welch, audio interview, December 1, 1992.
LW-v	Louie Welch, video interview, March 23, 1994.
MM	Marty McVey.
NYT	*New York Times.*
OK-a	Otis King, audio interview, November 8, 1989.
OK-v	Otis King, video interview, December 28, 1993.
PfR	Edgar Pfeil, senior assistant city attorney, Report of Investigation made by Legal Department into complaint of L. Drewy Stearnes [*sic*] (Eldrewey J. Stearnes, 3606 Rosedale, Houston, Texas) that he was mistreated by police officers of Houston Police Department while in their custody on August 23, 1959.
PYA	Progressive Youth Association.
QM-a	Quentin Mease, audio interviews, March 3 and 5, 1993.
QM-v	Quentin Mease, video interview, June 7, 1993.
RDS	Rudolph and Devona Stearnes, interviews, February 14, 1990; and

March 2, 1990. [Note: Rudolph and Devona spell their last name Stearnes. Eldrewey dropped the final *e* from Stearnes. To avoid confusing readers, Eldrewey's spelling — Stearns — is used for Devona and Rudolph in the text.]

RH   Robert Hutchings, interview, March 1991.

RS   Rudolph Stearnes, joint interviews, February 9 and 14, 1990; March 8, 1990; and April 1990, on trip to San Augustine. [Note: Rudolph and his wife, Devona, spell their last name Stearnes. Eldrewey dropped the final *e* from Stearnes. To avoid confusing readers, Eldrewey's spelling — Stearns — is used for Devona and Rudolph in the text.]

SC   Sally Coleman, interview, April 26, 1991.

SN-a   Dr. Samuel Nabrit, audio interview, February 10, 1993.

SN-v   Dr. Samuel Nabrit, video interview, August 1994.

SS   Shirley Stearns Survance, interview, April 4, 1991, and unpublished manuscript, "My Brother, Eldrewey Stearns."

TC   Thomas R. Cole.

TL   Ted Langham, interviews, January 16 and February 1, 1991.

TO   *Texas Observer*, Texas bimonthly, published in Austin.

TSU   Texas Southern University, Houston, Texas.

WL-a   Rev. William Lawson, audio interview, August 17, 1992.

WL-v   Rev. William Lawson, video interview, August 5, 1993.

Introduction

P. 1   soul is not rested: H. Raines, *My Soul Is Rested.*

P. 2   into a coherent unity: B. J. Cohler, "Personal Narrative and Life-Course," pp. 205–241; B. J. Cohler, "The Human Studies and the Life History," *Social Services Review* 62 (1988): 552–576; M. Freeman, "History, Narrative, and Life-Span Developmental Knowledge," *Human Development* 27 (1984): 1–9.

P. 2   ego integrity in later life: R. Butler, "The Life-Review: An Interpretation of Reminiscence in the Aged," Psychiatry 26 (1963): 65–76; M. Kaminsky, ed., *The Uses of Reminiscence.*

Chapter 1

P. 14   took him to the police station: PfR, p. 4.

P. 14   "he thought was wrong": Interview, EM.

P. 15   "officer about the law": Unpublished manuscript, ESLL.

P. 15   Harris County Council of Organizations (HCCO): HC, John Cash, "Negroes Renew Probe Demand," August 25, 1959; *HC,* "Negro Student Claims Two Cops Beat Him," August 26, 1959.

P. 16   "closer to the platform": Unpublished manuscript, ESLL.

P. 16 *police department:* Ibid.

P. 16 *"like I was in Hollywood":* Ibid.

P. 17 *to his fifth floor cell:* PfR, pp. 3–18.

P. 17 *"'Don't hit me no more'":* Unpublished manuscript, ESLL.

P. 17 *no more force than necessary:* PfR, p. 6.

P. 18 *"caused them to be here":* Ibid., p. 9.

P. 18 *"mouse pissin' on cotton":* Unpublished manuscript, ESLL.

P. 18 *hit or kick Stearns:* PfR, p. 13.

P. 19 *"and never look back":* Unpublished manuscript, ESLL.

P. 19 *"he had been mistreated":* PfR, p. 17.

P. 20 *who witnessed the beatings:* HP, "Student's Claim of Brutality Denied," February 26, 1960.

P. 20 *Stearns went too far:* Audio interview, OK-a.

P. 20 *no place to live:* Audio interview, OK-a; unpublished manuscript, ESLL.

P. 21 *African American population:* Audio interview, QM-a.

P. 21 *"getting out of line":* Unpublished manuscript, ESLL.

P. 22 *power between the races:* R. Blumberg, *Civil Rights*, Ch. 5; W. Chafe, *Civilities and Civil Rights*, Ch. 3; H. Sitkoff, *The Struggle for Black Equality*, Ch. 3. Within a year, student-led demonstrations in more than 100 cities had prompted at least some desegregation of public facilities.

P. 22 *"think of anything but money":* J. Gunther, cited by D. Carleton, *Red Scare*, p. 73.

P. 22 *a place of opportunity:* R. Fisher, "'Where Seldom Is Heard a Discouraging Word': The Political Economy of Houston, Texas," pp. 73–91; J. R. Feagin, *Free Enterprise City*; R. D. Thomas and R. W. Murray, *Pro-Growth Politics*.

P. 23 *"any city in the nation":* S. Friedman, unpublished manuscript.

P. 23 *legal bases of segregation:* D. C. Hine, "The Rise of the NAACP in Texas," pp. 393–416.

P. 24 *of the Constitution:* D. C. Hine, *Black Victory*.

P. 24 *Texas Southern University:* I. B. Bryant, *Texas Southern University*, p. 46; C. D. Wintz, "Texas Southern University," pp. 415–417.

P. 24 *with substantial funding:* Conflicts within Houston's black community over whether or not to support a separate black university are discussed in N. Sapper, "The Fall of the NAACP in Texas," pp. 53–68.

P. 24 *"Separate But Equal U":* unpublished manuscript, ESRR.

P. 25 *palpable fear of race war:* R. V. Haynes, *A Night of Violence*.

P. 25 *"North Carolina and Georgia":* Audio interview, QM-a.

P. 26 *to engage in public protest:* Audio interview, HH-a.

P. 26 *planned the travel route:* Interview, CL.

P. 27 *"we'll find somebody else":* Audio interview, WL-a.

P. 27 *"p. in history had turned":* Video interview, WL-v.

P. 27   *"cry of his newborn babe"*: Unpublished manuscript, ESLL.

P. 27   *"trouble for us all"*: Ibid.

P. 27   *"you gotta go"*: Interview, CL.

P. 28   *"you come with me"*: Unpublished manuscript, ESLL.

P. 29   *"get in the middle"*: HP, "TSU Students Fill Counter at Store: Supermarket Closes Lunch Bar during Quiet Demonstration," March 5, 1960; HC, "Negroes in Sit-down at 2d Houston Store," March 5, 1960, pp. 1, 5.

P. 29   *"Everybody stood around"*: Audio interview, HH-a.

P. 29   *"too much money involved"*: HP, "TSU Students Fill Counter at Store," March 5, 1960, pp. 1, 10.

P. 30   *the Mississippi River*: J. H. Laue, *Direct Action and Desegregation*, p. 80.

P. 30   *he said on his way out*: HP, Tommy Mahr, "Two Lunch Counters Closed as TSU Students Sit," March 5, 1960.

P. 30   *the Veterans Hospital*: HP, "TSU Student Group Widens Its Sit-down," March 6, 1960.

P. 31   *"I will not strike back"*: Audio interview, CG-a.

P. 31   *"diffused everything, tranquilized it"*: Video interview, CG-v.

P. 32   *and mass arrest*: T. Branch, *Parting the Waters*, pp. 278–282.

P. 32   *informed of the situation*: CG interview with Mack Hannah, November 23, 1992.

P. 32   *turned up nothing*: HP, "Newest Student Sitdown Move Ended Peacefully," March 8, 1960, p. 1.

P. 33   *"my head and shoulders"*: TO, "TSU Students 'Sit-ins,'" March 11, 1960, pp. 1, 3.

P. 33   *"and Western Civilization"*: Ibid.; "SA Stores Integrate; White Held in Cutting," March 18, 1960; *Austin American-Statesman*, "Houston 'KKK' Antic Tops Racial Incidents," March 9, 1960.

P. 34   *"stand with our students"*: F. K. Jensen, "The Sit-in Movement of 1960–61," p. 219, is quite inaccurate in his description of Nabrit's reaction. For an exact transcript of Dr. Sam Nabrit's speech, see Bryant, *Texas Southern University*, p. 103. Nabrit sent a transcribed copy of his speech to Bryant in 1974. See Bryant, Ch. 7, footnote 13, p. 127.

Chapter 2

P. 36   *as long as he was president*: Interview, CL.

P. 37   *"and act as a Christian"*: Audio interview, SN-a.

P. 37   *"calmly, intelligently, and fairly"*: HPr, "Mayor Talks to Police on Sitdowns," March 12, 1960, p. 1.

P. 37   *"by his public communication"*: Audio interview, SN-a; video interview, SN-v.

P. 37 *"what we can't do"*: Audio interview, EA-a.

P. 38 *"desperately to avoid"*: HP, "Mayor Cautions Students on Sit-down," March 16, 1960, p. 1.

P. 38 *services to anyone*: HC, "Mayor Says Demonstrators Can Be Arrested," March 15, 1960.

P. 38 *"nor promoting the activity"*: HP, "Mayor Cautions Students on Sitdown," March 16, 1960, p. 3.

P. 38 *his house for dinner*: Audio interview, OK-a; audio interview, EA-a.

P. 38 *"move in and handle it"*: Audio interview, OK-a.

P. 38 *"going to happen"*: Audio interview, CG-a.

P. 39 *"has to die for it"*: Unpublished manuscript, ESLL.

P. 39 *"to get hurt"*: Video interview, SN-v.

P. 39 *"to continue your struggle"*: T. Branch, *Parting the Waters*, p. 276.

P. 40 *"'the hell do we do now?'"*: Audio interview, CG-a; video interview, CG-v.

P. 40 *rather than call the police*: HP, "150 in Sitdowns; Lunch Counters Are Shut Down," March 23, 1960, pp. 1, 14.

P. 40 *"getting that kind of information"*: Audio interview, HH-a.

P. 41 *upstairs to the main floor*: HP, "Scuffle Stops Negroes at Courthouse Cafeteria," April 12, 1956.

P. 41 *building owned by the city*: Taping session, ES, Tape 20.

P. 41 *Friday morning at the YMCA*: Interview, JM.

P. 41 *"Back-Door-to-Go Service"*: HC, "Integration Ruled Out at City Hall Cafeteria," March 26, 1960, pp. 1, 4.

P. 41 *"needless pain we bear"*: Taping session, ES, Tape 22.

P. 42 *"so serve them"*: Audio interview, LW-a.

P. 42 *"he'll throw them out"*: Ibid.

P. 42 *"And defused the situation"*: Audio interview, August 8, 1990, GB-a.

P. 42 *business of those who boycotted*: Video interview, LW-v.

P. 43 *get away from the telephone*: HC, "Integration Ruled Out at City Hall Cafeteria," March 26, 1960, pp. 1, 4.

P. 43 *cafeteria reverted to segregation*: Taping session, ES, Tape 20b. Stearns remembers that Guy Boudois and Otis King were present during his phone conversation with Russell.

P. 43 *"community life in Little Rock"*: HP, "Mayor Considering Sitdown Study Panel: Conference on Solution Urged as Counter Incidents Continue," March 25, 1960, p. 14. On the history of the HCERR, see B. T. Day, "The Heart of Houston," pp. 1–31.

P. 44 *and power elite*: Carleton, *Red Scare*, Ch. 1; J. R. Feagin, *Free Enterprise City*, Chs. 4, 5.

P. 44 *his family would not be hurt*: Interview, CL.

P. 45 *"will be in good faith"*: This part of the letter appeared in HP, "Sitdown Group Asks Study Committee," March 27, 1960, pp. 1, 20.

P. 45 *"conference table with city merchants"*: This part of the letter appeared in *HPr*, "Mayor Will Order Bi-Racial Study," March 29, 1960, pp. 1–2.

P. 45 *"customers they wish to serve"*: *HPr*, "What Mayor Says about Sit-downs," March 28, 1960, pp. 1–2.

P. 46 *business as usual in the fall*: H. Sitkoff, *The Struggle for Black Equality*, p. 72.

P. 46 *to erupt into violence*: F. K. Jensen, "The Sit-in Movement of 1960–61," p. 217.

P. 46 *a majority voted against him*: Audio interview, SN-a.

P. 46 *privileges accorded to whites*: Interview, DLB.

P. 46 *"got any press"*: Video interview, SN-v.

P. 47 *"and a real Texan"*: Memorandum from AWW to the Citizens' Relations Committee, April 25, 1960, in possession of Ester King.

P. 47 *"soon tuned him out"*: Audio interview, EA-a.

P. 47 *"wrote them an ultimatum"*: Taping session, ES, Tape 21b.

P. 47 *sentiment of the student body*: HC, "Four Students Threaten New Sitdown Here," April 11, 1960.

P. 47 *"Student Leaders Battling among Selves"*: Pittsburgh Courier, April 23, 1960, p. 4.

P. 48 *Southern Christian Leadership Conference (SCLC)*: Taping session, ES, Tape 21a.

P. 48 *the entire segregated social structure*: Sitkoff, *Struggle for Black Equality*, p. 83.

P. 48 *"to implement the Constitution"*: Branch, *Parting the Waters*, p. 291.

P. 48 *"really solve their problems"*: Sitkoff, *Struggle for Black Equality*, p. 83.

P. 48 *his philosophy of nonviolence*: Ibid.

P. 49 *take to the streets again*: Taping session, ES, Tape 21b.

P. 49 *"wait a little longer"*: Ibid.

P. 49 *things would work themselves out*: Audio interview, OK-a.

P. 50 *"force that kept them going"*: Taping session, ES, Tape 21b.

P. 50 *" 'a splinter in their side' "*: Taping session, ES, Tape 22a.

P. 50 *"whole tactic had worked"*: Audio interview, OK-a.

P. 50 *turn on the television*: Taping session, ES, Tape 21b; audio interview, OK-a. Stearns remembers this phone call coming from Jimmy Lofton; King remembers it coming from Curtis Graves, which seems more likely.

P. 50 *Greyhound Bus Station*: Taping session, ES, Tape 21b; *HPr*, "Negroes Served at Bus Station," April 26, 1960, p. 4.

P. 51 *demonstration materials, and the like*: Unpublished manuscript, ESLL, Section 15, March 8 and 10, 1988.

P. 52 *"stand high in his class"*: James L. Blawie to Dean Harry Groves, November 6, 1957, student files of Texas Southern University, Houston, Texas.

P. 52 *"No question about it"*: Audio interview, EA-a.

P. 53 *"be no Eldrewey Stearns"*: Taping session, ES, Tape 21b.

P. 53 *declined a joint effort*: Audio interview, HH-a.

P. 53 *"another invisible barrier has fallen"*: FT, May 21, 1960.

P. 53 *in the black establishment*: Ester King's NAACP booklet, p. 46.

P. 54 *the committee in early June*: Jensen, "The Sit-in Movement of 1960–61," p. 217; HP, "Mayor's Bi-Racial Group to Disband: Subcommittee Head Expresses Surprise over Hamblen Move," June 10, 1960, pp. 1, 7.

P. 54 *other segregated businesses*: Taping session, ES, Tape 22b.

P. 54 *to protect the city*: R. Haynes, *A Night of Violence*.

P. 55 *integration for ten days*: Audio interview, JTJ-a. Born in Dallas in 1917, John T. Jones had come to Houston at age two or three and was educated in Houston Public Schools. During World War II, Jones served overseas in Northern Ireland, England, and North Africa before spending two long years as a prisoner of war. His uncle Jesse Jones, known mostly for his personal fortune, his international work with the Red Cross during World War I, and his prominent service in the Hoover and Roosevelt administrations, had also been a longtime supporter of what was then called Negro philanthropy. Jesse Jones had been a trustee of the Tuskegee Institute and a local champion of the United Negro College Fund. Through Dr. Frederick Patterson, the founder of the United Negro College Fund, Jones came to know Hobart Taylor, a prominent black businessman who came to work closely with John T. in the power brokers' quiet chess game of integration. When Jesse Jones died in 1956, John T. became publisher of the *Chronicle* and assumed control of the Houston Endowment.

P. 55 *"I could have kissed him"*: Interview, BD, notes in possession of author. Dundas's pivotal role is documented in his diary, in possession of his son, Robert Dundas, Jr.

P. 56 *"he did the right thing"*: Interview, JTJ-a.

P. 56 *"and threw you out"*: Video interview, HeH-v.

P. 56 *lunch counters in Houston*: Taping session, ES, Tape 22b.

P. 56 *"So?" asked Rather*: Taping session, ES, Tape 22b.

Chapter 3

P. 60 *"the Houston press clam-up"*: TO, "Houston Changes," September 2, 1960.

P. 60 *"SUBMITTED TO A CANDID WORLD"*: *Time*, "Blackout in Houston," September 12, 1960, p. 68.

P. 61 *"to talk about it too much"*: B. H. Bagdikian, "Houston's Shackled Press," p. 89. My descriptions of the *Houston Chronicle* and of Jones's meeting with Steven are adapted from Bagdikian's excellent article.

P. 61 *"rest of the [Negro] community"*: S. Friedman, "The Black Ghetto in Houston," p. 71.

P. 61   *"for one's rights is to sit down"*: T. Branch, *Parting the Waters*, p. 314.

P. 61   *shopped all their lives:* Ibid., p. 346.

P. 62   *"dump them in his lap"*: Ibid., p. 366.

P. 62   *white vote in Harris County:* C. Davidson, *Race and Class in Texas Politics*, Table 3.2, p. 34.

P. 62   *"Sweatt case to conclusion"*: Audio interview, GW-a.

P. 63   *"could manipulate the system"*: Audio interview, HK-a.

P. 64   *"as it related to politics"*: Ibid.

P. 64   *"down around Lyons Avenue"*: HC, "Negroes Stage Sit-in at Cafe, 48 Arrested," February 26, 1961, pp. 1, 20.

P. 65   *the Houston Medical Forum:* HC, "First Sit-iners Face Charges," February 25, 1961. Students arrested included Ronald Smith, Howard Gillory, Marvin Walker, Edythe Paige, Katy Gibbs, Nancy Smith, Horace Blair, Henry Allen, John Evans, Leo Bonner, Marion Moody, Robert Bolden, Robert Jones, and Eldrewey Stearns.

P. 65   *"attention for the process"*: Video interview, CG-v.

P. 66   *"Eldrewey could not control it"*: Audio interview, GW-v.

P. 66   *"table for them in the kitchen"*: HC, Walt Gray, "13 Demonstrators Fined $25 Each for 'Loitering' in Rail Station Cafe," March 24, 1961.

P. 67   *"'doing this for a cause'"*: Audio interview, CG-a.

P. 68   *"would not be hurt"*: Interview, JD.

P. 68   *"we'll build another Y"*: Audio interview, QM-a.

P. 68   *"sweepers and garagemen"*: HC, "Negroes Picket Office of Bell Telephone Co.," March 10, 1961.

P. 68   *motions for a new trial:* HC, Bill Porterfield, "Gains and Losses of Houston Integration Group Are Charted," June 28, 1961, pp. 1, 18.

P. 68   *Washington and King for their legal work:* The reasons for the HCCO's failure to pay Washington and King are not entirely clear. Attorney Aloysius M. Wickliff, chair of the HCCO fundraising committee to defend the students, believed that all money should be used or kept on hand to pay fines. George T. Nelson, longtime civil rights advocate and owner of the downtown Temple Barber Shop, was sympathetic to paying the lawyers for their work. See *I*, "Lawyers, Who Represented PYAers, Disgruntled Over 'Non-Payment,'" September 8, 1962, pp. 1, 8; *I*, "Lawyers Refused PYA Fund Pay," September 22, 1962, pp. 1, 8. In August 1964, Eldrewey Stearns filed a suit against the PYA on behalf of George Washington, who was seeking to collect $6,400 in legal fees for his defense of sit-in demonstrators. See *HC*, "Fee Suit for Sit-in Cases Filed," August 12, 1964, and *FT*, Varie Shields, "Attorney Who Handled Sit-in Legal Action Files Suit for Fees," August 15, 1964.

P. 69   *"what the NAACP is doing?"*: *I*, editorial page, "Will the NAACP Have to Move Over for the PYA?" June 17, 1961, p. 2.

P. 69   *"He did something really tremendous"*: Audio interview, EA-a.

P. 69   *the movement's militant leadership*: Audio interview, HH-a.

P. 69   *"love him for doing those things"*: Interview, AJ.

P. 70   *"down on the waterfront"*: Taping session, ES, Tape 29b.

P. 70   *"live demonstration to help"*: Interview, JD. Daniels describes his own experience in jail as a protester in "Trip to Jail Is Badge of Honor," *FT*, August 5, 1961.

P. 71   *"five hundred of my men with me"*: Interview, JD.

P. 71   *unlawful assembly charges were dropped*: Interview, JD; *HC*, "Gains, Losses," p. 18; *I*, "Duncan, ILA Head, Protests to City Council," June 10, 1961, pp. 1, 10.

P. 71   *"that's the way it was"*: Taping session, ES, Tape 29b.

P. 72   *Interstate Commerce Commission*: T. Branch, *Parting the Waters*, Chs. 11, 12.

P. 72   *"if you told them not to come"*: Audio interview, GW-a.

P. 73   *"all right in the morning"*: Taping session, ES, Tape 25a.

P. 73   *food service at Union Station*: *FT*, "Never in Houston!!!" July 29, 1961; *HP*, "Desegregation Order at Rail Station Cafe Sought," July 23, 1961; *HC*, "'Rider' Refuses Bond after Station Sit-in," July 23, 1961.

P. 73   *"'Christian in the morning'"*: Audio interview, GW-a.

P. 74   *"without going out of Houston"*: *HP*, "Cutrer's Aid in Sit-ins Requested," July 27, 1961; *HC*, "Attorney Asks Cutrer to Halt Sit-in Arrests," July 27, 1961. An unidentified article in John Bland's scrapbook, "Rights Fighter Turns Down Federal Post," says that George Washington, Jr., is thirty-two and "last October" successfully petitioned city integration.

P. 74   *"'they're doing the wrong thing'"*: Audio interview, GW-a.

P. 74   *dismissed the habeas corpus motion*: *HC*, "Sit-in Leader Told Loitering Arrests Slated," July 28, 1961.

P. 74   *released on $400 bond*: *HP*, "Stearns Is Out on Bond after Sit-in," July 31, 1961.

P. 75   *"everybody got along fine"*: *FT*, Varie Shields, "Freedom Riders Sought Cup of Coffee Here: Put Beliefs into Action . . . Beaten in County Jail," August 19, 1961; from John Bland's scrapbook; see photograph of Freedom Riders Robert Kaufmann, Stephen McNichols, and Joseph Stevenson being treated at Riverside General Hospital with Hamah King and George Washington, Jr.

P. 75   *"have the whole building rocking"*: Video interview, HH-v.

P. 75   *verdict directly opposed federal law*: *HPr*, "Freedom Riders on Trial Again," September 5, 1961, p. 1, and "18 Freedom Riders Fined $100 each," September 6, 1961, p. 1.

P. 75   *"to stop a peaceful demonstration"*: Audio interview, GW-a.

P. 76   *major league franchise to Houston*: G. Kirksey, "Houston, the Next Major League City," *Baseball Digest* (March 1959): 22; C. Nealon et al.,

"The Campaign for Major League Baseball in Houston," *Houston Review* 7 (1985): 2–46; B. O'Neal, *The Texas League*; E. W. Ray, *The Grand Huckster*.

P. 76   *integrated since 1954:* N. Sapper, "A Survey of the History of the Black People of Texas, 1930–1954," pp. 416–426.

P. 76   *construct a new stadium:* J. M. Carroll, "Houston Colt .45s — Houston Astros," pp. 240ff.; G. Kirksey, "Houston, the Next Major League City," pp. 21–26.

P. 77   *"I gave you my word, didn't I?":* Audio interview, QM-a.

P. 77   *"because we didn't know":* Video interview, QM-v.

P. 77   *the Houston Sports Association:* Ray, Grand Huckster, pp. 269ff.

P. 78   *"right side of God":* Taping session, ES, March 22, 1988.

P. 78   *a bond issue of $22 million:* Nealon et al., "Campaign for Major League Baseball in Houston," p. 37.

P. 78   *"cocked our guns and shot":* Video interview, QM-a.

P. 78   *"to face pretty quickly, aren't we?":* Video interview, JH-v.

P. 79   *without any local press coverage:* TO, "Hotels Act," April 14, 1962, p. 3; DT, "Houston Hotels Drop Color Bar," April 10, 1962; *New York Times*, "Major Houston Hotels Now Accept Negroes," April 10, 1962.

P. 79   *national convention business:* Houston was only one of many southern cities caught between the desire for hotel convention business and the practice of segregation. See *Business Week*, "Atlanta's Hotel Crisis," April 7, 1962, p. 128.

P. 79   *"it didn't turn out to be that way":* Video interview, JTJ-v.

P. 79   *"get back with the proper people":* Video interview, QM-v.

P. 79   *into effect without a hitch:* In July 1962, when Lloyd Wells, then a sportswriter and executive director of the *Informer*, went to see for himself "where we can and can't go on Houston's brilliant strip, called South Main, and in the downtown area," he found that almost every hotel was open for reservations but that some hotels maintained segregation in swimming pools. *I*, Lloyd Wells, "Informer Survey Finds Some Do Restrict Swimming Pools, Personal Reservations," July 21, 1962, p. 1.

P. 79   *"major league recognition":* I, "Colt Stadium, a Non-Segregated Institution," September 9, 1963, p. 10. (This article mistakenly dates the opening on April 10, 1961, whereas the actual opening was April 10, 1962.)

P. 80   *how much money you paid:* These vivid descriptions of opening day at the new Colt Stadium are taken from Carroll, "Houston Colt .45s — Houston Astros," pp. 239–240.

Chapter 4

P. 82   *"began to seem like a fantasy":* Phone interview with Ron Stone, September 1987.

P. 83   *"I would drink myself sober":* Taping session, ES, Tape 24b.

P. 84 "across the plains of America": Taping session, ES, 24a. Lent was February 15–April 2, 1961.

P. 84 "to put up with her?": Taping session, ES, Tape 24a.

P. 84 "'stop twisting around'": Taping session, ES, Tape 24a.

P. 84 "couldn't control myself": Unpublished manuscript, ESPR.

P. 85 "I got this bite from her": Taping session, ES, Tape 24a; unpublished manuscript, ESPR.

P. 85 "'don't let the man talk'": Taping session, ES, Tape 24a.

P. 85 "my station in Houston": Taping session, ES, Tape 24a.

P. 86 "That's the way it was": Taping session, ES, Tape 24b.

P. 86 "less I felt the pain": Taping session, ES, Tape 25a.

P. 86 officials of the Loew's Theater: I, "PYA Head to New York," April 15, 1961, p. 1.

P. 86 "started getting blurry": Taping session, ES, Tape 25a.

P. 86 known as the Freedom Rides: A. Meier and E. Rudwick, *CORE*. On James Farmer's Texas childhood and education, see J. Farmer, *Lay Bare the Heart*, pp. 51–65.

P. 87 "nobody's feelings to consider": Taping session, ES, Tape 24b.

P. 87 "sort of feeling his oats": Audio interview, SN-a.

P. 87 movement throughout the South: R. H. King, "Citizenship and Self-Respect," *Journal of American Studies* 22 (1988): 7–24.

P. 87 "equal use of public facilities": HC, "Gains and Losses of Integration Group Charted," June 28, 1961, pp. 1, 18.

P. 87 drop in his business: Ibid.; FT, "Rivals in Orlando Supermarket Row Present Their Arguments," June 17, 1961.

P. 88 "school of law this coming fall": Letter on PYA letterhead from ES to Dean Kenneth S. Tollett, July 3, 1961, from Texas Southern University student file.

P. 88 "'That's next for us all'": Audio interview, GW-a.

P. 88 "the mouth of some people": Audio interview, HH-a.

P. 88 "bills put in your pocket": Taping session, ES, Tape 23b.

P. 89 "haunt me in my absence": Taping session, ES, Tape 23a.

P. 89 "living off the movement": Audio interview, HH-a.

P. 89 "need to take a break": Taping session, ES, March 17, 1988.

P. 89 their financial support from Stearns: Audio interview, HH-a.

P. 89 "efforts have been effective": FT, "P.Y.A. Leader Quits, Mission Goes On," October 7, 1961.

P. 90 of the new leadership: HP, "Stearns, Who Led Sit-ins Here, Resigns Racial Post," September 30, 1961.

P. 90 costs of going to jail: HP, S. Friedman, "Negro Youth's Ex-Leader Says Movement Is 'Dying,'" October 2, 1961.

P. 90 "did not want all this known": Audio interview, HH-a.

P. 91 "more angry than in love": Unpublished manuscript, ESPR, March 17, 1988.

P. 91   *leaders in the United States:* The caption below Stearns's photograph reads: "Lider Racial en Estados Unidos," *El Porvenir*, n.d. I cannot decipher the headline from the tattered newspaper copy Stearns showed me.

P. 91   *"kept on getting more drunk":* Unpublished manuscript, ESPR.

P. 92   *"I had nothing but time":* Ibid.

P. 92   *"that action against me":* Ibid.

P. 92   *by tearing up the check:* Taping session, ES, Tape 27.

P. 92   *"contribution is needed desperately":* FT, "PYA . . . New Leader, Solid Program," December 30, 1961, p. 21.

P. 93   *declared him the winner:* Audio interview, HeH-a.

P. 93   *the foundation officers:* I, "Aid to PYA Is Suspended," January 27, 1962, pp. 1, 8.

P. 93   *whose cases were pending:* HC, "Pro-Integration Group Loses Backing in Feud," January 22, 1962.

P. 94   *the verge of a race war:* R. L. Blumberg, *Civil Rights*, pp. 115–122; T. Branch, *Parting the Waters*, Ch. 20; H. Sitkoff, *The Struggle for Black Equality*, Ch. 5.

P. 94   *North as well as the South:* NYT, Laymond Robinson, "Robert Kennedy Consults Negroes Here about North," May 25, 1963, pp. 1, 8; *NYT*, Robinson, "Robert Kennedy Fails to Sway Negroes at Secret Talks Here," May 26, 1963, pp. 1, 59.

P. 94   *a new civil rights bill:* The following four sources are from the *NYT*: Anthony Lewis, "Robert Kennedy Confers Today with Theatre Men on Race Issue," May 27, 1963, pp. 1, 19; Tom Wicker, "President Bids Governors Lead Rights Campaign," May 30, 1963, pp. 1, 9; "Businessmen Tell the President of Progress in Integration," June 5, 1963; "Head of Restaurant Group Asks Support on Integration," June 8, 1963, p. 23; J. H. Allan, "Businessmen Act on Integration after White House Conferences," June 15, 1963.

P. 95   *"he's going to work with us":* Video interview, QM-v.

P. 96   *"a good idea to change customs":* Video interview, JTJ-v.

P. 96   *seventy-five other theaters in Texas:* Interstate was a subsidiary of American Broadcasting–Paramount Theaters, which operated more than 200 theaters throughout the South. See *NYT*, Allan, "Businessmen Act on Integration after White House Conferences," June 15, 1963. Adams was one of four Texas businessmen who later attended a meeting with President Kennedy designed to spur immediate desegregation of southern businesses, many of which were owned by larger northern companies.

P. 96   *"gonna be responsible for it":* Audio interview, OK-a.

P. 96   *within thirty days:* Taping session, ES, Tape 28.

P. 97   *"start picketing again":* Ibid.

P. 97   *"for thirty more days":* Taping sessions, ES, Tape 28; ES, April 5, 1988.

P. 97   *"an old dog":* Taping session, ES, Tape 28.

P. 98   *"but nothing happened":* Video interview, JTJ-v.

P. 98   individuals over many years: FT, "It Takes More Than One Bullet to Win a War," July 13, 1963, p. 31.

P. 98   "effective and permanent way": I, Carter Wesley, "Ram's Horn," June 22, 1963, pp. 1, 8.

P. 98   and a prosperous economy: E. Jacoway and D. Colburn, eds., *Southern Businessmen and Desegregation*; D. L. Chappell, *Inside Agitators*; and J. Schutze, *The Accommodation*.

P. 99   "Negro militancy in Houston": TO, Saul Friedman, "Houston a Backwater of . . . ?" November 1963.

Chapter 5

P. 104   "goin' through the door": Interview, DS, July 1, 1988.

P. 105   "much time at home": Ibid.

P. 105   "And I say, 'A-a-aw'": Interview, RDS, March 2, 1993, from Tapes 1 and 2.

P. 105   condition was good: JSHR, Eldrewey Stearns, patient number 17748.

P. 105   "was a bastard, really": Taping session, ES, October 30, 1984.

P. 106   records fall silent: JSHR, February 1, March 14, 1932. ES's weight was recorded as nine pounds ten ounces; at eleven weeks he weighed fourteen pounds. The examining physician noted that ES's weight was above average for eleven weeks and recommended no further treatment. These records do not seem to indicate a "failure to thrive" or fundamental problem in the mother-child relationship. More likely, they reflect a "colicky" baby and DS's anxiety about her life situation in general and her newborn baby's health in particular.

P. 106   bingo, and horse betting: D. G. McComb, *Galveston*, pp. 161–162.

P. 106   "family in Galveston, Texas": Unpublished manuscript, ESFS.

P. 106   "Devona fed the family": Taping session, ES, Tape 5.

P. 107   "care where it went": Ibid.

P. 107   "face to sober him up": Ibid.

P. 107   "than darkness for sure": Ibid.

P. 107   exodus from the rural South: N. Lemann, *The Promised Land*. On the movement of black Texans from rural to urban areas between 1900 and 1950, see W. J. Brophy, *The Black Texan*, Ch. 1. Brophy shows that out-of-state migration was relatively low compared to other southern states and that migration from rural to urban areas *within* the state was of more significance. In 1900, the black population in Texas was 80.8 percent rural; by 1950, it was only 37.3 percent. This pattern was roughly equivalent to the movement of whites during the same period (pp. 13–16).

P. 107   the area during the 1820s: W. T. Chambers, "The Redlands of Central Eastern Texas," *Texas Geographic Magazine* 5:2 (Autumn 1991), 1–15; G. L. Crockett, *Two Centuries in East Texas*, pp. 79ff.

P. 108   *on foot or in wagons:* A. Barr, *Black Texans*, pp. 14ff.

P. 108   *place for the Texas Army:* Crockett, *Two Centuries in East Texas*, p. 121.

P. 108   *together a large plantation:* Story told by Crockett, *Two Centuries in East Texas*, p. 95; apparently first told to him by Judge William T. Davis of San Augustine, sometime in the early 1930s. Repeated by Joanna Phillips of San Augustine.

P. 108   *"away to pray any more":* Joanna Phillips, "History of Roberts Baptist Church," p. 2. I am grateful to Lon L. Garner and James Phillips, Mrs. Phillips's son, for letting me see this document.

P. 108   *Indian and African descent:* Ibid.

P. 109   *entrance to Roberts Community:* Interviews, RS, February 14 and March 2, 1990.

P. 109   *born September 13, 1885:* Records of San Augustine County Courthouse, listed on Mollie Cook's Certificate of Death, December 8, 1953. This is also the date cited in the Roberts Baptist Church obituary. RS's family Bible "Family Record" page gives the birth date as September 13, 1888. The later birth date seems unlikely, since it would mean that Mollie was married at age thirteen and gave birth to Rudolph at age fourteen.

P. 109   *paternity of their children:* J. Dollard, *Caste and Class in a Southern Town*; and D. Cohn, *Where I Was Born and Raised*, pp. 294ff. The United States was — and is — the only nation in the world that uses the "one-drop rule" to culturally and legally define a person as black. According to this rule, any person with a single drop of "black blood" (i.e., *any* known African black ancestry) is defined as black (or Negro, colored, African American) and assigned the status of this subordinate group. See also F. J. Davis, *Who Is Black?*; and J. Williamson, *New People*.

P. 109   *Sterne, Sternes, Stearns, Stearnes:* Corey's Certificate of Death lists his date of birth as December 2, 1880, and his father as Henry Sterns. I have relied on the census taken on June 25 and 26, 1880, which identifies Corey as having been born on June 12, into the household of Joe and Martha Stearns. A four-year-old boy, Austin, was also listed. See U.S. Manuscript Census for 1880, San Augustine County, Supervisor No. 1, Enumeration District No. 80, p. 34, lines 3–6.

P. 109   *twice in his life:* Interviews, RS, February 9 and 14, 1990.

P. 110   *"to deal with him":* Interviews, RS, February 14 and March 2, 1990.

P. 110   *movement for independence:* A. P. McDonald, "Adolphus Sterne: Mover and Shaker"; and A. P. McDonald, ed., *Hurrah for Texas: The Diary of Adolphus Sterne.*

P. 110   *history of the place:* Unpublished manuscript, ESFS. Unfortunately, Joanna Phillips died shortly before I got to talk with her. When Eldrewey, Rudolph, Eric Avery, and I arrived at the Garner Funeral Home in San Augustine in April 1990, Mrs. Phillips's freshly cut headstone was sitting in the driveway.

P. 110 *"I'm not kidding":* Interview, SS.

P. 110 *San Augustine County Courthouse:* For statistics on lynching in Texas between 1882 and 1927, see Brophy, *The Black Texan,* pp. 253–256. Also L. C. Goodwyn, "Populist Dreams and Negro Rights: East Texas as a Case Study," *American Historical Review* 76 (1971): 1435–1456.

P. 111 *"was some way out":* Interview, RS, February 9, 1990.

P. 111 *she raised herself:* Interviews, RS, February 9 and 14, 1990.

P. 111 *"can talk about it":* Interviews, RS, June 23, 1988, and February 14, 1990.

P. 111 *"whippin's . . . from nobody":* Interview, RS, February 14, 1990.

P. 111 *"sheriff after me":* Interview, RS, April 28, 1990.

P. 112 *"Last me a long time":* Ibid. See also B. O'Neal, "Bootlegging in Northeast Texas," *East Texas Historical Journal* 22:2 (1984): 13–20.

P. 112 *"outside of San Augustine":* Interview, RS, June 23, 1988.

P. 113 *"a half each way":* Unpublished manuscript, ESFS.

P. 113 *"squirrels and armadillos":* Taping session, ES, Tape 5.

P. 114 *"harvested cotton in town":* Unpublished manuscript, ESFS, and taping session, ES, Tape 5.

P. 114 *"at the same time":* Unpublished manuscript, ESFS.

P. 114 *"take the tomato":* Ibid.

P. 115 *"and drink himself":* Taping session, ES, Tape 5.

P. 115 *"go ahead and eat him":* Ibid.

P. 115 *"was the mockingbird":* Unpublished manuscript, ESFS.

P. 117 *"sawmill for a while":* Ibid., and taping session, ES, Tape 5.

P. 117 *"picked some cotton":* Unpublished manuscript, ESFS.

P. 117 *"any in my life":* Taping session, ES, Tape 5.

P. 117 *"women in San Augustine":* Unpublished manuscript, ESFS.

P. 118 *"the giant Goliath":* Ibid.

P. 119 *"still court loneliness":* Ibid.

P. 119 *"'good for the gander'":* Unpublished manuscript, ESFS.

P. 120 *"a Baptist preacher":* Ibid.

P. 121 *a church congregation:* Ibid.

P. 121 *"for my own good":* Ibid.

P. 122 *"to my eyes again":* Ibid.

P. 123 *"see their brother":* Ibid.

P. 124 *"lookin' at me":* Interview, DS, July 1, 1988.

P. 124 *"so far away":* Unpublished manuscript, ESFS.

Chapter 6

P. 126 *"And this child has been ill":* Interview, DS, November 18, 1991.

P. 127 *"can't be your brother":* Interview, JG.

P. 127 *"as a backyard well":* Unpublished manuscript, ESSP.

P. 128 *"where the rabbit come in!":* Interview, JG.

P. 128   *"look like a rabbit"*: Unpublished manuscript, ESSP.
P. 128   *"He didn't hold back"*: Interview, GS.
P. 128   *"legend in that family"*: Unpublished manuscript, ESSP.
P. 128   *"the kids loved him"*: Interview, GS.
P. 129   Macedonia Baptist Church: Interview, JT. See also B. C. Armstead, Jr., papers at Rosenberg Library, Galveston, Texas.
P. 130   *"no doubt about it"*: Unpublished manuscript, ESSP.
P. 130   *"'You see!' I saw enough"*: Ibid.
P. 130   or parading on horseback: K. M. Stampp, *The Peculiar Institution*; E. Fornell, *The Galveston Era*, pp. 115–125; R. B. Campbell, *An Empire for Slavery*.
P. 131   *"slammed the door behind me"*: Unpublished manuscript, ESSP.
P. 131   *"all the luxuries"*: Ibid.
P. 132   *"quit the Boy Scouts"*: Ibid.
P. 132   took off down the alley: Interview, JG.
P. 132   *"not to blab a word"*: Unpublished manuscript, ESSP.
P. 132   putting the alcohol away: Interview, DS.
P. 133   *"nothing but white foam"*: Unpublished manuscript, ESSP.
P. 133   *"'knife in my son's head?'"*: Interview, DS.
P. 134   bring them cigarettes: Unpublished manuscript, ESSP.
P. 134   *"Certainly not me"*: Ibid.
P. 134   *"not another one like him"*: Interview, DS.
P. 135   been a racial brawl: Unpublished manuscript, ESSP.
P. 135   card games, and roulette: Ibid.
P. 136   *"'run, nigger, run'"*: Ibid.
P. 137   last day at the Watermelon Garden: Ibid.
P. 138   *"ran home by myself"*: Ibid.
P. 138   *"though I wanted him dead"*: Ibid.

Chapter 7

P. 140   *"everyone else was doing"*: Unpublished manuscript, ESH.
P. 140   a *"Mecca"* for blacks: Interview, BL.
P. 140   drew especially large crowds: Interview, JF.
P. 140   their numbers too: Ibid.
P. 140   *"corner delinquents"*: Interview, HHS.
P. 141   Central High School in 1949: Ibid.
P. 141   through the back door: Taping session, ES, Tape 1; interview, HHS.
P. 141   his spot as a waiter: Interview, HHS.
P. 142   tails, black tie, and vest: Unpublished manuscript, ESH.
P. 142   ignored the warning: Ibid.
P. 142   *"whenever he caught him drunk"*: Ibid.
P. 142   *"Shorty can handle me"*: Ibid.
P. 142   *"back to partial sobriety"*: Ibid.

P. 143   *"falling out of bed"*: Ibid.

P. 143   *"get you home. Goodnight"*: Ibid.

P. 143   *the principal's office*: Ibid.

P. 143   *John Sealy Hospital*: Ibid.

P. 144   *"take me home at night"*: Ibid.

P. 144   *flowing into her household*: Interview, DS.

P. 144   *"I became his master"*: Taping session, ES, Tape 1; unpublished manuscript, ESH.

P. 144   *way in the world*: Interview, TL.

P. 144   *sell to their friends*: Unpublished manuscript, ESH.

P. 145   *"what hovel you had"*: Interview, TL, February 1, 1991.

P. 145   *reorganized as a social club*: Interview, RH.

P. 145   *accounts for the year*: Ibid.

P. 146   *"anything was possible"*: Unpublished manuscript, ESH.

P. 146   *"best drinks in America"*: Ibid.

P. 146   *"had to give something"*: Ibid.

P. 146   *"three girls broke down"*: Interview, TL, February 1, 1991.

P. 147   *"of the clap. Go ahead!"*: Unpublished manuscript, ESH.

P. 147   *"like a black woman"*: Ibid.

P. 148   *returned to a whorehouse again*: Ibid.

P. 148   *"for the taking"*: Ibid.

P. 148   *"original Negro gourmet dish"*: Ibid.

P. 149   *"coon, coon, coon"*: Ibid.

P. 149   *unless Gus was sober*: Ibid.

P. 149   *ranged from 72 to 80*: Galveston Public School Records: Central High School.

P. 149   *they nicknamed "Ichabod"*: Interview, TL.

P. 150   *"if you are black, stay back"*: Unpublished manuscript, ESH.

P. 150   *"don't you know that?"*: Ibid.

P. 150   *"to the bar to celebrate"*: Unpublished manuscript, ESH, revision.

P. 150   *"to use the white toilets"*: Ibid.

P. 151   *"cocked then for a law career"*: Ibid.

P. 151   *"sit back and listen to him"*: Interview, TL.

P. 151   *"our eyes ever on our objectives"*: Unpublished manuscript, ESH.

P. 152   *"wavering and threatening to sink"*: Ibid.

P. 152   *"after leaving him the way I did"*: Unpublished manuscript, ESH, revision.

Chapter 8

P. 156   *"know what he was doing"*: FT, "Attorney Says Stearns Not Responsible," March 25, 1967, p. 6; interview, JKC.

P. 157   *"not only now," Sher told the court*: "Defendant's Application on

Behalf of Accused to Try Issue of Insanity in Advance of Trial on the Merits," *State of Texas v. Eldrewey Stearns,* Case No. 124,944, p. 7, Harris County Courthouse, Criminal Records Division.

P. 157 *"out of touch with reality"*: Ibid., p. 16.

P. 157 *psychiatric help for Stearns:* Ibid., Theodore Hogrobrooks's testimony, pp. 19–23.

P. 158 *State Hospital as soon as possible:* "Minutes of the Criminal District Court No. 5 of Harris County, Texas," March 16, 1967, vol. 7, p. 367.

P. 158 *"alert eyes will smile again":* FT, Sonny Wells, "Declared Insane, Found Not Guilty on Worthless Check Rap," March 25, 1967, p. 6.

P. 158 *treatment for manic-depressive illness:* The first time that manic-depressive illness (or bipolar disorder) appears in Eldrewey's medical records is when he was temporarily committed to Austin State Hospital from September 29 to October 30, 1981. Copy of Austin State Hospital medical records in author's possession.

P. 159 *it is largely ignorant:* B. J. Cohler and T. R. Cole, "Studying Older Lives," pp. 61–76.

P. 160 *stigma of mental illness:* D. R. Williams, "African American Mental Health," *African American Research Perspectives* 2:1 (Spring 1995): 8–16.

P. 160 *"energy and productivity":* F. K. Goodwin and K. R. Jamison, *Manic-Depressive Illness,* p. 3.

P. 160 *"the point where it started":* J. D. Campbell, *Manic-Depressive Disease,* pp. 112–113.

P. 161 *"taken advantage of":* Cited by Goodwin and Jamison, *Manic-Depressive Illness,* p. 51.

P. 162 *as much as four decades:* Goodwin and Jamison, *Manic-Depressive Illness,* pp. 128–136; and R. W. Gibson, M. B. Cohen, and R. A. Cohen, "On the Dynamics of the Manic-Depressive Personality," *American Journal of Psychiatry* 115 (1959): 1102.

P. 162 *not allow them to rest:* My description of hypomanic and manic states is taken from Goodwin and Jamison, *Manic-Depressive Illness,* pp. 22–35.

P. 163 *and an increased sexual drive:* Ibid., p. 310.

P. 163 *"of the underlying emotion":* W. Mayer-Gross, E. Slater, and M. Roth, *Clinical Psychiatry,* p. 209, as cited by Goodwin and Jamison, *Manic-Depressive Illness,* p. 37.

P. 164 *strengthening influence of friendship:* Ibid., p. 302.

P. 164 *family members by alienating them:* Observations and studies by E. Kraeplin (1921), R. W. Gibson (1963), and D. S. Janowsky and his colleagues (1970–1974) are summarized and cited by Goodwin and Jamison, *Manic-Depressive Illness,* pp. 302–303.

P. 166 *"like a lawyer, you know":* Taping session, ES, Tape 33.

P. 166 *he failed to repay:* ES letter to Faurice and Jessie Prince. On letterhead: Law Offices of Chargois and Stearnes [*sic*]. No date. "Dear Mr. Prince: No I haven't forgotten you — cases on T. D. will enable me to begin paying you in full rather than the monthly schedule — As soon as I can get a big loan through . . . I will more than bring up my back payments. And this is a written promise to pay all interest for lateness — Thanks, Stearns. P.S. To be definite, by the end of next week, I shall bring to you at least $300."

P. 166   from District 22 in Houston: HC, "E. J. Stearns to Run for Legislature," February 7, 1966; and *HP*, "Stearns in District 22 House Race," February 7, 1966.

P. 166   to run as an independent: Letter to ES from Kenneth Tollett, castigating him for borrowing money from a white supporter and failing to pay it back. From ES's file at TSU.

P. 167   "you'd collect it": Taping session, ES, May 17, 1988.

P. 167   "to run for dogcatcher": Ibid.

P. 167   "for a few days, you know": Ibid.

P. 167   the Harris County sheriff: Letter from C. R. Miller to Judge Sam Davis, July 26, 1967: Austin State Hospital Records, Case #59914.

P. 167   in his courtroom: Interview, MM.

P. 167   "somewhere burning in hell": Taping session, ES, Tape 51.

P. 167   Davis ordered his release: Judgment in Case #124944, Minutes of the 179th District Court of Harris County, October 18, 1967, vol. 8, p. 191.

P. 168   "that would be my therapy": Taping session, ES, Tape 51.

P. 168   "they were of a different race": Taping session, ES, August 18, 1988.

P. 168   staying at his establishment: Memo to the Director of the FBI, Washington, D.C., from a Mr. Legat in Mexico City, June 20, 1968. Obtained through a Freedom of Information request.

P. 168   advised caution in contacting him: From FBI memos and letters dated June 20, July 12, October 24, October 29, and December 19, 1968. In author's possession.

P. 169   second-class citizenship: For a few years, Stearns handed out leaflets urging people to contribute time and money to his mobilization efforts. The address on the Black Emergence Day letterhead was 14 E. 28th St., Suite 650, New York. Copies in author's possession.

P. 169   "'that is the only way'": M. Bott, "Doctor Stearns Plans New Push to Bring Races Together," *Galveston Daily News*, June 24, 1973, p. 7-A.

P. 169   "emerge from the center": *Chicago Tribune*, Emmett George, "Black Dreams of Making Oct 1 Day to Remember," December 26, 1974, section 7.

P. 170   "pleading eyes of Eldrewey Stearns": *FT*, Sonny Wells, "Declared Insane, Found Not Guilty on Worthless Check Rap," March 25, 1967, p. 6.

P. 170   "in a common cause": "Lawyer Leads Boycott of Arab, Chinese, & Korean Merchants," *San Francisco Courier*, May 12, 1979, p. 3.

P. 170   "Tear Out Their Hole": Taping session, ES, "South African Vendetta," October 11 and 28, 1988.

P. 170 intent to commit rape: These records were obtained through a Freedom of Information request and contain Stearns's FBI arrest record, #764-455-D. In author's possession.

P. 171 he was released: Saint Elizabeth's Hospital Record, Patient Record 98,049, June 4–July 8, 1970, Washington, D.C. In possession of author.

P. 172 "and didn't get made": Interview, AJ.

P. 173 "stars above and earth below": Eldrewey memorized this poem in high school.

P. 173 "trying to say 'thank you'": Interview, FGB.

P. 174 "all the way back to Houston": Ibid.

P. 174 at the Houston VA Hospital: On this hospitalization, Eldrewey was diagnosed with schizophrenia. He was treated both with the antipsychotic medication Haldol and with lithium. Houston Veterans' Administration Medical Center, Medical Records; copy of discharge summary in author's possession.

P. 175 "any additional problems": From a handwritten memoir by Shirley Stearns, "My Brother Eldrewey: There Is One in Every Family" (26 pp., 1990). Copy in author's possession.

P. 176 "wouldn't have to suffer": Phone conversation, DS, August 17, 1990. Signed affidavit and Social Security disability file in author's possession.

Chapter 9

P. 186 "warm and understanding": L. Edel, *Writing Lives.*

P. 189 "wonderin' about it": RS, personal communication.

P. 194 motivating the public figure: L. Edel, *Writing Lives: Principia Biographica,* pp. 29–30.

P. 197 they aren't all there: M. Kaminsky, "Discourse and Self-Formation," *American Journal of Psychoanalysis* 54:4 (1994): 293–316.

P. 198 experience of being inferior: For an excellent analysis of these issues in American life, see P. Berman, "The Other and Almost the Same."

P. 199 to face it directly: See S. H. Baron and C. Pletsch, eds., *Introspection in Biography;* and G. Goraitis and G. Pollock, *Psychoanalytic Studies of Biography.*

P. 200 exclusive truths and destinies: For an excellent discussion of the tension between cosmopolitanism and pluralism in multiculturalism, see D. Hollinger, *Postethnic America,* Ch. 4.

P. 200 and hidden in others: J. Scott, "Multiculturalism and the Politics of Identity," *October* 61 (Summer 1992): 12–19.

P. 200 cultural definition of black: F. J. Davis, *Who Is Black?*

P. 201 "looking glass of the white mind": Taping session, ES, Tape 31A, p. 10.

P. 201 *"from my own presence"*: F. Fanon, "Black Skin, White Masks," pp. 109–110; also H. K. Bhabha, "Interrogating Identity," pp. 183–209.

P. 202 *"race, but only one"*: G. Nash, "The Hidden History of Mestizo America," *Journal of American History* 82:3 (December 1995): 960.

P. 202 *their children as white or black*: See, for example, L. Funderburg, *Black, White, Other*; G. H. Williams, *Life on the Color Line*.

P. 202 *than by prescribed descent*: Nash, "Hidden History of Mestizo America," pp. 941–964.

P. 202 *soul is still not rested*: H. Raines, *My Soul Is Rested*.

P. 202 *must be remembered*: See B. Myerhoff, *Remembered Lives*.

Armstead, Bert Carson, Jr. Papers at Rosenberg Library.

Bagdikian, Ben H. "Houston's Shackled Press." *Atlantic Monthly* (August 1966).

Baron, Samuel H., and Carl Pletsch, eds. *Introspection in Biography*. Hillsdale, N.J.: Analytic Press, subs. Lawrence Erlbaum Assocs., 1985.

Barr, Alwyn. *Black Texans: A History of Heroes in Texas: 1528–1971*. Austin, Tex.: Jenkins, 1973.

Beeth, Howard, and Cary D. Wintz, eds. *Black Dixie: Afro-Texan History and Culture in Houston*. College Station: Texas A & M Press, 1992.

Berman, Paul. "The Other and Almost the Same." In Paul Berman, ed., *Blacks and Jews: Alliances and Arguments*, pp. 1–28. New York: Delacorte, 1994.

Bhabha, Homi K. "Interrogating Identity: the Postcolonial Prerogative." In David Goldberg, ed., *Anatomy of Racism*, pp. 183–209.

Blumberg, Rhoda Lois. *Civil Rights: The 1960s Freedom Struggle*. Revised edition. Boston: Twayne, 1984.

Bott, Margaret. "Doctor Stearns Plans New Push to Bring Races Together." *Galveston Daily News*, June 24, 1973.

Bradford, E. *Nelson: The Essential Hero*. London: Granada, 1979.

Branch, Taylor. *Parting the Waters: America in the King Years, 1954–1963*. New York: Simon and Schuster, 1988.

Brophy, William Joseph. "The Black Texan 1900–1950: A Quantitative History." Ph.D. dissertation, Vanderbilt University, 1974.

Bryant, Ira B. *Texas Southern University: Its Antecedents, Politics, Origin, and Future*. Houston, Tex.: D. Armstrong, 1975.

Bullard, Robert D. *Invisible Houston*. College Station: Texas A & M Press, 1987.

Butler, Robert. "The Life-Review: An Interpretation of Reminiscence in the Aged." *Psychiatry* 26 (1963): 65–76.

Campbell, J. D. *Manic-Depressive Disease: Clinical and Psychiatric Significance*. Philadelphia: J. B. Lippincott, 1953.

Campbell, Randolph B. *An Empire for Slavery*. Baton Rouge: Louisiana State University Press, 1989.

Carleton, Don. *Red Scare: Right-Wing Hysteria, Fifties Fanaticism, and Their Legacy in Texas*. Austin: Texas Monthly Press, 1985.

Carroll, John M. "Houston Colt .45s — Houston Astros: From Showbiz to Serious Baseball Business." In Peter C. Bjarkman, ed., *Encyclopedia of Major League Baseball Team Histories: National League*, pp. 234–258. Westport, Conn.: Meckler, 1991.

Chafe, William H. *Civilities and Civil Rights: Greensboro, North Carolina, and the Black Struggle for Freedom*. New York: Oxford University Press, 1980.

Chambers, William T. "The Redlands of Central Texas." *Texas Geographic Magazine* 5:2 (Autumn 1941): 1–15.

Chappell, David L. *Inside Agitators: White Southerners in the Civil Rights Movement*. Baltimore: Johns Hopkins University Press, 1994.

Cohler, Bertram J. "The Human Studies and the Life History." *Social Services Review* 62 (1988): 205–241.

———. "Personal Narrative and Life-Course." In P. Baltes and O. G. Brim, Jr., eds., *Life-Span Development and Behavior*, vol. 4. New York: Academic Press, 1982.

Cohler, Bertram J., and Thomas R. Cole. "Studying Older Lives: Reciprocal Acts of Telling and Listening." In James E. Birren et al., eds., *Aging and Biography*, pp. 61–76. New York: Springer, 1996.

Cohn, David. *Where I Was Born and Raised*. South Bend, Ind.: University of Notre Dame Press, 1967.

Crockett, George L. *Two Centuries in East Texas*. Dallas: Southwest Press, 1932.

Davidson, Chandler. "Negro Politics and the Rise of the Civil Rights Movement in Houston, TX." Ph.D. dissertation, Department of Sociology, Princeton University, 1968.

———. *Race and Class in Texas Politics*. Princeton, N.J.: Princeton University Press, 1990.

Davis, F. James. *Who Is Black? One Nation's Definition*. University Park: Pennsylvania State University Press, 1991.

Day, Barbara Thompson. "The Heart of Houston: The Early History of the Houston Council on Human Relations." *Houston Review* 8 (1986): 1–31.

Dollard, John. *Caste and Class in a Southern Town*. New Haven, Conn.: Yale University Press, 1937.

Edel, Leon. *Writing Lives: Principia Biographica*. New York: Norton, 1959/1984.

Fanon, Frantz. "The Fact of Blackness." In David Goldberg, ed., *Anatomy of Racism*, pp. 108–126.

Farmer, James. *Lay Bare the Heart: An Autobiography of the Civil Rights Movement*. New York: Arbor House, 1985.

Feagin, Joe R. *Free Enterprise City: Houston in Political and Economic Perspective*. New Brunswick, N.J.: Rutgers University Press, 1988.

Fisher, Robert. "'Where Seldom Is Heard a Discouraging Word': The Political Economy of Houston, Texas." *American Studies* 33: 73–91.

Fornell, Earl. *The Galveston Era: The Texas Crescent on the Eve of Secession*. Austin: University of Texas Press, 1961.

Freeman, Mark. "History, Narrative, and Life-Span Developmental Knowledge." *Human Development* 27 (1984): 1–9.

Friedman, Saul. "The Black Ghetto in Houston." Unpublished manuscript (98 pp.). Houston, 1965.

Funderburg, Lise. *Black, White, Other: Biracial Americans Talk about Race and Identity*. New York: Quill/Morrow, 1994.

Gibson, Robert W., Mabel B. Cohen, and Robert A. Cohen. "On the

Dynamics of the Manic-Depressive Personality." *American Journal of Psychiatry* 115 (1959): 1102.

Gillette, Michael L. "The Rise of the NAACP in Texas." *Southwestern Historical Quarterly* 81 (April 1978): 393–416.

Goldberg, David Theo, ed. *Anatomy of Racism*. Minneapolis: University of Minnesota Press, 1990.

Goodwin, Frederick K., and Kay Redfield Jamison. *Manic-Depressive Illness*. New York: Oxford, 1990.

Goodwyn, Lawrence C. "Populist Dreams and Negro Rights: East Texas as a Case Study." *American Historical Review* 76 (1971): 1435–1456.

Goraitis, G., and G. Pollock, eds. *Psychoanalytic Studies of Biography*. Madison, Conn.: International Press, 1987.

Haynes, Robert V. *A Night of Violence: The Houston Riot of 1917*. Baton Rouge: Louisiana State University Press, 1976.

Hill, Christopher. *God's Englishman*. London: Weidenfeld and Nicolson, 1970.

Hine, Darlene Clark. *Black Victory: The Rise and Fall of the White Primary in Texas*. Millwood, N.Y.: KTO Press, 1979.

Hollinger, David. *Postethnic America: Beyond Multiculturalism*. New York: Basic Books, 1995.

Jacoway, Elizabeth, and David Colburn, eds. *Southern Businessmen and Desegregation*. Baton Rouge: Louisiana State Press, 1982.

Jensen, F. Kenneth. "The Sit-in Movement of 1960–61." In Howard Beeth and Cary D. Wintz, eds., *Black Dixie*, pp. 211–222.

Kaminsky, Marc. "Discourse and Self-Formation: The Concept of 'Mentsh' in Modern Yiddish Culture." *American Journal of Psychoanalysis* 54:4 (1994): 293–316.

———, ed. *The Uses of Reminiscence: New Ways of Working with Older Adults*. New York: Haworth, 1984.

King, Richard H. "Citizenship and Self-Respect: The Experience of Politics in the Civil Rights Movement." *Journal of American Studies* 22 (1988): 7–24.

Kirksey, George. "Houston, the Next Major League City." *Baseball Digest* (March 1959): 21–26.

Laue, James H. *Direct Action and Desegregation: 1960–1962*. Brooklyn, N.Y.: Carlson, 1989.

Lemann, Nicholas. *The Promised Land: The Great Black Migration and How it Changed America*. New York: Alfred Knopf, 1991.

Malcolm X. *The Autobiography of Malcolm X: With the Assistance of Alex Haley*. Ed. Alex Haley and M. S. Handler. New York: Ballantine, 1987/1992.

Mayer-Gross, W., E. Slater, and M. Roth. *Clinical Psychiatry*. 2nd edition. London: Cassell, 1960.

McComb, David G. *Galveston: A History*. Austin: University of Texas Press, 1986.

McDonald. Archie P. "Adolphus Sterne: Mover and Shaker." In *The Bicentennial Commemorative History of Nacogdoches*. Nacogdoches: Jaycees, 1976.

———, ed. *Hurrah for Texas: The Diary of Adolphus Sterne, 1838–1851*. Austin: Eakin Press, 1986.

Meier, August, and Elliot Rudwick. *CORE: A Study in the Civil Rights Movement, 1942–1968*. New York: Oxford University Press, 1973.

Myerhoff, Barbara. *Remembered Lives: The Work of Ritual Storytelling and Growing Older*. Ed. Marc Kaminsky. Ann Arbor: University of Michigan Press, 1992.

Nash, Gary. "The Hidden History of Mestizo America." *Journal of American History* (December 1995): 941–962.

Nealon, Clark; Robert Nottebard, Stanley Siegel, and James Tinsley. "The Campaign for Major League Baseball in Houston." *Houston Review: History and Culture of the Gulf Coast* 7 (1985): 2–46.

O'Neal, Bill. "Bootlegging in Northeast Texas." *East Texas Historical Journal* 22:2 (1984): 13–20.

———. *The Texas League, 1888–1987, Century of Baseball*. Austin, Tex.: Eakin Press, 1987.

Phillips. Joanna. "History of Roberts Baptist Church, 1872–1972." Mimeograph, San Augustine, Texas, 1972.

Pitre, Merline. "A Note on the Historiography of Blacks in the Reconstruction of Texas." *Journal of Negro History* 66:4 (Winter 1981–1982): 340–348.

Pringle, Henry. *Theodore Roosevelt: A Biography*. New York: Harcourt, Brace, 1931.

Raines, Howell. *My Soul Is Rested: Movement Days in the Deep South Remembered*. New York: G. P. Putnam, 1977.

Ramsdell, Charles. *Reconstruction in Texas*. Reprint of 1910 ed. Lib. Bdg. Rprt. Serv., 1993.

Ray, Edgar W. *The Grand Huckster: Houston's Judge Roy Hofheinz, Genius of the Astrodome*. Memphis, Tenn.: Memphis State University, 1980.

Rice, Lawrence. *The Negro in Texas, 1874–1900*. Baton Rouge: Louisiana State University Press, 1971.

Rosengarten, Theodore. *All God's Dangers: The Life of Nate Shaw*. New York: Random, 1984.

Sapper, Neil. "The Fall of the NAACP in Texas." *Houston Review* 8:2 (1985).

———. "A Survey of the History of the Black People of Texas, 1930–1954." Ph.D. dissertation, Department of History, Texas Tech University, 1972.

Schutze, Jim. *The Accommodation: The Politics of Race in an American City*. New York: Citadel Press, 1987.

Scott, Joan. "Multiculturalism and the Politics of Identity." *October* 61 (Summer 1992).

Sitkoff, Harvard. *The Struggle for Black Equality: 1954–1992.* Revised edition. New York: Hill and Wang, 1993.

Stampp, Kenneth M. *The Peculiar Institution: Slavery in the Antebellum South.* New York: Vintage Books, 1955.

Storr, Anthony. *Churchill's Black Dog, Kafka's Mice and Other Phenomena of the Human Mind.* New York: Grove, 1988.

Thomas, Robert D., and Richard W. Murray. *ProGrowth Politics: Change and Governance in Houston.* Berkeley, Calif.: Institute of Government Studies, 1991.

Williams, David R. "African American Mental Health: Persistent Questions and Paradoxical Findings." *African American Research Perspectives* 2:1 (Spring 1995).

Williams, Gregory Howard. *Life on the Color Line: The True Story of a White Boy Who Discovered He Was Black.* New York: Plume/Truman Talley Books, 1995.

Williamson, Joel. *New People: Miscegenation and Mulattoes in the United States.* New York: Free Press, 1980.

Wintz, Cary D. "Texas Southern University." In *The New Handbook of Texas,* vol. 6, pp. 415–417. Austin: Texas State Historical Association, 1996.